A PHILOSOPHY OF HUMAN HOPE

STUDIES IN PHILOSOPHY AND RELIGION

1. FREUND, E.R. *Franz Rosenzweig's Philosophy of Existence: An Analysis of* The Star of Redemption. 1979. ISBN 90 247 2091 5.
2. OLSON, A.M. *Transcendence and Hermeneutics: An Interpretation of the Philosophy of Karl Jaspers*. 1979. ISBN 90 247 2092 3.
3. VERDU, A. *The Philosophy of Buddhism*. 1981. ISBN 90 247 2224 1.
4. OLIVER, H.H. *A Relational Metaphysic*. 1981. ISBN 90 247 2457 0.
5. ARAPURA, J.G. *Gnosis and the Question of Thought in Vedānta*. 1985. ISBN 90 247 3061 9.
6. HOROSZ, W. and CLEMENTS, T. (eds.) *Religion and Human Purpose*. 1987. ISBN 90 247 3000 7.
7. SIA, S. *God in Process Thought*. 1985. ISBN 90 247 3103 8.
8. KOBLER, J.F. *Vatican II and Phenomenology*. 1985. ISBN 90 247 3193 3.
9. GODFREY, J.J. *A Philosophy of Human Hope*. 1987. ISBN 90 247 3353 7.
10. PERRETT, R.W. *Death and Immortality*. 1987. ISBN 90 247 3440 1.

A PHILOSOPHY OF HUMAN HOPE

JOSEPH J. GODFREY

Saint Joseph's University

1987 **MARTINUS NIJHOFF PUBLISHERS**
a member of the KLUWER ACADEMIC PUBLISHERS GROUP
DORDRECHT / BOSTON / LANCASTER

Distributors

for the United States and Canada: Kluwer Academic Publishers, P.O. Box 358, Accord Station, Hingham, MA 02018-0358, USA
for the UK and Ireland: Kluwer Academic Publishers, MTP Press Limited, Falcon House, Queen Square, Lancaster LA1 1RN, UK
for all other countries: Kluwer Academic Publishers Group, Distribution Center, P.O. Box 322, 3300 AH Dordrecht, The Netherlands

Library of Congress Cataloging in Publication Data

Godfrey, Joseph J. (Joseph John), 1938-
A philosophy of human hope.

(Studies in philosophy and religion ; 9)
Bibliography: p.
1. Hope. I. Title. II. Series: Studies in philosophy and religion (Martinus Nijhoff Publishers) ; v. 9.
BD216.G63 1986 128 86-8666
ISBN 90-247-3353-7
ISBN 90-247-3354-5 (pbk.)

ISBN 90-247-3353-7 (hardback)
ISBN 90-247-2346-9 (series)

Copyright

PRINTED IN THE NETHERLANDS

ἀλλὰ τῶν μὲν θείων τὰ πολλά
ἀπιστίηι
διαφυγγάνει μὴ γιγνώσκεσθαι.

Most of what is divine
we miss for lack of trust.

– Heraclitus

TABLE OF CONTENTS

PREFACE

Few reference works in philosophy have articles on hope. Few also are systematic or large-scale philosophical studies of hope. Hope is admitted to be important in people's lives, but as a topic for study, hope has largely been left to psychologists and theologians. For the most part philosophers treat hope *en passant*.

My aim is to outline a general theory of hope, to explore its structure, forms, goals, reasonableness, and implications, and to trace the implications of such a theory for atheism or theism.

What has been written is quite disparate. Some see hope in an individualistic, often existential, way, and some in a social and political way. Hope is proposed by some as essentially atheistic, and by others as incomprehensible outside of one or another kind of theism. Is it possible to think consistently and at the same time comprehensively about the phenomenon of human hoping? Or is it several phenomena? How could there be such diverse understandings of so central a human experience? On what rational basis could people differ over whether hope is linked to God?

What I offer here is a systematic analysis, but one worked out in dialogue with Ernst Bloch, Immanuel Kant, and Gabriel Marcel. Ernst Bloch of course was a Marxist and officially an atheist, Gabriel Marcel a Christian theist, and Immanuel Kant was a theist, but not in a conventional way. Kant recognized as central the question "What may I hope?" but he addressed only how hope is a subjective state implying certain beliefs; his understanding is different from that proposed in a line of Thornton Wilder and in Christian scriptures' Letter to the Hebrews: Wilder calls one kind of hope an organ of apprehension, not just a climate of the mind; and the Letter to the Hebrews speaks of hope not only as an anchor of the soul, but also as entering into the inner shrine behind the curtain (Heb 6:17). Hope is somehow prehensile, enabling a person to in some sense know what would, without hope, be beyond that person's grasp.

I saw a need for a study like this more than a decade ago when I read essays on hope by Christian theologians. Some drew on Marxist thought, often that of Ernst Bloch. Some drew on existentialist thought, usually that of Gabriel Marcel. I wondered whether a unified understanding could be put together. More recently, I have begun to be familiar with non-western religious thought, where I encounter the proposal that hoping and wishing are weaknesses of character. Wanting things is the source of human pain. Desirelessness is desirable. Desire can seem to be self-centered, covetous, and open to all manner of wishful thinking and self-deception. Since hope is usually taken as including desire, perhaps at least some hopes are vices, not virtues.

This essay on hope is philosophical rather than theological. It sets forth a systematic and comprehensive study of hope, yet includes survey and assessment of paradigmatic writers on hope. It presents a sustained argument for the view of hope it proposes. It distinguishes and relates two kinds of hope, one with an aim or target and one which is a disposition without focus. The essay focuses on hope becoming "sound" rather than becoming "justified." It gives careful analysis to the trust that characterizes sound hope. Hope's trust has implications to the degree that certain models for reality apply. The essay uses such model-supported analysis to trace hope's implications for differing kinds of theism as well as atheism. It is the level of ontological models that is largely decisive for hope's being understood in an atheistic or theistic way: the subject-object model for understanding trust commits one to either an atheism or an instrumental theism, while the intersubjective model is open to theism of a personalistic and non-instrumental sort.

Inasmuch as there is both sustained argument and survey, this essay can be read in two ways or even three: solely for the argument, omitting the summaries of Bloch, Kant, and Marcel; or comprehensively for the full reasons for the argument, taking account of insights Bloch, Kant, and Marcel provide; or even starting from the epilogue, for those who would begin with seeing what consequences my thought might have for religion and theology.

This analysis has connections with religious thought that has made much of hope. I think of Macquarrie, Moltmann, Pannenberg, and more recently theologians dealing with hope in existential or social-ethics ways, as well as liberation theologians, and the studies on trust by Küng and Donald Evans. Particularly significant for understanding what I may soundly hope for is my contrast between social system and community. This contrast is suggestive for ethics and political thought, inasmuch as what hopes are aimed at are forms of social existence. Important for any religious doctrine of immanence and transcendence is my notion of *embodiment*, suggestive of religious doctrines of incarnation: Marcel employs the contrast between absolute Thou and empirical thou, but I argue that *both* are "indicated" for the grounding of intersubjectively understood trust insofar as such trust is without reservation. (A different but related sense of "embodiment" is used in chapter 9, to indicate how what I may in general hope for can find fulfillment only in particular ways.)

My exploration begins and ends with the story of Zeus, Prometheus, and Pandora. The story is symbolic of our human search for an account of ourselves, of our own hopes and lack of hope, and of what we may reasonably hope for and hope in.

The Principle of Hope, the excellent translation of Ernst Bloch's *Das Prinzip Hoffnung* by Neville Plaice, Stephen Plaice, and Paul Knight (Cambridge MA: MIT Press, 1986), was nog available when I wrote this book, and so passages from *Das Prinzip Hoffnung* are my own translations, unless I cite some other source.

For permissions to quote from *Homo Viator: Introduction to a Metaphysic of Hope* by Gabriel Marcel, translated by Emma Craufurd, I am grateful to Harper & Row, Publishers, Inc., and to Victor Gollancz Ltd.

Donald Evans was midwife to the first version of this study in the 1970s. Among those who in major ways were muses and critics at various stages were Lorna Green, Emil Fackenheim, Graeme Nicholson, Elizabeth Linehan, RSM, and Patrick Earl, SJ. For help in editing, typing, and proofreading the text I am deeply indebted to many, among them Mary Aloysius Kerr, IBVM, Joan Franks, OP, Jean Gill, Ethel Ritter, Carolyn McNasby, Joy Ansky, James Karustis, Michael Blee, SJ, Joseph Feeney, SJ, and especially Joanne Devlin. I am grateful to Dean Thomas McFadden and to the Board on Faculty Research of Saint Joseph's University, and to the Kirby Endowment Fund, for financial support in bringing this work to completion. To my colleagues and friends in the philosophy department, and especially to the university's Jesuit community, I am most grateful for their collegial and personal support.

I dedicate this essay to my friends – my brethren and sisters, my parents, teachers and students – with whom I hope.

INTRODUCTION

Long before time began, a young girl of many endowments could not resist opening a casket that contained what she knew not. When Pandora – for that was her name – opened a crack between lid and casket, out swarmed a cloud of ills which infest the earth yet. It was too late to re-close the box. She swung the lid full open, and found inside something that had not escaped. It was *elpis*, hope.

In another story, there were two brothers. One was Prometheus, and he became very famous, storming the heavens and snatching from Zeus and the gods the fire which he brought back to earth to serve the needs of men. The gods became very angry, and Prometheus ended his days chained to a rock, with an eagle continually consuming his liver. His brother, less well-known, was Epimetheus (we may translate his name Second Thoughts). Epimetheus' wisdom led him to take in marriage the hand of a young girl who had brought no gift for men like his brother's fire; in fact, she it was that loosed upon the world swarms of troubles. Prometheus advised against the marriage. But Pandora did have in her dowry a casket, and in that casket was the single gift, hope.

Did Epimetheus marry the girl for her wealth? Does her dowry contain a blessing or a curse? Hope has been evaluated in diverse ways.[1] It has been judged a blessing, in personal, political, psychotherapeutic, and religious contexts. Friedrich Nietzsche called hope "the worst of evils." Fritz Buri described hopes as useful, "appropriate to the degree that they awaken in us the significance of the moment and give us courage to take up the tasks we face." And from the depths of Auschwitz Tadeusz Borowski judged hopes useless or even harmful: "We were never taught to rid ourselves of hope, and that is why we are dying in the gas-chambers."

There are, however, different kinds of hope. A line of Thornton Wilder identifies this essay's subject-matter: "Hope (deep-grounded hope, not those sporadic cries and promptings wrung from us in extremity that more resemble

1. Friedrich Nietzsche, in *Human, All-too-Human,* as quoted by Karl Menninger, "Hope," *The American Journal of Psychiatry* 116 (December 1959): 481-91 (quotation is from p. 483); Fritz Buri, *Unterricht in christlichem* Glauben (Bern, 1957), pp. 91f., as quoted in Harold H. Oliver, "Hope and Knowledge: the Epistemic Status of Religious Language," *Cultural Hermeneutics* 2 (1974): 85; Tadeusz Borowski, a writer and Auschwitz inmate cited by Manes Sperber in *than a Tear in the Sea* (Bergen Belsen Memorial Press, 1967), p. xiii, as quoted by Emil Fackenheim, *God's Presence in History: Jewish Affirmations and Philosophical Reflections* (New York: New York University Press and London: University of London Press, 1970), p. 104.

despair), is a climate of the mind and an organ of apprehension."[2] It is deep-grounded hope that is the subject-matter of this essay. And its analysis is aimed at understanding under just what conditions such hope is a climate of the mind, and under what conditions it is an organ of apprehension.

This is a philosophical study of deep-grounded hope. It is systematic and comprehensive, but it also emphasizes aspects of hope sometimes neglected in philosophical discussion. Hope does have cognitional conditions, implied beliefs; but its conative side has desirings of different kinds, and its affective side, hope-in or trust, also requires careful reflection. Some hope is harmful and some not; some is curse and some blessing. I use "sound" to refer to hope that is positively linked to human well-being. Such an approach does have room for concern about warranted or justified hopes, but takes account not only of the *what* of hope but of the *how* as well.

I apply my analysis to the question whether some kind of hope is an organ of apprehension in the matter of theism and atheism. Does Pandora's dowry have anything to do with Prometheus and Zeus? Does analysis of deep-grounded hope incline towards – is it suasive towards – atheism or theism?

Hope has traditionally shown up in the listings as a theological virtue, given by God and relating persons directly to God. How then is it an appropriate subject for a philosophical treatise? It does show up in human speech, activity, experience. Whether philosophers place it in a religious context or not, it has been treated as a human passion or emotion or affect.[3] Let theologians classify it as they wish; it is no more foreign to philosophical consideration – thought it seems to have been sojourning abroad – than believing or loving. Paul Ricoeur has observed that, even if hope be conceded to the theologians, it has nevertheless a counterpart as topic for philosophers.[4] Indeed, according to Josef Pieper, the structure of hope is the same as the structure of man – and the same as the structure of philosophy.[5] Analysis of hope, then, is a topic for philosophy – not just analysis of "religious hopes," and not just for philosophy of religion.

Three philosophers, Immanuel Kant, Ernst Bloch, and Gabriel Marcel, have devoted substantial discussions to hope, and to connections among

2. Thorton Wilder, *The Eighth Day* (New York: Harper & Row, 1967), p. 57.

3. David Hume treats it as a direct passion in *A Treatise of Human Nature,* Bk. II, 'pt. III, Sec. IX; in his *Summa Theologiae,* Thomas Aquinas treats hope as a passion (I-II, q. 40), as among virtues which are theological (I-II, qq. 52-57), and in its own particularity as a theological virtue (II-II, qq. 17-22).

4. Paul Ricoeur, "Hope and the Structure of Philosophical Systems," American Catholic Philosophical Assocation, *Proceedings for the Year of 1970,* pp. 55-69, esp. pp. 6l, 64, 69.

5. Joseph Pieper, "The Philosophic Act," in his *Leisure the Basis of Culture,* trans. Alexander Dru (New York: Random House, Panetheon Books, 1963), pp. 102-107.

hope, religion, and unbelief or belief in God. While I present the philosophy of hope of each of these, to a large extent on its own terms, it is because each offers paradigmatic distinctions, analyses, and arguments that they figure as contributors to the dialectical movement of my analysis.

This analysis of hope can be applied to other topics besides atheism and theism, although such application is not carried out here. What I understand by the terms system and communion are suggestive for social and political philosophy and for ethics. The "altruism" of hope has links with the question of meaning in the philosophy of history. Work in psychology and philosophical anthropology should mesh with or challenge the frameworks of this essay which are based upon, respectively, the primacy of the self as subject, an approach which takes hope as essentially an attitude, and the primacy of the interpersonal, an approach which takes hope as essentially a relation. This essay does sketch ontological models of a subject-object sort and an intersubjective sort; metaphysical thinking might be able to shed further light on the compatibility and applicability of these models.

The movement and argument of this essay is as follows. Part I is preparatory. It surveys hope descriptively and analytically, in terms of its language, what it is aimed at, its desiring, satisfaction, imagining, and projecting, its beliefs concerning possibility and desirability, its character as a subjective feeling, its core of trust, its historical and transhistorical, individual, and social ranges. Hope has cognitional, conative, and affective aspects.

Such mapping is for the sake of developing an analysis of basic deep-grounded hope in Part II. But a distinction becomes necessary and is argued for, between two equally significant kinds of hope: hope that has an aim and is one's deepest hope – ultimate hope – and a kind of hope without aim, one which is a tone or basic disposition with which one faces the future – fundamental hope. The deep hoping of Bloch, Kant, and Marcel can be explored in this light, and their reflections clarify and give depth to the distinction and the structures that relate these two kinds of hope. These philosophers converge concerning the goal of hope: it has a social, not an individual form. I explore such social form as, on the one hand, social "system," and, on the other hand, "communion."

If ultimate hope, aimed at a social target and exercised in the face of obstacle and finitude, is to be at least formally sound, it must be characterized by a certain kind of desiring and reckoning or believing. Fundamental hope, distinguished from ultimate hope, has as its core the refusal to judge "All is lost, I am lost." Yet fundamental hope cannot obtain without at least some minimal aimed ultimate hope.

Sound ultimate hope and fundamental hope have implications, and these are explained and argued in Part III. The principal implications of hope depend on their being understood, however, in terms of some ontological model of reality. I sketch two such models, the subject-object or will-nature model, consonant with the thought of Bloch and Kant, and the intersubjective model, consonant with the thought of Marcel. In the will-nature model, the principal relationship to reality is an agent's utilization of objects; in the intersubjective model, the principal relationship is a self's appreciative presence to a thou.

The immediate implications of sound ultimate hope are beliefs about possibility, adequate agency, and worth. Sound ultimate hope also implies certain kinds of readiness on the part of the one who hopes, as well as implying trust. The immediate implication of fundamental hope is trust.

Hope's trust, if correctly understood on the will-nature model, implies belief – that what is needed is available as instrument. But if it is correctly understood on the intersubjective model, hope's trust implies reality – of a thou, since such trust requires co-grounding. To have such trust is not merely to believe that certain things are so, but actually to be in touch with what grounds hope's trust. Under these conditions hope is a cognitive experience, an organ of apprehension.

Applied to atheism and theism, this essay's analysis recognizes that a sound social hope does not imply theism if human and natural powers are sufficient. If they are judged insufficient, then hope implies at least belief-that sufficient powers are available. Immanuel Kant's position may be stronger than such an implied – postulated – belief-that, yet Kant's agency is instrumental, as is consistent with the will-nature model: God gives fairminded assistance. But if the intersubjective model applies to hope's trust, a person has thereby what I call presential cognitive access to the real as thou. And if such hope is unshakable, unconditional, or absolute, it is less plausible to judge any empirical thou and I as adequate for such hope's grounding; indeed it is plausible to understand such ground to include absolute Thou.

On the intersubjective model, then, deep-grounded hope is not simply a climate of the mind; it is an organ of apprehension: it implies presence of, reality of, a thou. And if such hope can survive any disappointment, such hope's strength both implies the reality of an empirical thou and indicates presence of thou beyond the empirical. Thus, in explaining the grounding of absolute hope, neither Zeus by himself, nor Prometheus, Epimetheus, and Pandora by themselves, suffice.

PART I

ANALYSIS OF HOPE

CHAPTER 1

HOPE TALK

> One might observe a child and wait until one day he manifests a hope; and then one could say "Today he hoped for the first time." But surely that sounds queer! Although it would be quite natural to say "Today he said 'I hope' for the first time."
>
> Ludwig Wittgenstein, *Zettel*

Hope shows up in our song and poetry, in our politics and religion, and in our very ordinary speech. Sometimes it is plainly expressed; more often it is veiled in images: to be a winner, a lover, to be saved, to build a just society. And, often as words and images are used for hopes, more often still hope comes across quite wordlessly; only a manner of being silent seems to fit the hope of some people.

Later we can look at images and silence; at the outset we can learn from the ordinary speech of hope.

Perhaps the most frequent manner of speaking of hope takes the following forms: "I hope to finish this essay"; or "She hopes for a job near the city"; or "Do you really hope that he'll be on time?" In such locutions, there is something that follows the hope-verb – "to finish," "for a job," "that he'll be on time." Each of these ways of expressing what it is that is hoped can be translated without significant loss of meaning into the form "I hope that P," where "P" expresses in propositional form the content of the hope.[1] So common are these ways of speaking, each convertible to the form "I hope that P," that this form of hope-locution is taken as the standard use.[2] But taking this form as standard should not be allowed to mask significant aspects of hope-talk illuminated by analysis of other usages.

Hope is sometimes a noun:[3] "There's no hope for him"; "That poor fellow hasn't a hope"; "Your employer won't do anything, so your brother is your only hope." Such noun-uses suggest two things at this preliminary level. The first is that hope frequently means chance, or odds-in-one's-favor. Having a hope means having some likelihood of favorable outcome, frequently based

1. Not every proposition can be a sentence radical after a hope-verb, e.g., "I hope that I will be disappointed."

2. E.g., in J.P. Day, "Hope," *American Philosophical Quarterly* 6 (1969): 97.

3. In French, hope is two nouns, *espoir* and *espérance*. The former is definite; the latter, closer to a general attitude. Ths difference is very important, and will be examined later.

upon resources under the command of the hoper. But sometimes the hope is based on others' resources. Thus, "having not a hope" can mean either "there's nothing the poor fellow can do," or "there's nothing, or no one, to come to the fellow's aid"; as a consequence of both cases, he hasn't a chance. But (and this is the second point) this expression "no one to come to aid" recalls the locution quoted above,"... your brother *is* your only hope." Here we glimpse a contrast between *having* a hope, in the sense of having one's own or others' resources, and *being* a hope, in the sense, at this stage vague, that one person can *be* another's hope, with emphasis not immediately placed on just what resources the helper has.

There is another verb-usage of hope that should be located on a map of hope. The expression is "I hope in you." Its sense is not easily reducible to that of the form "I hope that P." What is hoped-for is not prominent in this expression; it is the personal relationship that is expressed. Such speech is often in a religious context, e.g., Psalm 25, or in a context of intimacy. Often as not it would not be expressed but would be real nonetheless.

The last hope-locution that claims attention is neither verb nor noun, but adjective: "Despite disappointment of my every wish, I am still hopeful." A person can speak meaningfully of being hopeful without even implicitly suggesting what it is for which he or she hopes. Hope is here an attitude, and can thus be distinguished – though perhaps not separated – from specific things hoped-for or specific persons hoped-in.

So far we have noticed a few ways in which people use hope-words in speaking. Of course hoping is something which does not require speech. It is a kind of "doing" in which this term, taken at this stage in a very broad sense, includes activity, action, state, attitude, feeling, performance, and so forth – whatever it is that is sometimes manifested in words but can also be expressed without words in gesture, in decision, in waiting, in silence, or in an entire manner of life. In this essay I will usually use the gerund form "hoping" to refer to whatever is being done when one hopes, whatever is conveyed by the active verb-forms of "to hope." The noun "hope" (or, more precisely, "a hope," or "the hope") will usually be used to refer to what is hoped for, hoping's objective or object, its content, its "target," the X in "I hope for X." And on occasion, "hope" will be used where the context makes it clear that hoping and its object are not being considered separately.

The chapters that follow identify features expressed in these various ways of speaking of hope. There is analysis of hope that has an aim or target: such hopes have an objective; they also characteristically exhibit desiring and believing possible, and sometimes they involve imagining. On the other hand, there is the "being hopeful" that seems objectless, and there is also what is expressed as "hope-in." Finally, some hopes have a social or utopian orientation, one which includes some further features necessary, as all the other features are, for plumbing the deep grounded hopes that are the central subject-matter of this essay.

CHAPTER 2

HOPE'S OBJECTIVES

Work without hope draws nectar in a sieve,
And hope without an object cannot live.

Coleridge, *Work Without Hope*

Our reflection on hope that has an aim or target begins with the features of such targets. With apologies to Coleridge, however, hope does not, strictly speaking, have an "object." What is hoped for is not a thing or an item, but rather a state of affairs or an event. Hope for a job is hope for my having a job; and similarly (when I'm lost in deep woods at sunset) hope for a light or hope for a trail is hope that I'll see the light, find the trail. I hope, not that the hoped-for exist, but that it be in a certain kind of relationship with myself or others. I hope, not simply that there *be* a target, but that I hit it. Thus it is preferable for clarity's sake to use hope-that rather than hope-for as the precise expression of hope, and to understand the targets of hoping not as things but as states of affairs or events – not as objects, but as objectives.

A second opening remark concerns hope's future orientation. In this essay the context of hoping is essentially the future. There are, of course, expressions of retrospective or present hope, as in "I hope you had a good night's sleep," or "I'm ten minutes late; I hope I don't have a parking ticket." But the pattern of hope-locutions is so heavily that of the future that I do not hesitate to regard other usages as not of major significance for this essay.

It seems that the key feature of any hope's objective is that it be definite, and this for two reasons. If a hope be not definite, how then could one recognize that it is satisfied? How could a person make sense of hope unless he could say what would count as fulfillment or disappointment?[1] Furthermore, there is a tradition of reflection on hoping that holds strongly to hope's modesty. Not everything should be hoped for. Some things are impossible and hopeless. What becomes important is the drawing of a clear and stable line between what is hopeless and what can be hoped for. Hopes

1. The basis for such a question is the position that hoping involves wanting or desiring. Anthony Kenny, for example, says, "In the standard case, what is wanted can be both described and attempted" and "No one can intelligibly say that he wants something if he cannot also say what counts as getting what he wants." *Action, Emotion, and Will* (London: Routledge & Kegan Paul, and New York: Humanities Press, 1963), pp. 123, 112.

should be accurate.[2] Such accuracy means a hope that is definite in what is desired and believed possible. If hope is sound or at its best when it is thus moderate or modest, then it is of paramount importance that a hope be definite in its focus.

Some hopes are definite by being unique. When the hoped-for is unique, there is no problem recognizing whether such a hope is fulfilled or disappointed. Examples of such unique hopes are: to come out of this impending surgery alive; to get the job for which I was just interviewed; to pass a particular examination. But there are grey areas even here, and they follow the outlines of any theory of referring to a unique event, thing, or state of affairs. Frequently the context implicitly supplies the determinations which verbal expression does not show. My aim in calling attention to unique objects of hoping is to indicate one extreme on a scale of hopes' definiteness. Generally, however, in a subject matter such as this, and for reasons which will become evident later, there are kinds of precision which analysis of hopes and hoping does not permit. For the present, a rather clumsy but serviceable way of putting it would be to say that hopes can be arranged on a continuum beginning with the definite as unique.

Most often, hopes are definite according to *types*. Here what is hoped for is an instance of a certain type; any instance will do, but only such instances as those which are convertible to an item of this type will fulfill the hope.[3] Unique features are of secondary importance.

Yet coming as a surd in any typology of hopes is what I will call the surprise. What is hoped for is verbalized as definite in one direction, but finds fulfillment in another. A person may say, "I'd like to get a job that would put me in contact with lots of people." But the only job offered him is one most solitary, like putting the numbers on the spines of books acquired by a small library. But the person finds out that "This is just what I really wanted." This type of example has led some philosophers to argue that our desires – and by extension our hopes – become specified only with their fulfillment; there is no meaningful way of saying "I want X"; we can only say "I wanted X," and this when we find out that it is X that assuaged our

2. William Lynch makes this point very strongly when he stresses the importance of keeping separate that which can be hoped for and that which is hopeless. *Images of Hope* (Notre Dame and London: University of Notre Dame Press, 1974), pp. 47-62.

3. Paralleling what Anthony Kenny says concerning specification of desires, we can say: hoping for X is definite if and only if (a) anything which is an X will fulfill the hope; and (b) nothing which is not an X will fulfill the hope better or equally well. *Action, Emotion, and Will*, p. 114.

uneasiness.[4] I think it is wiser to take a difference between what we say we want and what subsequently turns out to be our satisfaction as a case of not knowing what we want, rather than as an indication that we cannot know what we want. To be in touch with our desires and to know what they are is a good thing, a fine human achievement.

Whether what is hoped for be unique or an instance of a type, any definite objective bears some relationship to present or past situations. Indeed, it is only insofar as such a future event or state of affairs has some conceptual links with what is already determinate that it can be described. There are basically three such relationships. I hope for *repetition*, for what I have experienced before: "I hope to see you again." Or, I hope for *reversal*: my past or present situation is to my objective as a photographic negative is to a print: "I hope I'll never see that charlatan again." Hopes for vindication and for liberation from captivity are such reversal hopes, as also, in part, are Marxist overcoming of alienation and Christian "death shall be no more." Or, mine may be a hope of *super-abundance*.[5] Its structure is "once again, but more, much more." It occurs in contexts like hope for a better job, for a fuller life, for the classless society, for the kingdom of God. In these cases, there is (1) a content that gives some idea of what the hope is for; there is (2) a negation of the limits of that content as it presently stands; but there is (3) the surpassing of the positive aspect of that content in ways which cannot be precisely described. Expression of the hoped-for is usually therefore not literal. This hope of superabundance is often found in utopian and religious discourse about the future.

But once our delineation of what is hoped for includes surprise and superabundance, we have departed from understanding hope's objective in ways thoroughly definite. Gabriel Marcel, as we shall see, describes hope's target as different and better, "a transfiguration," and Ernst Bloch makes much of a hope that he labels explosive and incognito.

Bloch puts a third label on his full hope, "total," and in our present context we can note as much: some objectives differ from others in being more comprehensive. Hope for a better job is less comprehensive than hope for a fuller life, or Kant's hope for the highest good.

But operating as an undertow to this emphasis on aimed hope's definiteness is an apparent movement of hope towards shifting and lability on the one hand, and towards vagueness on the other, that is, towards being a hope for

4. This is, for example, Bertrand Russell's understanding in the third chapter of *The Analysis of Mind* (London: George Allen and Unwin, and New York: Macmillan, 1921), as summarized and quoted by Anthony Kenny, *Action*, pp. 103-4.

5. On hope of superabundance, see Paul Ricoeur, "Hope and the Structure of Philosophical Systems," pp. 58-59, 69, as well as the thought of Ernst Bloch and Gabriel Marcel.

nothing in particular, objectless, or – in a loose sense of the word – cosmic. These latter experiences will be assessed in reflection on hope's desiring and on hope as a feeling.

A fruitful way of understanding what hope's objectives have in common derives from taking hope, at least aimed hope, as having and act-and-object structure. Acts are specified by their objects, and by the differences of their objects they are differentiated. What would categorize hope's objects would be those formal features that are a necessary condition for any hope, those features that characterize a hope's objective and in the absence of which we have something other than hope. Aquinas described the formal object of hope as "what is agreeable, future, arduous, and possible of attainment"; other thinkers take a similar approach.[6] But is difficulty ("*arduum*" – "steep") an essential feature of aimed hope's objectives?

Those who speak of hope as a very basic human attitude speak often of the obstacles to fulfillment of such hope. The notion of blockage and difficulty attends Marxist discussion of the overcoming of alienation; it characterizes Marcel's description of the context in which hope may arise, a context of an impossibility of rising to a certain fulness of life. More often than not, when people speak of hope they usually understand a certain lack of easy solution, e.g., hope for the rescue of trapped miners, or hope for the end of a war. There are, on the other hand, hope locutions that appear in situations quite free of constraints: one has to stretch the imagination to conjure up the difficulties attending a hope voiced at a cocktail party, "I *do* hope you'll have some of this cheese"! Such garden-party hope-locutions do not so much convict *arduum* of inappropriateness as reveal the shallowness of some hopes.

So, I will stick with *difficulty* as a characteristic of objectives of deep aimed hope, and use hopes quite free of difficulty as tokens of such hopes' superficiality. There are hopes that are trivial; it is not of such that this essay intends to speak. Such trivial hopes lack not only the *arduum* of attainment but just as often the ardor of desire.[7] The hoper could hardly care less. But my focus is on hope when there is obstacle, when the one who hopes cares a great deal, and when a great deal is at stake. What this essay will label "ultimate hope" is of this sort.

6. Aquinas, *Summa Theologiae* I-II, q. 40, a. 2. A similar formulation can be assembled from, for example, David Hume's *A Treatise of Human Nature*, Bk. II, Pt. III, Sec. IX. or J.P. Day, "Hope," *American Philosophical Quarterly* 6 (1969): 89-102.

7. But note the possibility that an object of explicit hope, or at least of conscious hope, may, although trivial, symbolize something much more significant. For example, a teenage girl's desperate hope that *he* will finally *notice me*. See Bloch's notion of real-symbol and this essay's notion of ultimate hope's complexity.

CHAPTER 3

HOPING, DESIRING, AND BEING SATISFIED

The hopes we develop are a measure of our maturity.

Karl and Jeanetta Lyle Menninger *Love Against Hate*

With the topic of hope's desiring, we begin reflection on hope's subjective side. Such reflection takes aimed hope to be a kind of doing, a kind of act, or perhaps also a kind of attitude. The subjective side of hope includes its conative aspect, its cognitional aspect, and its affective aspect. This last includes hope as feeling or emotion; the cognitional side, in this introductory analysis, includes hoping's imagining and believing. Its conative side is the focus of this section, devoted to how hoping includes desiring and, with desiring, different ways of satisfying such desires. There are many words that can express what hope's desiring is doing. A partial lexicon would include wishing, dreaming, wanting, willing, needing, and perhaps lacking; words like pressure, drive, impulse, and appetite (the scholastic *appetitus*) might also be included.[1] In the present context, all the words mentioned will be taken as indicating some sort of stirring in some sort of direction.[2]

Let us consider the following examples of desiring; desiring a milkshake; desiring something to eat; desiring a second career; desiring wisdom; desiring happiness; desiring pleasure; desiring Jane; desiring God; desiring freedom for my country; desiring nothing. (The word "desiring" sounds awkward in some of these contexts; "wanting" or other words can just as easily be used.) Reflection on these examples can bring out some important features about desiring, satisfaction, and disappointment.

Desiring a milkshake and desiring something to eat are two cases of hunger. One is specific: a milkshake. The other is general. But there is one common feature: the advent of what is desired brings the departure of the desire.

1. Note that some of these words are used when one is presuming consciousness, deliberation, and freedom, e.g., willing, while others do not suggest consciousness or freedom necessarily, e.g., drive, impulse.

2. The lexicon also divides into movement (1) "from behind," as is suggested by "drive" when the term is taken as indicating a tension seeking release, and (2) "from ahead" as in "I dream of retiring to a farm in the country." Both kinds of movement are included in the present discussion. The distinctions I am about to make will divide these terms in various ways, but I will content myself with making the distinctions, and will not always return to the lexicon composed here to locate every term mentioned here with respect to the new distinction.

Desires and satisfactions like these function on the homeostatic model: the desire disappears when the desire is satisfied.[3]

Desiring a second career raises the question of whether desiring shifts and thereby casts light on the shifting or lability of hoping mentioned earlier. Suppose that after a number of years in one career, I set it aside and pursue a new one. Maybe the desiring of achievement in the first career was fulfilled, maybe it was disappointed, maybe its outcome was indifferent. Can we ask whether there is here *one* desiring of achievement which continues over first and second careers, or *two* desirings (one succeeding the first), or one desiring that *shifts*? Though this question sounds otiose, its structure parallels that of questions about Plato's Eros, and touches upon the unity and plurality of hope's desiring. And regardless how the "one desiring or two" question is answered, regardless of how "one desiring that shifts" might be understood, the one thing that is clear is that *I* have shifted. How to enumerate desirings is secondary to reflection on the phenomenon that, with the first career's outcome fulfilling or disappointing or indifferent, I have in this case gone on to new vistas and desires. Desiring a second career illustrates a shifting which is at least *my* shifting, whether or not it is felicitously termed *desiring's* shifting.

But reflection on such desiring unearths a second issue, that of "partial satisfaction." It suggests that, if we are dealing with one desiring, there can be cusps in the line of its fulfillment, of which one can truly say "satisfaction" yet not "complete satisfaction."[4] On a deeper level the issue is whether human kind can ever be fully satisfied with anything less than, in some sense, everything.

3. "Homeostatic" here includes both resolution to zero-level tension and resolution to optimum-level tension (not necessarily "zero").

4. Here is as good a place as any to point out the ambiguity that attends such terms as "satisfaction," "fulfillment," and "realization." All three are used to refer to the occurrence of the wished-for outcome of desire or hope. But a distinction must be made between the psychological state and the factual outcome, i.e., between "I feel satisfied" and "The conditions I insisted on were satisfied." The distinction is essentially between feelings of contentment – a psychological state – and factual outcome – an ontological situation. These two coalesce in the case that what I desire is a kind of feeling in myself; when the feeling comes, how I feel *is* the factual outcome. But they are often different, as in the case of a man who says of his career, "What I hoped for has been realized, but I am still not satisfied." "Realization" more readily refers to factual outcome; "satisfaction" can refer to both, as also can "fulfillment." In this essay I will not adopt a rigid distinction in usage, e.g., using "satisfaction" only for one's feeling, for such a policy would often founder on awkward expressions that distract from the point being made. The context will convey which sense, the psychological or the ontological, is intended.

But when we reflect on desiring wisdom, something new emerges. Desiring something to eat fits a homeostatic model: the advent of food brings the departure of the hunger. But the advent of wisdom does not slake the thirst for wisdom; it increases it. Desiring is augmented with its satisfaction. Here it is not a matter quite of part and whole; it is not quite that the satisfaction wears its "limited" label on its sleeve. There seems rather to be a sense of complete satisfaction, of rest and enjoyment, of cessation of striving, of having arrived at insight, understanding, comprehension, yet this completeness is shadowed by a yet further possible completeness. It is as if wisdom were a mysterious onion: removing its outer layer reveals inside an even bigger onion, and within that, one even (and ever) larger.[5] What we have here is desiring that does not fit the homeostatic model, nor is it accurately analyzed as one aimed at partial-and-total-fulfillment, especially if part and whole are understood in quantitative fashion. Desiring wisdom is a desiring that can grow, yet each realization is sensed as complete. Its growing seems irreducible to the second-career-desiring previously examined.

What has been said of desiring wisdom holds in general also for desiring happiness. Advent of what is desired does not bring cessation of desire; desiring continues. But it continues with a difference. Happiness, like wisdom, is not an event but a state. We can contrast the *getting* or attaining with the *keeping* of such a state; the getting would be worth it, even if it did not last. This contrast is helpful because it illuminates the transitory and tragic character of much that people desire. We desire an attainment, an event, and hunger to transmute it into a state, like Goethe's *Faust*: "*Verweile doch, du bist so schön*" ("Tarry awhile, thou art so fair"). But we also sometimes strive and win, only to become bored with the victory.

Desiring pleasure is complicated. It is not my intention to enter into the labyrinthine senses of words like pleasure or enjoyment. If pleasure is taken in the Aristotelian sense of unimpeded operation, then desiring pleasure (if it is usefully distinguishable from the desire for successful activity) continues in the same way that desiring happiness continues. On the other hand, pleasure often has the sense of "fleeting pleasures," the pursuit of which inevitably brings a decline in enjoyment when they are repeatedly attained. Furthermore, both pleasure and its cousin happiness can be taken either as characterizing one's self, or as characterizing one's involvement in the world. Thus both words are used when someone is seeking a pleasant feeling, a euphoria or "good trip," or, on the other hand, when someone is seeking a kind of personal and social existence that is situated in a world of people and nations,

5. For this image I am indebted to Rosemary Haughton, *The Mystery of Sexuality* (London: Darton, Longman & Todd, 1973), Chap. III, "The Layers of the Onion," esp. pp. 33-37.

e.g., I cannot be happy when even one person is unjustly imprisoned. We can call the first situation a state-of-*self* and the second a state-of-*affairs*; either way, what is desired is a state that continues. Focusing on pleasure and happiness allows us to notice the difference between a state-of-self (a feeling) and a state-of-affairs. Desiring can continue with both.

These animadversions suggest elements of a schema dealing with the terminating or continuing of desiring, dependent on different types of satisfaction. One type is homeostatic: satisfaction brings an end to desiring. What is usually involved here is a consumption that relieves a hunger, a release of tension. A second type is satisfaction that continues by possession: I get and keep, I *have*. A third type is satisfaction that continues as union or being.[6] I do not have happiness like I have a car; rather I *am* happy, I *am* wise. My point is not to construct a theory of satisfaction. But noticing these three types of satisfaction – consumption or homeostasis, possession, and union or being – enables us to understand the manners in which desiring can be terminated or continue. The point is not that some desirings are short-range and others long.[7] The point is that desirings differ in type, and these types of desirings are noticeable via types of their satisfaction. Consumption, possession, and union or being will figure in this essay's analysis of types of ultimate hopes' desirings and of the ways in which such hopes may be fulfilled.

Desiring Jane – expressed as "I want you," or "I love you," but as often unexpressed – exhibits many features of desiring already glimpsed. It differs from other desires previously discussed in that its object is a person. Desire for Jane can be just like other desires: the aim of such desire can be possession, or can be a state of union or being. Desiring Jane is as polymorphous in its nuances as loving Jane. But this example can bring into especially clear light the contrast between desiring (loving) someone for herself and desiring someone as an instrument or means to something else. In concrete situations, human motives are usually mixed, but clarifying them in the abstract can be of help. Thus, I can desire Jane as a gratification for my ego, as a prop for my security, as revenge against her boyfriend, or as a token of my social status. If such be the case, she is a means to my self-

6. The first and third types of satisfaction are illustrated by Rollo May's discussion of sex and eros, contrasted inasmuch as the former seeks release and the latter union with the beloved. There is also a contrast of movement "from behind" with movement "from ahead," comparing Freud and Plato. See May's *Love and Will*, pp. 87-88. And there are very helpful contributions to understanding satisfaction as union or being in Abraham Maslow's exploration of peak experiences. See *Toward a Psychology of Being*, 2d ed., (New York: D. Van Nostrand, 1968), Chaps. 6-7, 71-114.

7. *Pace* Ernst Bloch on "expectation-affect" [*Erwartungsaffekt*] and Aquinas as Kenny presents him.

enhancement, and such desire for her fades when a more promising means appears. But desire for Jane could be something quite different: I may want her for herself, so that she and I may become we. My point here is not to sketch the various kinds of human loving under the rubric of desire. My point is that the desiring involved in hoping may be, especially in the case of persons, directed at the formation of a we. Such a movement toward union was adumbrated when earlier I suggested three possible kinds of satisfaction, homeostasis or consumption, possession, and union or being. But when we are speaking of a person, it is easier to grasp how desire for the person-as-instrument is different from desire for the person for union.

The principal reason why this aspect of desire-for is taken up here is that earlier I said that hope-for is regularly equivalent to hope-that: hope for something to eat is hope that I find and eat some food. The object of hope is a state of affairs or an event, not just an object *tout court*. If this is true of hope-for, then it would seem to be true of hoping's component, desire. Desire-for is equivalent to desire-*that*; the verb is followed by a clause that expresses a state of affairs or event. But possession and union are different kinds of states of affairs. Here I anticipate somewhat, and prepare the ground for discussion of a kind of hope elaborated by Gabriel Marcel. He speaks of hope-for-us. In the present context, we can speak of desire-for-us, and what this might mean is clarified if we see how desiring Jane might be aimed, not at possession or instrumentality, but at union. Desiring Jane can be desiring that she and I become a we. It is precisely this desiring of a person that moves towards "community" that is the sense highlighted here.

The next two desires, for God, and for the liberation of my country, reveal something about history. Desire for God might conceivably be satisfied quite without reference to history, in direct communion of the soul with its Source. Liberation of my country, on the other hand, finds its desire surrounded by a network of past and present conditions that shape its satisfaction. The conditions that shape satisfaction of desire for God are putatively "vertical"; the future liberation of my country is thoroughly ahead, "horizontal." But if we add nuances to the ready contrast between the "vertical" and the "horizontal," if we consider desire for the kingdom of God, or for the classless society, we find that several facets of desire's satisfaction emerge. The first is that both the kingdom of God and the classless society are "final." They are not followed by any further stage or progress (whereas liberation of my country can be). At least they are final in the sense that they either terminate history, or inaugurate a whole new kind of history. Secondly, a final future of this type may raise questions like: "What about me? What I desire will take place only after I die. Is it right for me to desire what can't be satisfied *for me*? Or is there some way in which I can share in the absolute future, though I die too early for it?" Thirdly, such expressions as the kingdom of God and the classless society, at least as they are elaborated, sketch out the future in *imaginative* terms. What does constitute satisfaction – or disappointment – when desire is of such a vague and distant goal? Fourthly, these futures, besides being absolute in some sense of final, and besides being possibly beyond my own individual reach, and besides being imaginatively expressed, are total.[8] There is no legitimate desire which doesn't find its place in the compass of such a vision.

A final desire and its satisfaction: to desire nothing. What I desire is to have no desires. Satisfaction of my desire is extinction of my desires. This may stem from the homeostatic model: all my needs are met. Or it may stem from another model: to desire anything is unworthy of a human; therefore human fulfillment is achieved with abolition of desire. This desire-to-desire-nothing is usually situated within a context that distinguishes between unconscious needs and conscious desires, and takes the latter to be essentially of a particularly covetous or alienating sort.[9]

So far, a schematization of desiring has proceeded "one desire at a time." But people are creatures of many desires. As noted earlier, what is aimed at in hope is often not constant. Inconstancy is due often enough to the fact that many desires are found in the human heart at the same time. Some outline of this manifold character of hope's desiring is now in order.

The plurality of hope's desirings can be ordered according to different kinds of human needs. (Later we shall look at how desires differ in time.) The work of A. H. Maslow is very helpful in this area, not in the least because his writing gathers many other researches into the kinds of human needs and desires.[10] He gathers human needs into several categories: physiological needs, safety needs, belongingness and love needs, esteem needs, self-actualization needs, cognitive needs, and aesthetic needs. The accuracy and comprehensiveness of the list is not as important as his point that when the needs occurring earliest on the list are not met in some basic way, such needs become the prime desire of the subject. "It is quite true," Maslow observes, "that man lives by bread alone – when there is no bread."[11] But when there is bread, other and higher needs emerge and dominate the organism, more or less in the order indicated above. He argues that "the basic human needs are

8. These characteristics of desiring – as oriented toward what is final, as longing for what is possibly beyond my participating, as representing the future in imaginative or symbolic terms, and as total – will receive further attention in the chapter "Hope, Society, and History."

9. Such an understanding of desiring is reflected in Ernst Bloch's discussion of Buddha (*Prinzip Hoffnung*, Chap. 54) and in Schopenhauer and Zen.

10. Abraham H. Maslow, *Motivation and Personality*, 2d ed., (New York: Harper & Row, 1970), pp. 35-58.

11. Ibid., p. 38.

organized into a hierarchy of relative prepotency," such that the first or lower must be to some degree satisfied before the higher appear. Yet the order shifts: certain levels in the hierarchy may, in some people, be reversed; others disappear, as in cases of severe economic or psychological deprivation. Further, there are some people who, for the sake of higher values, can sacrifice fulfillment on many other levels, and this especially if basic needs have been gratified in the early years of life. The person whose needs have been met early in life is able to endure deprivation in later years.[12]

Maslow's overview, here given only the most sketchy summary, confirms an understanding of basic human needs, and therefore of conscious desires, as a *plurality*. Relative emphasis within this plurality is according to a hierarchy of prepotency: when the more basic are satisfied, the others emerge more strongly. And when satisfaction for a basic need is lacking, desire to fulfill that need becomes dominant: paradise is banquet for the hungry; paradise becomes home for one who is fed but lacks roof and roots. Maslow makes the point that specific behaviour is usually multimotivated; returning home may be for the sake of food and security and love and respect. And even though Maslow does not discuss the point, it would seem that if several needs can motivate one behaviour pattern, so several needs can motivate *conflicting* behaviour tendencies.

If Maslow's type of reflection is sound – and there are many others who would take the same track – then human desiring may be plural, converging or diverging, but in any case multiple. Therefore human hoping can be multiple, even conflictual, and substantially affected by whether certain types of hopes are fulfilled or not.

The plurality of hope's desiring extends over *time*; what is the hope of one age is something else later. Yet it is hope nonetheless. This is one central insight into hope that stems from the work of Erik Erikson. Consideration of the unity and plurality of hope and desire through the periods of human development and life is assisted enormously by his writings.[13] He has evolved

12. Ibid., p. 53. Yet Maslow adds that habituation seems to support endurance of deprivation. Those who experienced relative starvation seem better able to endure lack of food. But perhaps deprivation or other frustration must be *meaningful*. Erik Erikson and Viktor Frankl both maintain that frustation can be borne if it is meaningful. Frankl is much drawn to Nietzsche's saying, "He who has a *why* to live can bear with almost any *how*." Viktor E. Frankl, *Man's Search for Meaning: An Introduction to Logotherapy* (New York: Washington Square Press, 1963), p. xiii; Erik H. Erikson, *Childhood and Society*, 2d ed. rev. and enl. (New York: W.W. Norton & Co., 1963), pp. 249-50.

13. Some writings of Erik H. Erikson helpful for this essay's analysis are: *Childhood and Society*, 2d ed. rev. and enl. (New York: W.W. Norton & Co., and Toronto: George J. McLeod, 1963), *Identity: Youth and Crisis,* Austen Riggs

a well-known schema of crisis phases in personal development that span the entire lifetime. The outcome of each of these successive phases in human growth is important for the next phase and the growth to come. Each successive phase has its predominant human strength to be established: Hope, Willpower, Purpose, Competence, Fidelity, Love, Care, Wisdom.[14] Each of these virtues (Erikson intends the word's root meaning, "strength") is the favorable ratio achieved between two polar attitudes, e.g., in the case of Hope, between Basic Trust and Basic Mistrust. The relation between the polar attitudes and their outcome – if favorable, hope – will be discussed later.[15] What is important for the present discussion is that each of these strengths, while being the favorable outcome of *one* specific stage, is also to be found *at every stage in human development*.[16] Thus, hope is the favorable outcome of the developmental phase of infancy; its emergence is very dependent on maternal presence. But as a human strength it should be found at every stage of human growth, yet found not in the form it took as the outcome of infancy.

Consequently, if hoping involves desiring, we can expect the desirings of infancy to be different from those of adolescence, and these from those of maturity. Common sense shows this, and Erikson's development of Freudian insights cautions against a reductionism of all desires to the infantile. Pathological or fixated desires may be so reducible, but not the desires that can be found at the various periods of human life in an appropriately maturing person.

Monograph No. 7 (New York: W.W. Norton & Co., and Toronto: George J. McLeod, 1968); *Insight and Responsibility: Lectures on the Ethical Implications of Psychoanalytic Insight* (New York: W.W. Norton & Co., and Toronto: George J. McLeod, 1964); "Life Cycle," in *International Encyclopedia of the Social Sciences*, ed. David L. Sills (New York: Macmillan Co. & Free Press, 1968) 9: 286-92; "The Roots of Virtue," in *The Humanist Frame*, ed. Julian Huxley (London: Allen and Unwin, 1961), pp. 225-46; *Young Man Luther: A Study in Psychoanalysis and History*, Austen Riggs Monograph No. 4 (New York: W.W. Norton & Co., 1958).

14. Erikson, *Childhood*, p. 274.

15. Erikson's notion of basic trust, its bipolar context, and its bearing on this essay's notion of hope-in, are set forth in chapter 7.

16. To my knowledge Erikson has given detailed account only of the adolescent strength Fidelity, the favorable outcome of the conflict between identity and role diffusion; he traces back to childhood and infancy the precursors of identity. In parallel fashion, a detailed account of hope would trace the trust-mistrust crisis, dominant in infancy, through its modalities in later stages. Erikson has found, in the adolescent crisis of identity versus identity-confusion, the presence of the trust-vs.-mistrust crisis of infancy; he labels it "time perspective vs. time diffusion." *Psychological Issues* I, 1 (1959), p. 120.

If this insight of Erikson is added to those of Maslow, we have psychological confirmation for a view that hope's desire is plural yet unified, at least in normal human development. My desiring can shift not only according to satisfaction or deprivation of basic human needs, and be perhaps itself a conflict of desires; it also changes according to age; indeed, if it fails to shift, it expresses a fixation at a level inappropriate for the given stage and detrimental to human growth. The contributions of Maslow and Erikson constitute elements of a psychological theory of hoping.[17] Such psychological theory finds congruent expression in some philosophical theories of human existence which take explicit account of levels in human beings from which various types of movement – can we call them desires or hopes? – arise. There is, for example, Marcel's distinction between genuine personal hope in the face of death and what he calls an organic refusal to die.[18] A full philosophical account of human hope's desiring awaits a full philosophical account of human existence. But I believe there is enough evidence to proceed with the understanding that hope's desiring may well include a plurality of desires which nonetheless do not lose their character as desire.

The coda to this survey of desire is the manner of desires' *integration*. The first point I would make is that desires can become educated. The drives, needs, and inclinations that well up in human living are, or can become, gradually shaped by factors of experience, education, authority, satisfaction or disappointment. Desiderative aspects that move spontaneously can be gradually drawn or turned to that which is most appropriate as satisfaction for them. John Macmurray and others make a parallel point when they argue that emotions are not to be suppressed, but are to be educated, made more rational.[19] Hoping should be accurate. This same "education" process is the gist of Freud's fine and well-known distinction between primary and secondary processes. The latter are the energy transformations brought about by reality-testing, contributions from parents, peers, and the appeal of social allegiances. A further aspect of the achievement of secondary processes is the separating out of those areas where help can be found from those where there is no help: not all things are possible, and the impossible must not contaminate the possible.[20] The second point is to take notice of the issue of

17. Ezra Stotland also brings together a lot of experimental data regarding hope. *The Psychology of Hope: An Integration of Experimental, Clinical, and Social Approaches* (San Francisco: Jossey-Bass, 1969).

18. *Homo Viator*, pp. 49, 36.

19. John Macmurray, *Reason and Emotion* (London: Faber & Faber, 1962), "Education of the Emotions," pp. 67-77; and "Developing Emotions," *Saturday Review* 41 (1958): 22ff. See also Robert C. Solomon, *The Passions: The Myth and Nature of Human Emotion* (Garden City, N.Y.: Anchor Press/Doubleday, 1977).

resolving conflicting desires. Such desires might be called – to alter a phrase from sociology – conative dissonance. One type of such dissonance is internal: to wish for what one does not really desire. (Hoping based upon such tension would be one type of unsound hoping, irrespective of what the object of that hoping is.) A type of such dissonance may obtain between different levels or aspects of a person. Thus we have Plato's soul with its three aspects, *logistikon, thumoeides*, and *epithumētikon*,[21] and Kant's contrast between sensuous inclination or desire (hope as phenomenal) and what is involved in practical moral action (hope as noumenal).[22]

A full doctrine of the resolution of conflicting desires, carried out in the world of society as well as in the world of the personal interior, is a mammoth task. Suffice it to say here that anyone who attempts a full theory of hope must bring forth a theory of desire that encompasses all these aspects: types of desiring and manners of satisfaction, levels of needs, stages of human development, aspects of the human person, various human desires as mistaken and well taken, and the resolution of their conflicts.

For purposes of this essay, however, we should especially keep in mind the ways in which desiring and therefore hoping may be satisfied – in consumption or homeostasis and in possession, both of which are essentially manners of using or utilization, and in union, a manner of being.

20. William Lynch (*Images of Hope*) is very good in analysing these areas, and in presenting the traps that seduce one into impossibility. On primary and secondary processes, see Lynch, pp. 181-83, and Charles Brenner, *An Elementary Textbook of Psychoanalysis* (Garden City, N.Y.: Doubleday, 1957), pp. 49ff.

21. Reason, high spirit, and appetite or desire. *Republic*, Book IV, 435-42. The Phaedrus (246f) presents the image of the charioteer with a team of winged steeds, one upward-winging, the other down.

22. Kant's distinction between *virtus phaenomenon* and *virtus noumenon*, and the relation of both to *Willkür*, is summarized and traced by John R. Silber in his essay "The Ethical Significance of Kant's *Religion*," contained in Immanuel Kant, *Religion Within the Limits of Reason Alone*, trans. with Introduction and Notes by Theodore M. Greene and Hoyt H. Hudson (New York: Harper & Row, Harper Torchbooks, 1960), pp. xcv-xcvi. The distinction seems to be applicable to hope insofar as the latter involves willing.

CHAPTER 4

HOPING, IMAGINING, AND PROJECTING

Hopes are but the dreams of those who are awake.

Pindar

"That's only your imagination." "That's just wishful thinking." There are ways of understanding hope which concede its prevalence but question its soundness. It would be, in the phrase Sartre used in another context, a "useless passion," one quite real, to be sure, but without fulfillment or release. One could take the view that it is useless *tout court*, a lamentable but ineradicable feature of human existence. It is alienating; it turns us away from the real present to the never-to-arrive future.[1] Or it could be lamentable and alienating, but *necessary*, an escape, a shield to blunt the hard teeth of today: "Human kind cannot bear very much reality" (T. S. Eliot). The judgment, albeit from different rationales, comes to the same: hoping on its cognitional side is out of touch with reality.

Such a judgment has a special impact inasmuch as hope deals with the future. If hoping deals with what is presumably very much like the past, then hoping can have a definiteness that aligns it more or less neatly with the course of past events. But if what is at issue is a hoping that reaches for a future very different from the past, the images of that hope and the manner in which that hoping proceeds will be discontinuous with what has gone before. If imagination is the mental representation or grasping of what cannot be found in the here and now nor in the past, then some kinds of hoping are certainly out of touch with reality, if reality is limited to what is or has been.

I certainly do not claim that all hoping is "in touch." Surely some hopes are pure fantasy, and turn us to "pie in the sky." But there may be hopes that are attuned to reality, even when hoping is directed to an imagined future. In the present context, I make an attempt to stake out a territory for hoping that is not the same as the territory for fantasizing. The question whether such a territory is empty or is populated is referred in individual instances to the reader's own experience and, in the argument of this essay, to later sections.

Clearly there are some coordinates for non-fantastic hoping. When hope's desiring is consciously in tune with human needs, and is matched by genuine likelihood of desire's fulfillment, then such a hoping has an accuracy about it that can hardly be called fantasy. It is a measured hope, with its psychic

1. As in the gas-chamber situation mentioned in the Introduction.

hunger stretching no farther than the fulfillment within reach. Such hoping is of course good, but is hardly the hoping that comes to mind when imagining and projecting are mentioned.

But when we speak of hoping which goes beyond the contours of the past and present, it is important to outline just how the question of imagining as sound or illusory should be posed. An image may help here. The stick-and-carrot technique of driving a mule-cart is a familiar picture. There are those who would maintain that in human living there is only the stick: we move by *vis a tergo* (force from the rear). Versions of this explain such *vis* as fate, biological or social determinisms, what we eat, what our parents were like, what our culture is like and so forth. There is a lot of truth in this, and perhaps one of the baldest expressions of it is Freud's saying that man is "lived by the unconscious."[2]

The issue of imagination and projection is not that there is no carrot. On the contrary, there is a long tradition, perhaps most eloquently expressed by Plato as Eros, describing how we are drawn by what is before us. The question is: *where does the carrot come from*? In the standard picture of the carrot-led mule, we see that the carrot hangs from a stick firmly held behind the mule's head by its driver. The carrot is real in one sense of the word; but it is not a reality like that of barn and fodder farther down the road. Obtaining the carrot is a fiction useful for getting the mule moving. Perhaps the same can be said of some hopes. But hoping for the carrot and hoping for the fodder are quite different. They differ as projection differs from anticipation. This can be clarified at least negatively by a closer look at what projection means.

Historically, the root of the issue is seen clearly in Feuerbach. God, as Feuerbach understood the matter, is a projection of humanity. The excellences that people recognized as God are really descriptions of the capabilities of *humanity*. What people have done is to have gathered and summed up all of what they might be, and hypostatized this outside themselves in what they call God. What man is not, God is. The structure of this projection is that of taking as real and external to humanity the good attributes of humanity.[3]

2. As quoted by Rollo May, *Love and Will*, p. 183.

3. "Man's conception of God is the human individual's conception of his own species, that God as the total of all realities or perfections is nothing other than the total of the attributes of the species – dispersed among men and realizing themselves in the course of world history – compendiously combined for the benefit of the limited individual." Ludwig Feuerbach, *Principles of the Philosophy of the Future*. trans. Manfred H. Vogel (Indianapolis: Bobbs-Merrill, 1966), # 12, p. 17.

Man in Feuerbach here is man-as-species. It is not in the final analysis clear whether man-as-species, called by Feuerbach *ens realissimum*, is mankind as ideal, or mankind as the aggregate of past, present, and future achievements in history. If the former,

But in psychological discourse the sense of projection often employed is not that of projection of what is good, but of what is bad. Projection means "the attribution to other people and to objects of one's own ideas, feelings, or attitudes, *esp.*: the externalization of blame, guilt, or responsibility for one's thoughts or actions as an unconscious mechanism to defend the ego against anxiety ('delusions of persecution are based on the mechanism of projection')."[4] This psychological sense of projection is more germane to understanding fear than hope; it is the Feuerbachian sense of projection – the external localization of what is *good* – that yields a sense applicable to hope.

There is no doubt that some hopes are like carrots, thoroughly driver-arranged. Perhaps others are like guiding stars – things to steer by or towards, but in themselves quite unattainable. Perhaps others are like mirages, appearing occasionally under special circumstances, but with a quite natural explanation. But the possibility must be held open that perhaps there are others, like vistas glimpsed from a mountaintop – "silent, upon a peak in Darien" – that are neither mirages not guiding stars but *anticipations*. They glimpse a land (or Cortez's ocean) that can be reached.

This essay will not chart the reaches of imagination and image. But it helps to keep the definition of imagination open. It can be construction or fabrication, presumably illusory; but it can also be anticipatory and receptive. In beginning a survey of the cognitional side of hope, the issue should not be foreclosed by an understanding which by definition prejudges hoping to be either sound or illusory.

then man-as-species may be as much an alienating projection as God-as-*ens realissimum*. This is Marx's criticism of Feuerbach.

The Feuerbachian conversion of theology to anthropology shifts man's future from God to Man. This approach returns in the writings of Ernst Bloch.

4. *Webster's Third New International Dictionary of the English Language, Unabridged* (1961), p. 1814. See also Erikson, *Childhood and Society*, pp. 248-49.

CHAPTER 5

HOPING, POSSIBILITY, DESIRABILITY, AND BELIEF

Hope is the passion for the possible.

Søren Kierkegaard

The cognitional side of hoping may include imagining, but it must include assessments of possibility and, I argue, desirability. Hoping thus involves beliefs about the possibility and the worth of what is hoped for.

I do not intend to take up discussion of possibility over the whole range of its meanings; nor will I do so with its related term, probability. The considerations I offer here will be general; they will become precise only in the one case this essay deals with, the possibility of what is *ultimately* hoped-for. The hoped-for is in some ways *possible*, in some ways *impossible*, and – in some hopes – *inevitable*. A word first about impossibility and inevitability.

Gabriel Marcel maintains that hope, if it is not trivial, is situated – as despair also is – within a context where there is an "impossibility, not necessarily of moving or even of acting in a manner which is relatively free, but *of rising to a certain fullness of life*.[1] This is at least a felt impossibility. The obstacle may be in one's environment, like prison bars; it may be also – and maybe solely – within one's spirit, as in some psychic disorders. But in any case, there is blockage across the way toward fulfillment. Such blockage is more or less removable. The more insuperable it is, the more hope becomes desperation. But the more readily the blockage is swept aside, the more hope approaches confidence, optimism, assurance. I suppose it is acceptable to use the word "hope" when the hoped-for is a sure thing. (But do I really *hope* to draw my next breath – unless, that is, maybe, I *cannot*.) It does seem, however, that hope is more properly found where the future is veiled, and where the present contains elements set to thwart movement toward the goal. So, while "hope" may be used to title the attitude of confident expectation, or the attitude of trapped desperation, I think it more suitably fits a sort of middle ground, one where I am in bondage, yet glimpse a way out.

There is also, however, a sense of hope where some outcome is *inevitable*. In Christianity, Judaism, and Marxism there is the doctrine that the final condition is already basically established: the Kingdom of God will be finally real, the Messiah will come, the classless society is historically inevitable. Such

1. *Homo Viator*, p. 30.

religious hope or Marxist hope is directed towards a future which is not barely logically possible, but in some way inchoatively achieved. The future is not indeterminate; the victory is already won. People can now enter into its anticipation, share proleptically in its reality, contribute to its arrival. What is still open is whether and how I shall participate in such a future: Is this future open for me?

With such observations on the relative impossibility of the hoped-for, and on the believed inevitability of some religious and non-religious eschatological hopes, we can consider the *possibility* of what is hoped for. This possibility is not to be identified with probability. The sense of possibility under discussion here is twofold. That is possible which is not logically contradictory. In this sense, it is possible that all people be well-fed, that someone who has died return to life, that disease be eliminated. This sense of possible is of course required for hope, but more central to hope's analysis is a second sense of possibility: that is possible which has extant one of the realities that can bring about what is hoped for.[2] For example, to hope reasonably for a parking space in the city core, it is required that there *be some* parking spaces. They may be full; but I cannot hope for a parking space if I know that all parking has been eliminated from the city's core. There has to be at least one lot, or at least one space. If there is nothing actually extant which is capable of bringing about what I hope for, then – if I know this – I cannot hope. Hope can only be for what is in this minimal sense possible.[3]

Probability is another matter. Granting the above, with probability the question shifts to the context of *sound* hoping, and then takes up the matter of the *accuracy of estimation of likelihood*. Sound hoping depends on careful calculation of future events; I do not allow myself to hope for what is unlikely.[4]

But a general conclusion can be drawn without details of probability theory. One can hope only for what is believed possible. One's hoping is more sound the more it includes accurate calculation of likelihood.

2. More technically, one conjunct of the necessary condition is known to exist and be operative.

3. Non-contradictory possibility is often called logical possibility. The possibility that permits hope, based upon what is real, is sometimes called physical possibility.

4. I use the more homey word "unlikely" to avoid the more distinction-laden "probability." "Probability" and "probably" have both the sense of "more likely than not" (better than 50% chance) and "some chance, but not much" (probability greater than zero). Further, probability is of two kinds, mathematical or statistical, and inductive. For the point being developed here, further discussion is not necessary, but is available (see J.P. Day, "Anatomy of Hope and Fear," *Mind*, New Series 79 (July 1970): 369-384, for references to Russell, Carnap, and Kneale). Sound hoping does require such sophistication.

The possibility of what is hoped for is believed possibility.[5] The term "belief" takes note of the fact that the possibility in question is possibility-as-thought; the question whether such estimation is borne out by world or personal conditions is left open.[6]

But hoping's *desiring* also requires believing, and does so in perhaps more than one way. The one who hopes must at least believe that what is hoped for is good. Whatever is hoped for is taken to be good, taken, in the scholastic phrase, *sub ratione boni* (under the aspect of good). This does not mean that what is hoped for is unqualifiedly good; it does mean that, whatever it is, the aspect of it according to which it is desired is an aspect which is taken as good. To desire cigarettes, for example, is to want them not precisely insofar as they are a health hazard, but despite the hazard. Thus, to hope, insofar as it involves desiring, entails that the hoped-for be believed to be good, at least in the sense of desirable. Believed desirability characterizes the object of hoping just as surely as believed possibility does. But at times believing also characterizes desiring itself. In earlier discussion of desire, we observed that there were levels of desiring in human beings, and that such levels could conflict. If desiring can obtain at several levels, and some of these levels can be conscious and even reflective – recall Freud's secondary processes and Macmurray's "education" of emotions – then we can sometimes know what we really want, know what our desires actually are.

No attempt will be made in this chapter, which is essentially a mapping or cataloguing, to indicate criteria for sound or unsound beliefs regarding desirability and possibility. But we can note here that Ernst Bloch is at great pains to point out differences between several kinds of possibility, to elucidate objectively real possibility [*das objectiv-real Mögliche*] and distinguish it from other kinds.[7] And Immanuel Kant's notion of postulation is a way in which reason fills in cognitional conditions required for hoping, though not in the form of theoretical beliefs. Gabriel Marcel focuses on the question whether one may hope when reasons for hoping are insufficient. His response employs some distinctions we shall examine later, but here we should note that he

5. That such possibility is believed possibility is noted by Day ("Hope," p. 101), by Anthony Kenny ("The description of the formal object of a mental attitude such as an emotion, unlike a description of the formal object of a non-intensional action, must contain reference to a belief" [*Action, Emotion, and Will*, pp. 193-94]), and, in analogous fashion, by Aquinas ("*apprehensionem boni futuri ardui possibilis adipisci*" [*Summa Theologiae* I-II, q. 40, a. 2]).

6. The senses of "believing" are very complex, here as in other contexts. Here it ranges from "to be of the opinion" to "to hold" or "to be convinced of" or "to know." No attempt is made in this section to sort out the linguistic and epistemological questions involved.

7. See this essay's presentation of Bloch on pp. 74-76.

makes use of a distinction between hope and "the calculating faculty," and I would urge that such a "faculty" covers not only calculation of probabilities but also reckoning of worth: insufficient reasons may pertain to the worth of the hoped-for as well as to its likelihood, and desire may outstrip judgment of desirability.

To sum up: aimed hope, then, is of a desiderative-calculative sort. Its objective arguably needs some kind of definiteness. Its subjective side includes forms of conation, desirings with satisfactions of a consuming, possessing, or unitive sort; it also includes a cognitional or believing side that may be imaginative or projective, but must include beliefs about possibility and desirability.

But an affective strand of hope: what sense can be made of that?

CHAPTER 6

HOPE AS FEELING

I cannot resist a feeling of hope.

Franz Kafka, *Letters to Felice*

What sense can be made of hope as a feeling or emotion? Is hope a mood, an affect, a passion of the soul, a psychological state? Is it a generic disposition or attitude? Is it a state of mind, or a "climate of the mind"? These questions overlap where the subjective side of hope appears to be as much *affective* as conative or cognitional.

Answers to these questions depend on what is meant by feeling or emotion, and on what the term "hope" is used to refer to. Two approaches to such questions are promising. One asks whether indeed hope is an emotion; many have considered it such. The other asks whether it is a feeling.

From one point of view, it is impossible to answer definitively whether hope is an emotion; from another perspective, it is not necessary. But something can be learned from entertaining the question.

Perhaps hoping is *not* an emotion. Such a conclusion stems from a particular understanding of emotion, one according to which emotion is an aspect of a subject which is constituted by (or recognized by means of) the regular concurrence of three observable elements – the same characteristic sensation, the same physical symptom, and the same behavior pattern.[1] According to such an understanding, hoping would be the name for the simultaneous occurrence of a standard sensation (let's say, conscious well-being), a standard physical symptom (let's say, slightly increased pulse), and a standard behavior pattern (for example, physical approach). If this is what an emotion is or how an emotion is recognized, then hoping is not an emotion because there is no one pattern of sensation and symptom and behavior associated with people's claims that they hope for something. Compare, for example, a hope to catch the bus you see, a hope to be found and rescued, and a hope to succeed in your life's work. In these three hopings, there is no pattern of simultaneous occurrence of the same sensation, the same physical symptom, and the same behavior pattern. If emotion is constituted or recognized by such patterns, then hoping is not an emotion; the subjective

1. J.P. Day, in "Hope," *American Philosophical Quarterly* 6 (1969): 89-102, employs these three observable elements as criteria. Broader bases are outlined by William P. Alston in "Emotion and Feeling," *Encyclopedia of Philosophy* (New York: Macmillian & Free Press, 1967) 2: 479-486.

features of hoping do not readily meet the conditions for calling hoping an emotion.[2]

But an emotion is often understood to include *intentionality*. This means that emotions are, with some degree of consciousness, aimed at something or someone, have a focus or "target."[3] Some hold that it is precisely the general features of such targets that identify emotions; this is expressed more formally in the principle that emotions are specified by their objects.[4] Even if we concede constant patterns in what is observable, we must still know the object if we are to identify the emotion. For example, suppose the physiology and behavior of hoping and fearing are the same: there might be the same strain and sweat and speed of someone running, but before we could speak of fear or hope we would have to know whether he is fleeing from or sprinting toward something. The intentional object of hoping is usually said to include the elements gathered in Aquinas' classic definition: hoping's intentional object is "what is agreeable, future, arduous, and possible of attainment."[5] If the intentional object is neither desirable nor possible, there is no justification for speaking of hope. (This of course says nothing about *real* desirability or possibility; the object's desirability and possibility are in the first instance "mental," not "extramental.") If the definition of emotion includes intentionality, then, inasmuch as at least some hoping is intentional, at least such hoping can be recognized as an emotion. Such hoping has the act-and-object structure of aimed hope noted earlier. Calling such aimed hope an emotion adds recognition of its passionate nature, the ardor of its desire.

But there is also another kind of feeling in hopes, a simple steadfastness or an objectless expectancy. The language of hope offers an intransitive "I am

2. Thus concludes J.P. Day, while recognizing nonetheless that most philosophers, including Aristotle, Aquinas, Descartes, and Hume take hope to be an emotion.

3. Cf. Ludwig Wittgenstein, *Philosophical Investigations*, § 476.

4. There is a difference between holding that *all* emotions are specified by objects and holding that emotions are *generally* specified by objects. Anthony Kenny, in *Action, Emotion, and Will* (London: Routledge & Kegan Paul, and New York: Humanities Press, 1963) holds the stronger position (pp. 60-62, 73); putatively objectless emotions have latent objects, or are derivative. Kenny's formulation, and his argument that connections between emotion and object are essential or non-contingent, have been challenged by J.R.S. Wilson in his *Emotion and Object* (Cambridge: Cambridge University Press, 1972), Chs. IV and V. That emotions *generally* have or should have objects that specify them is held by J.P. Day in "Hope" and, in a different context, by Rollo May in *Love and Will* (New York: W.W. Norton, 1969), p. 91. George A. Schrader, in his "The Structure of Emotion," takes a position close to Kenny's but from a phenomenological standpoint. His essay appears in *Invitation to Phenomenology*, ed. James M. Edie (Chicago: Quadrangle, 1965), pp. 252-265.

5. Aquinas, *Summa Theologiae* I-II, q. 40, a. 2.

hopeful." A psychiatrist, for example, may note a patient's more hopeful frame of mind, or more markedly hopeful affect. Such hope seems to be aimless, "cosmic." Often enough it emerges through disappointment: "Despite the failure of every effort on my part, I am still hopeful." Insofar as such an attitude can obtain without enumerable resources, prospects, or possibilities, it is a hoping without an intentional object or objective. Such objectless hoping might be called "vague," but this term connotes a superficiality and fickleness quite foreign to it. Two contrasts illuminate what this putatively purely emotional or dispositional hoping is. Hope is often contrasted with fear, and fear is usually fear of something specific; in this context, hope would also be specific. But hope is also contrasted with despair, and these attitudes are unfocused, or, perhaps, taken with respect to "everything." No one item, or series of items however long, suffices to locate precisely that which is feared or hoped. Such fear has been termed *Angst* in Freud and Heidegger; in Freud, however, being afraid of we know not what can be a mask for a quite specific but hidden fear. Heidegger takes *Angst* as a disposition in the face of the world.[6] The positive counterpart of this, perhaps *espérance* rather than *espoir*, is the objectless hoping to be highlighted here.

This hope without an objective may be what Emily Dickinson had in mind when she wrote:

"Hope" is the thing with feathers –
That perches in the soul –
And sings the tune without the words –
And never stops – at all –[7]

"Hope" she puts in quotes; shall the objectless hope here under discussion bear the same name as aimed desiderative-calculative hope? And such "hope" does not *do* anything; it just "perches in the soul." And – wordlessly – sings.

Such is the hope that will come to be labeled in this essay as "fundamental hope."

6. Freud, *Collected Works* 18: 12; Heidegger, *Being and Time*, Section 40.

7. *The Complete Poems of Emily Dickinson*, ed. Thomas H. Johnson (Boston: Little, Brown & Co., 1960), p. 116.

CHAPTER 7

HOPE-IN

Those who hope in you shall not be disappointed.

Psalm 25 (Grail)

A hope which is aimed at an objective is essentially a desiderative-calculative hope. Differing from such a hope, there seems to be a disposition which is not aimed at any objective. Where does such reflective analysis leave the hope-in expressed in, for example, Gabriel Marcel's "I hope in thee for us," or in expressions like "My hope is in you"? Such a hope seems to be transitive or intentional, inasmuch as it is *in* or "toward" something or someone. Thus, it seems not to be hope as a disposition without *any* focus.

There are two possible understandings of hope-in. One is that it is indeed a form of desiderative-calculative hope, a form that gives expression to the resource that figures in the calculation while leaving tacit the objective desired and believed possible. It thereby expresses something like the reason, cause, or ground of the hope, leaving its other elements in the background. Thus it would be desiderative-calculative hope viewed "from beneath," from the perspective of its perceived basis. The other understanding – one perhaps related to the first – is that hope-in is essentially trust-in: such hoping is in fact trusting.[1]

Here the argument will be: hope-in is *not* desiderative-calculative in usual senses of such terms; it *is* closely bound up with trust; but such trust – and a related feature, mutuality – have key relationships to kinds of desiring and kinds of calculation appropriate to aimed hope. This initial reflection contrasts hope-in with desire and with calculation, and urges that certain types of desiring and calculation require a background of hope-in, trust, mutuality, and cannot take place without such support. The issues are joined through Marcel's maintaining that hoping and desiring are distinct, and that hoping affects what is possible and therefore alters the process of calculating.

Hoping and desiring, Marcel maintains, *are quite distinct*.[2] Desire is always

1. For example, J.P. Day, following Aquinas ("Hope," pp. 97-98).

2. The principal writings of Marcel that supply philosophical analysis of hope, referred to in this chapter, in chapter 12, and in chapter 18, are as follows: *Being and Having: An Existentialist Diary* (New York: Harper & Row, Harper Torchbooks, 1965); "Desire and Hope," in *Readings in Existential Phemenology*, ed. Nathaniel Lawrence and Daniel O'Connor (Englewood Cliffs, N.J.: Prentice-Hall, 1967), pp. 277-285; *The Existential Background of Human Dignity* (Cambridge, MA: Harvard

specific; "to desire is always to *desire something*."[3] There can be hopings which involve desire, as in "I hope for X." But there can be hoping for which the ultimate unavailability of X does not mean that, when this becomes known, the person necessarily ceases to hope. He or she *does cease to expect X*. The kind of hope that Marcel attempts to illumine is one where, for example, a person, finally certain that he is about to die, and accepting this, still holds an attitude that can be called neither defiance nor capitulation.[4] If desire is specific, such a hope is not specific. If desire is covetous and egotistical, this hope is not. For example, hope as desiderative is hope for an event or state of affairs in accord with one's own will. I desire an ice cream cone (to be eaten), a promotion (to bring me greater prestige and income), a wife (to have as mine). The coloration of this hoping's desire is basically one of *having*, of *possession*. The hope that Marcel explains is one that is capable of rising beyond a failure to possess its object. The more one's hoping is tied to specifics and possession, the less one's hoping is what Marcel is pointing to. But the more one's hoping is able to live beyond disappointment without diminishment of life, the more one's hoping is the hope Marcel calls attention

University Press, 1963); *Homo Viator: Introduction to a Metaphysic of Hope*, trans. Emma Craufurd (New York: Harper & Row, Harper Torchbooks, 1962, and London: Victor Gollancz, 1951, a translation of *Homo Viator: prolégomènes à une métaphysique de l'espérance* (Paris: Aubier, 1944, 1963); *The Mystery of Being*, vol. 1: *Reflection & Mystery*; vol. 2: *Faith & Reality* (Chicago: Henry Regnery, Gateway Edition, 1960); *The Philosophy of Existentialism*, trans. Manya Harari (New York: Philosophical Library, 1949, and Citadel Press, 1971); *Presence and Immortality*, trans. Michael A. Machado & rev. by Henry J. Koren (Pittsburgh: Duquesne University Press, 1967); "Theism and Personal Relationships," *Cross Currents* 1 (1950): 35-42; *Tragic Wisdom and Beyond, Including Conversations between Paul Ricoeur and Gabriel Marcel*, trans. Stephen Jolin and Peter McCormick (Evanston: Nothwestern University Press, 1973).

These writings are abbreviated as follows:

BH	*Being and Having*
DH	"Desire and Hope"
EBHD	*Existential Background of Human Dignity*
HV	*Homo Viator*
MB 1, 2	*Mystery of Being*, vols. 1, 2
PE	*Philosophy of Existentialism*
PI	*Presence and Immortality*
TPR	"Theism and Personal Relationships"
TW	*Tragic Wisdom and Beyond*

3. MB 2, 181. On desiring's distinctness, see HV 66-67; MB 2, 176-82; "Hope and Desire."

4. HV 37-38. Elisabeth Kübler-Ross has chronicled such hope in *On Death and Dying* (New York: Macmillan, and London: Collier-Macmillan, 1969), chaps. 7 and 8.

to. Marcel's argument is that there is a non-desirous hope, which is hope in a person. His formula is not "I hope for this" but "I hope in you." Hope-in-you is conceivable without specific demands, the disappointment of which will not vitiate the bond that links I and you together. Hope-in is a form of non-possessive love.

Hope-in is also understood by contrasting it with calculation. Hope-that has as one component a belief about the possibility of what is hoped for. Hope-in takes effect on a plane different from that on which hope-that reckons likelihood. Hope-in, rather than being determined by evidence, shapes the evidence; it brings it about that certain aspects of a situation shall count as evidence. In this sense, there is a hoping that determines what is possible, so that not to hope is to affect what is possible.[5] In forms of psychotherapy employing insight, for example, what decides the issue of recovery is not just what the patient has come to see about herself, her history, and so forth; what is crucial at the point of such insight is the relationship she has with the therapist. The positive character of this relationship is crucial for the patient's improvement.[6] There are many cases, especially in relations between persons, of an attitude establishing just how the facts shall bear on the future, or whether certain facts shall be allowed to bear at all. In such cases it is not far off the mark to say that hope determines what is possible. Marcel's thesis is that there can be a hope – a hope-in – which can shape what is possible rather than be held within possibility's boundaries.

5. For Marcel's analysis of how hope affects what is possible, see pp. 114-16.

6. Note that the relationship does not determine what is believed possible, though it may also affect belief. The point being made is that the relationship affects what personal growth can occur. The importance of this relationship is argued by William Lynch:

"It is a moment of trust. Trust transforms the evidence. Before the moment of trust, evidence suggested that an attack was on,... Now, the same evidence, with trust behind it, is transformed... In a sense, *the relationship comes first and the evidence comes second.*" (*Images*, p. 106.)

Lynch quotes Freud in support:

"It might happen that [the patient] would decide for a repetition of the previous outcome and allow that which had been raised into consciousness to slip back again under repression. The outcome in this struggle is not decided by his intellectual insight... but slowly by his relationship to the physician." (S. Freud, *A General Introduction to Psychoanalysis* [New York: Liveright, 1935], p. 387.)

Support for this conviction about the importance of relationship comes from a work gathering and organizing a great deal of clinical and experimental data on hope-issues Ezra Stotland concludes that persons are assisted by what he calls hopeful "schémas" (propositions, convictions, or hypotheses), and such schemas are invoked sometimes by events and sometimes by *communication from another*. (*The Psychology of Hope*, esp. chap. 9, p. 147 and chap. 7, pp. 114-115.)

Marcel's own argument for a hope that is in a sense not desiderative-calculative, but rather one which goes beyond possessive and fixating desire, and which, by not holding any series of calculations as final, does affect the outcome – this argument will be reviewed later. Here we simply take note of his insistence on the difference: hope-in is not analysable into desiderative-calculative hope.

But *is* it the case that hope-in is not a form of desiderative-calculative hope? If they are different, hope-in must not be simply a defective form of desiderative-calculative hope: it must not be one which fails to calculate thoroughly or is out of touch with sound desiring. How hope-in differs from desiring and calculation, yet is nonetheless related to each of these, can be seen through the psychological insights of Erik Erikson and William Lynch.

Erikson has contributed much to understanding personal growth in psychosexual and psychosocial contexts. His epigenetic model of eight stages of human development not only maps out a process from birth to death, but does so via the resolution of dynamic tensions in each phase of life. Each of his eight stages of human life is characterized by one predominant conflict of dispositions with one vital strength as favorable outcome. It is the stage of infancy that claims our attention now, for its outcome is hope.

The poles of the conflict in infancy are two – basic trust and basic mistrust. Favorable outcome of a stage's crisis means the predominance of one disposition over the other – in this case of infancy, of basic trust over basic mistrust. Speaking of stage and crisis rightly suggests a specific time-span during which the conflict appears, but it is incorrect to suppose that outcome or resolution is a once-and-for-all event. Erikson speaks of "the firm establishment of *enduring patterns* for the solution of the nuclear conflict of basic trust versus basic mistrust";[7] the conflict does not go away, but sound patterns for dealing with it can be established. Previous reference to Erikson highlighted his position that the sound patterns, the establishing of which is central to one stage, are nevertheless relevant to each and all stages of life, although each such vital strength has a different form in each stage. Here we stress that the strength is always in a bipolar context. Basic trust is always "shadowed" and challenged by basic mistrust.

> But even under the most favorable circumstances, this [infancy] stage seems to introduce into psychic life (and become prototypical for) a sense of inner division and universal nostalgia for a paradise forfeited. It is against this powerful combination of a sense of having been deprived, of having been divided, and of having been abandoned – that basic trust must maintain itself throughout life.[8]

7. *Childhood*, p. 249. Emphasis added.
8. *Childhood*, p. 250. The negative pole must not be forgotten in a rush to convert

This continuing tension is reflected in one of Erikson's phrasings of infancy's strength: "Basic Trust vs. Basic Mistrust: Drive and *Hope*"; the strength is "the lasting outcome of the 'favorable ratios.'"[9] With this said about the enduringly bipolar context, we should take a look at the positive pole's disposition, basic trust.

Basic trust is an attitude of the infant to the whole world, primarily in the person of its mother. The infant must be able to trust its mother. Together with this maternal trust there is also development of the infant's trust of itself, and encompassing both is "the trusted framework of their culture's life style."[10] Such trust - if its maternal ground is available - is basic both inasmuch as it is the first general attitude, and inasmuch as it underlies and makes possible further developments. Even in infancy basic trust is compatible with frustration. What is required is a general somatic reliability of the mother, quite compatible with mother's absences. There can be frustration of urges, provided frustration is meaningful, i.e., situated within a larger context of belongingness.[11] And it is against the background of basic trust that the child begins to develop specific trusts and specific distrusts.[12]

Erikson's understanding of hope as the predominance of basic trust over basic mistrust lends some support to the idea that there might be a hope that is hope-in, a hope that is non-desiderative and non-calculative. If we may bring Erikson's understanding to bear, and focus on infancy-originated hope, the following tentative conclusions emerge.[13] This hope is essentially basic

any of these strengths into an achievement scale. Such is the tendency of a success ideology, and risks becoming a maladaptive optimism. *Childhood*, pp. 273-74; *Insight and Responsibility*, p. 118.

9. *Childhood*, p. 274.

10. Ibid., p. 249. Erikson looks for cultural and institutional frameworks for each individual psychological strength, and intends to link the social and the psychic realms in his work (*Insight and Responsibility*, pp. 148-55; "Life Cycle," pp. 286-92; and *Childhood*, pp. 278-79).

Regarding self-trust, Erikson notes that the infant must be able to "trust oneself and the capacity of one's own organs to cope with urges;... trustworthy enough so that the providers will not need to be on guard lest they be nipped." *Childhood*, p. 248.

11. Ibid., pp. 249-50.

12. In an equivalent context in *Insight and Responsibility* (p. 142), Erikson remarks, "The disposition, to be sure, is for Hope, not for a particular variety of prescribed hopes." With basic hope established, the infant is able to grow in discriminating among specific hopes, fulfillments, and disappointments. *Insight*, p. 117.

13. To these conclusions should be added the emphasis of the earlier discussion: the reason why Erikson's infant hope is so important for our discussion is that hope is the developmental turning point that characterizes the infant stage but is found as well in different forms *at every stage* of human development. What mature hope might be can be guessed in contrast to the despair that figures in Erikson's formulation of the eighth

trust. It is founded in the primordial relationship of infant to trust-worthy maternal persons, with the infant's concomitant self-trust, and within the society's cultural context that supports mother and child. Hope as the predominance of basic trust over basic mistrust is hope "shadowed" by that which threatens it; as a human strength it is an enduring pattern for handling the tension between dispositions that are all-encompassing. But even where all-encompassing disposition is involved, we have observable difference between basic disposition and specific trusts or hopes. Indeed, it is precisely insofar as the difference obtains between this hope and specific cases that the hypothesis involving hope-in is supported by Erikson's analysis: his hope is non-calculative insofar as basic trust is a disposition in some sense *prior* to the infant's learning to reckon what and who in particular is trustworthy; and it is non-desiderative insofar as basic trust is compatible with frustration of particular desires and is therefore different from any one or all such urges.

Erikson offers as definition: hope is "the enduring belief in the attainability of fervent wishes, in spite of the dark urges and rages which mark the beginning of existence."[14] This formulation is helpful, because it captures the bipolar "in spite of" character of this hope. But it also seems to resist assimilation to hope-in because its terminology recalls calculation ("belief in the attainability of") and desire ("fervent wishes"). Less terminologically and more substantially considered, it seems that trust may yet turn out to be desiderative-calculative: it is just that the reckoning is cosmic – the mother is the whole world – and the desiring is either serially specific, or is just generalized desire to avoid discomfort. Thus infant hope as Erikson understands it would really be a concrete form of desiderative-calculative hoping, from which hope-in is only apparently different.

Towards two kinds of desire

A way out of this apparent reductive impasse lies in some further reflection on what wishing involves. There may be different types of "fervent wishes," some of which are desiderative and others closer to what Marcel intends to point out.

The work of William Lynch is helpful here. He takes up a very key point that Freud made, and uses it to differentiate between what he terms "wishes" and "examined wishes."[15] Freud distinguished between primary processes

and final stage: "Ego-Integrity vs. Despair: Renunciation and *Wisdom*." *Childhood*, p. 274. On hope's perduring developmental importance, and clues to sound and unsound forms it can take, see *Insight*, pp. 116, 118, 140, 155; *Childhood*, pp. 250, 269, 271-73, 278-79.

14. *Insight*, p. 118.

15. *Images*, pp. 181-84.

and secondary processes. The former are movements and desires that are blunt, imperious, and tolerate no delay. But at another psychic level, such drives can be examined, integrated with each other, and appropriated. They can become no longer "a drive within me," but *my wish*. In this very ordinary movement of primary processes into secondary, desires are ideally brought into touch with the full range of myself and my world.

What Lynch says of wish can be applied to desire. Desire can be distinguished into desire (primary) and examined desires. Yet the difficulty remains, although now situated on two levels. Both the (primary) desire and examined desire can be merely more nuanced species of what Marcel claimed is *not* involved in genuine hoping.

Lynch has a theme that is most germane to the possibility of non-desiderative hoping. It can be found through his differentiation of Absolute Wish from Willful Act.[16] The need to make such a distinction arose for him when he was trying to elaborate an understanding of human wishing as a foundation for a theory of hope that would assist both the well and the ill. In trying to explain a wishing that would stand against apathy, everything he described sounded like willfulness.[17] For the sake of the mentally ill, he hoped to bring into relief a simple wishing characterized by unconditionality and freedom. The line he moved toward was that of recognizing the Willful Act as an act of *reaction*. The Willful Act is determined by what another wants. It may be an act of conformity: "This is what you want, and therefore I want it too." It may be an act of rebellion: "This is what you want; I want the opposite." The phenomenon of willfulness is characterized by the determination of movement only *appearing* to be autonomous. In fact the will of another is always consulted.[18]

In contrast to the Willful Act Lynch describes the Absolute Wish. As a wish, it is a desire or a movement towards. It is absolute because it is not dependent on the will of another. The Willful Act expresses itself in this form: I would like some tea, *if* I think you would like me to have some tea, or *if* you would think less of me if I preferred a drink (*or* I would *not* like some tea if you think only the British drink tea or if you think tea is a stimulant and sound people do not need stimulants). The Absolute Wish is simple: I'd like some tea. Period. It is free of all the conditions that hedge a choice that

16. *Images*, pt. 2, chap. 2, pp. 143-157.

17. *Images*, p. 15. He acknowledges the assistance of Dr. Leslie Farber, and the analysis which later became Farber's *The Ways of the Will: Essays Toward a Psychology and Psychopathology of Will* (New York and Evanston, Ill.: Harper & Row, 1968).

18. Erikson lends support to this analysis when is observes that what he calls Initiative is not to be confused with *a self-will which acts in defiance or protested independence. Childhood*, p. 155.

is willful. But – and here is the signal feature of Lynch's analysis often overlooked by others – *the simple absolute wish requires a context of mutuality*. Lynch explains it like this:

> What accounts for the possibility of an absolutely autonomous act of wishing that simply wishes a thing and is at peace with itself in doing so is some relationship of mutuality. Let us imagine that the individual has achieved a satisfactory relationship or set of relationships of friendship or love. Granted such a relationship, the individual does whatever he wishes so long as the range of action does not put him outside the relationship. In saying this I am only trying to find a way of explicating the sentence of St. Augustine: *Ama et fac quod vis*: Love and do what you will.[19]

If we are friends, whether I have coffee or tea or nothing is dependent on nothing more than on what I'd prefer.[20] But without such a relationship of mutuality, my choice must be evaluated: is it a proof of love? An act of rebellion? Is that what you want me to want? Is this what I, as opposed to you, want precisely as *opposed*?

This analysis of wishing is readily applied to hoping's desire. There can be simple absolute desire; there can be willful desire. Willful desire encompasses both "I want what *you* want," and "I want (vis-à-vis you) what *I* want." Simple absolute desire is "I want a cup of tea." And therefore there can be a simple absolute hope: "I hope for a cup of tea." Period. Simplicity is made possible when the hope is situated within some relationship of mutuality.

Objections

A number of objections spring immediately to mind. Lynch's analysis, preoccupied with the atrophied wishing of the mentally ill, rests on objects categorized at the outset of this essay as trivial. Hope for a cup of tea is hardly a deep, important, or essential hope. And such examples hardly do justice to the nuances of ardor or fundamentality indicated by Erikson ("fervent wishes") or Kierkegaard ("Hope is the passion for the possible"). Yet I maintain that Lynch's conceptual framework can bear the weight of more fervent wishes. Let us say a man hopes ardently to save his marriage, or get a promotion, or make a scientific discovery. Lynch's analysis permits viewing

19. *Images*, p. 151. Rollo May notices and applauds the same observation. *Love and Will*, pp. 215ff.

20. He who has a real friend, Lynch observes, need not consult him. *Images*, p. 152. But care should be taken to distinguish desiring in submission (I want a piece of that ruined cake only because you want me to want it) from desiring a token of union (I want a piece of that ruined cake; I know it's a disaster, but you made it, and I love you). The former is a defeat in a contest of wills; the latter occurs in mutuality.

such hopes either as willful or as absolute wish. He does suggest one principle that may show a way of carrying this argument forward. He writes:

> Thus a man who is really wishing needs nothing but the object of his wish. For the willful act the object only happens to be there and is of no value save as an instrument for the satisfaction of his willful needs.[21]

These are deeper waters. What this implies is not only that the hoped-for may be desired for itself, simply "the object of his wish." It also implies that the hoped-for may be instrumental in *two* ways. It may be instrumental to something else, and this latter is desired on its own merits. Or it may be an instrument or token of yielding to or rebelling against someone else's will, in which case it has no value save as an instrument for the satisfaction of *willful* needs. Desiring willfully is not necessarily bad. As Lynch suggests, perhaps many games are rooted in such a disposition: in chess, for example, I want to find a move, not for its own value, but to block you, to prevent your castling. But when living is taken as a game of winners and losers, then my promotion, my discovery, my spouse approaches being purely an instrument for my relation to the will of another; they have no value of their own. Did I do what you wanted me to do? Or do I want to do what *I* want to do?

Important for this essay's later notion of ultimate hope is Lynch's distinction between willful desiring and simple absolute desiring, the latter governed not by another's desiring but by the merits of what is desired. For our present context, it is important to note that simple wishing or desiring can take place only within a relation of mutuality. If this is so, and if we incorporate the framework of Erikson on hope, the following conclusions emerge for desiderative-calculative-hope-that, hope-in, trust, and mutuality.

From infancy into adulthood, there is development in desiring or wanting and in reckoning. This development occurs over specific wants and reckonings. But distinct from this is the human strength Erikson calls hope, a strength that changes through the years but remains constituted by the psycho-social balance of basic trust over basic mistrust, neither of which are specific. This non-specific trust has affinities, it seems, with hope-in.

Of the two types of desiring we can derive from Lynch's thought, simple absolute desiring is the one that takes what is desired on its merits. But for such desiring to obtain, a relationship of mutuality is required. "In the presence of" friends one can simply want something, without dependence on the will of the friends. This relationship of mutuality has, it seems, affinities

21. *Images*, p. 154. If we compare Lynch's point to earlier discussion of emotion's act-and-object structure, we find that the object is the *necessary* condition for the act of wishing, while it is only *contingently* related to the willful act ("only happens to be there").

with hope-in as non-possessive love.

Thus, three themes are sounded, each to be made more precise later in discovering hope's implications in Part III. First, beneath at least some specific desirings there is trust or mutuality; there is some plausibility, then, in understanding hope-in as trust and/or mutuality. Second, trust seems to be an "attitude"; mutuality seems to connote relationship"; "attitude" and "relationship" will figure significantly in probing hope's implications. Third, the word "hope" has been taken as future-oriented, while trust seems to have the present as its context. Again, the relation of hope to both future and present is part of the implications of ultimate and fundamental hope. For the present, we can say that the hope of hope-in is simply the way in which trusting love faces the future.

CHAPTER 8

HOPE, SOCIETY, AND HISTORY

He who is joined with all the living has hope,
for a living dog is better than a dead lion.

Ecclesiastes 9:4

A catalogue of hopes frequently concludes with the one most comprehensive, a state in which all mankind's sound desires and real needs are fulfilled. Such a conception is a *utopia*, and usually emphasizes that human beings are truly human only within society, and thus the full measure of happiness can be taken only if it is a social order that is measured. Ernst Bloch has such an emphasis, as does Immanuel Kant; More's *Utopia* and Plato's *Republic* show such emphasis as well – in contrast, for example, to Schopenhauer's nirvana.

Reflections on hope developed so far can be brought to bear on hope in a social and historical context, and such analysis prepares immediately for one of this essay's central themes, ultimate hope. About social as well as other hopes, questions arise concerning imagination, possibility, the types of desire and satisfaction involved, and the relation of satisfaction on a societal level to that of individual desires and needs.

Sometimes a social order is considered as not really practical; it serves essentially as a measuring rod or a star to steer by. Its character of being no-place (*ou topos*) does not seriously compromise its usefulness. But sometimes a social order is taken as really possible: it is the classless society, the kingdom of God, the messianic age, or heaven. In every case it is a comprehensive conception: the totality of human fulfillment is achieved therein, usually in a superabundant way.

Prior to the present discussion the paradigm case of hoping has been first-person-singular: I hope. "Utopia" raises the issue of collective hope: We hope; or I hope that we.... Is there a useful contrast between a first-person-singular hope and what I will now call *societal* hope, and thus between individual satisfaction and collective satisfaction?

Whether a useful contrast is possible depends on the comprehensivity of any individual's hope. If first-person-singular-hope is hope-for-me (*tout seul*), then there is a contrast, one parallel to that between egoism and altruism, individual fulfillment and general good. If there can be a conflict between individual and societal good, then there can be a conflict – and thus a distinction – between individual and societal hope. Given such a conflict, societal hope is presumably more comprehensive. But some theories of human existence would argue that such conflict is resolvable. If so, then individual and societal hope can be one: sound hoping would then mean that what the individual hopes for and what others hope for are the same.

Yet there is one way in which individual and societal hoping may be contrasted, according to the satisfaction envisioned. Abstractly, the issue is one of those involved in "altruistic" hoping. *I* hope that *you* may live better, knowing that *I will not share in it*. My hoping is for what I know is not possible; not possible, that is, *for me*, but possible for you. My hoping desires your fulfillment, knowing that such fulfillment will not be mine; indeed, it may cost me mine, as in my hoping for the liberation of our country. It would be the hope of Ecclesiastes' "dead lion." This is the situation of Bloch's Red Hero, giving his life for the revolution.[1] It recalls the attitude of St. Paul, ready to be separated from salvation if this would promote the salvation of his brethren.[2]

Note what is at stake here. The cases are not those of sacrificing a lesser good for a greater. The *greatest* good is at stake in both cases: life in the classless society, or life in the kingdom of God; both the Red Hero and St. Paul are willing to have their hope for others' full life fulfilled at the cost of their own.[3] Here we are speaking of that which is hoped for as total, yet it seems possible for society only on the condition that individuals are ready to hope for it with knowledge that they cannot share in it. Both the hope of the Red Hero and the hope of St. Paul are altruistic and sacrificial: each says "I hope for what you may obtain, even though my hoping will cost me my fulfillment as it furthers yours." For both the Red Hero and St. Paul the same question obtains: can the societal total hope of each, that others benefit at the expense of each, be reconciled with the presumed needs and desires and consequent total *individual* hopes of each?

Yet there is a difference between the hope of the Red Hero and that of St. Paul. Both are altruistic and sacrificial, both are total; but the former is for fulfillment that is historical and the latter aims at transhistorical fulfillment. If a hope is total and historical, it raises the question of whether, upon such hope's realization, there will be anything more to hope for, expect, or work for. "Superabundance" may thus re-enter the conceptual framework of such a hope. But if a total hope is transhistorical, to be realized beyond history,

1. *Prinzip Hoffung*, p. 1378.

2. Romans 9:3. Recall Moses, ready to be erased from the book of life if his fellows are not forgiven by God (Exodus 32:32).

3. Whether it is ethical to prefer others' interests over one's own is of course highly disputed. Further, the classless society and the kingdom of God can be understood in such a way that it is not possible for an individual to fail to share in the goal if he is ready to give up everything to secure it for others.

"at the end of time," or "beyond time," "in eternity," then the question arises why there are intervals and lifetimes and centuries at all; history seems quite unnecessary, and therefore equally pointless would be any action that takes seriously into account what has already taken place or what can reasonably be expected in history.[4]

We now have identified further features of aimed hope. If its objective is societal, some account of its historical-transhistorical features must be given, as well as of the individual or altruistic benefits hoped for.

The features of aimed hope sketched so far – its objective, its patterns of desire and satisfaction, imagination and calculation, its individual and societal targets – and the features of hope as feeling and of hope-in have been charted in order now to be applied to this essay's central concepts of ultimate hope and fundamental hope. These will now be elucidated, in dialogue with the principal philosophers of this essay.

4. See Philip Merlan, "Eschatology, Sacred and Profane," *Journal of the History of Philosophy* 9 (April 1971): 193-203.

PART II

ULTIMATE HOPE AND FUNDAMENTAL HOPE

INTRODUCTION

The analysis of hope just concluded stopped short of the two kinds of hope that are the subject matter of this part. That analysis, however, is propaedeutic to exposition and argument concerning ultimate hope and fundamental hope. The reason why these notions are developed is that relationships between theism or atheism and hope are not best explored through pedestrian or garden-variety hopes; this is the conviction of the philosophers this essay deals with, and that supposed for this essay's own argument. The hope under reflection henceforth is a hope that is deeper, more important, larger, closer to the human core, more encompassing of the total human context, more significant in human history. Why such reflection requires not one but two notions of more basic hope will become clear as the exposition proceeds.

The method of Part I consisted of analysis and clarification of elements involved in hope. Hope's objective or hoped-for side and its subjective or hoping side were examined. Analysis dealt with imagination, possibility, and hope-in, and treated the latter especially in the context of the difference between simple absolute desire and willful desire. Several issues were raised concerning hope as ideal or realizable, individual and societal, historical and transhistorical.

The method of Part II involves hypothesis and dialectic. Chapter 9 offers a preliminary characterization of ultimate hope and fundamental hope. Chapters 10, 11, and 12 examine the contributions of Ernst Bloch, Immanuel Kant, and Gabriel Marcel to an understanding of hope in general and of these two notions of hope in particular. In chapter 13, more thoroughly formulated notions of ultimate hope and fundamental hope, reworked in give-and-take with the three philosophers' exposition and argument, are set forth. Their clear definition sets the stage for inquiry into their implications concerning theism and atheism.

CHAPTER 9

ULTIMATE HOPE AND FUNDAMENTAL HOPE: PRELIMINARY CHARACTERIZATION

Ultimate hope

Our first brush with ultimate hope comes when we notice that some hopes are deeper, more important, more comprehensive, more heartfelt, than others. The comparative degree is what we notice, but the superlative degree is what is decisive for the core element in describing ultimate hope. Ultimate hope is one's highest, one's deepest hope. I hope for something with all my heart; my hope is for this more than anything else in the world – such is its language. Yet language may be lacking: my deepest hope may be too deep for words. Indeed it may be too deep for me even to recognize it.

Ultimate hope is hope that has an aim, a target, an objective. It is therefore like any previously analyzed hope in that it is desire of or movement towards what is believed desirable and believed possible although difficult to obtain, but *ultimate hope* differs from other hopes insofar as it *is superordinate to all other hopes.* The key term "superordination" requires careful elaboration.

One hope is superordinate to another if the first "outranks" the second. What this means is that the movement or activity of oneself that hope is, contains the one hope *in preference to* the other if they are such that there can be a conflict between them.

Preference may show itself inasmuch as action stemming from hope stems from the one rather than the other; or, if one moves in one direction and then feels guilt, this guilt may be a sign that the hope pointing in the other direction is the weightier. It is not necessarily the hope most readily on the lips of the one who hopes that can be presumed to be the more important; deeper analysis may bring out predominance of another desiring and believing than the one expressed. The weightier of the two, the preferred, is a candidate for ultimate hope. But – and this is the central point – only that which wins out over all other hopes is actually the ultimate one. Ultimate hope is superordinate to *all* other hopes. "All" here is the de facto all in one person or group at one time.

There is no claim here that everybody has some ultimate hope. A person might vacillate between two hopes, unresolved in preference. Or a person might truly have no ultimate hope: there is nothing which he or she holds as really good and also really possible and does desire in a way that takes precedence over other hopes.

> I said to my soul, be still, and wait without hope

For hope would be hope for the wrong thing;...[1]

Such a person may be so discouraged, so shaken, so betrayed, so transported by joy, so afflicted by *taedium vitae*, that ultimate hope cannot be discerned.

This preliminary characterization of ultimate hope does not vary according to whether it is located on the level of the conscious, the pre-conscious, or the unconscious.[2] Furthermore, it does not presume that one's ultimate hope is a matter of free choice; nor does it presume the opposite. It points to the *result* of a process of determining superordination or preference without implying how such determination is reached.

It is crucial here not to take this "preference" in terms simply of the *what* that is hoped for. Often hope does differ from hope as one objective differs from another: one objective is believed more desirable, or is believed more likely. Indeed, one hope may be preferred because, though the good involved is less than another good, it is possible – the greater good is beyond reach. Calculation of possibility and of desirability both bear on a hope's being preferred, and consequently on hope's super- or sub-ordination. There are *reasons why* one may be superordinate. But a hope may be superordinate, not for the weight of reasons like this, but because of quite different factors. An ultimate hope may be mine because others have instructed me that it should be mine, and I hold it so because I defer to their judgment; superordination may be motivated in such a way. But the reasons for hope, and its motivation, must be distinguished from the de facto or phenomenological superordination of a hope. It is the latter that is the distinguishing feature of ultimate hope, though the former may account for its being so.

"Superordination," therefore, refers to the outcome of the process of determining which of two or more hopes predominates in some way over others where incompatibility between them is operative. Because it does not refer directly to the objective that is hoped for, superordination characterizes primarily the hope, and only secondarily the constituent elements of the hope – believed desirability and believed possibility of what is hoped for.[3]

1. T.S. Eliot, "East Coker," *Four Quartets*.

2. In this respect it follows a lead of Kierkegaard where in *Sickness Unto Death* (p. 162) he titles a section: "Despair regarded in such a way that one does not reflect whether it is conscious or not,..." *Fear and Trembling and The Sickness unto Death*, trans. with introductions and notes by Walter Lowrie (Princeton, N.J.: Princeton University Press, 1968).

3. Another approach to superordination is possible: one could say that a hope is ultimate if its *realization* is believed to be fulfilling of *all* my needs. Such a hope is included in my notion, and would figure insofar as the looked-for fulfillment is the *reason why* my ultimate hope is superordinate. But there could also be other reasons

Does everyone have the same ultimate hope? This essay takes no position on this matter. Some may argue for hope's unity, understanding hope to have implicit objectives and explicit highly symbolic expression. This may be the case. But rather obvious is the *variety* of what people actually say they hope for deep down, and this variety persists well beneath the level of words. It seems better, therefore, in framing a hypothesis that includes ultimate hope, to take full account from the outset of the variegated hopes people express and exhibit. Human desires can stem from different levels, different needs, and different stages of human maturity.[4] Insofar as such analysis of differing desires bears upon ultimate hope, such a plurality of desire argues that ultimate hope stemming from this will be plural over changing circumstances and years. At any one time there can be at most one such hope, but as time goes on the person's ultimate hope will be manifold.[5]

But whether ultimate hope is judged serially heterogeneous, manifold, or basically one, the analysis of this essay is germane.

A question of ultimate hope's unity raises the question of how ultimate hope can be *complex*. The same question arises when, attending to the role incompatibility plays in defining superordination, we ask how two hopes can be both compatible and ultimate. The obvious tack is that they are "parts" of one ultimate hope. Present logical analysis of complex ultimate hope is for the sake of preparing conceptual tools both for dealing with the analyses of totality and hope in Ernst Bloch and Immanuel Kant, and for this essay's more comprehensive treatment of ultimate hope.

A fruitful way of analysing how ultimate hope can be complex is to do it in terms of part and whole: How can one hope be part of another? With regard to hope *tout court,* i.e., prescinding from its being distinguished into elements of desire and possibility, we can say that one hope has another as

why a hope is superordinate, including the view that its realization, while hardly *all*-fulfilling, is the only outcome believed possible. Maybe the most that Sisyphus can hope for is a cool breeze. Maybe life is nasty, brutish, and short.

4. Such levels, needs, and stages are surveyed in part I, chapter 3, Hoping, Desiring, and Being Satisfied.

5. This approach to ultimate hope's plurality and change over time depends on determining whether the different stages do or do not have one overarching or undergirding hope as their pre-eminent factor according to the organic-complexity model of ultimate hope about to be sketched. If there is no pre-eminent factor, then hope's changes are simply plural; if there is, then the succeeding stages embody the constant, more abstract, factor within the one ultimate hope. This is one consequence of leaving open the question whether there is in man just one ultimate drive, desire, *élan*, or *Ursprung*. Ernst Bloch, as we shall see, argues for hopes' underlying unity.

"part" if we can recognize that one hope-expression entails the second.[6] An ultimate hope is complex if certain hopes are not disparate with respect to it but are related to it in some way that does not admit choice between it and them. Such relations, which constitute the complexity of the ultimate hope, are the basis for one hope-expression entailing another, and are the criteria for deciding that a certain hope is or is not "part" of an ultimate hope.

These relations obtain between elements of hope's objective; hence analysis of complexity focuses on complexity in what is hoped for. These relations can fit several models.

A first set of relations obtains when what is hoped for in an ultimate hope is a simple *aggregate*. The hoped-for is the sum of several objectives, let us say A, B, C, and D. If the hoped-for is the sum of these – let us call it "O" – then hope-for-O is superordinate to hope-for-X,[7] and hope-for-O entails hope-for-B. Hope-for-B is not superordinate to hope-for-C; they are believed compatible. And one would not say that hope-for-O is superordinate to hope-for-B, since superordination obtains only where there can be a conflict between hopes. Hope-for-O is complex insofar as O has A and B and C and D as parts of an aggregate; therefore hope-for-B is "part of" hope-for-O.

A second set of relations obtains when what is hoped for is an *ordered* aggregate. The hoped-for consists of several objectives, B and C and D, but in the order A. The order, A, could be, for example, serial: B is hoped for only as first to be fulfilled, then C, then D; or it could be simultaneous. The order, however, is essentially spatio-temporal. If the whole hoped-for is O, then hope-for-O includes hope-for-B-C-D and hope-for-A, but A is not part of O the way B, C, and D are parts; it is the order of the parts. O is a whole with B and C and D as parts, but ordered according to A. A makes B-C-D to be the constellation whereby O differs from another possible ultimate hope, also made up of B and C and D as parts.

Somewhat different from the first and second models is a third, one where *means* are involved. Speaking precisely, it makes no sense to say that one *hope* is a means to another *hope*. But if one *objective* is a means to another *objective*, then we can sketch an ultimate hope where its complexity is due to instrumentality. I may, for example, hope for an exit visa for myself and my family. Though getting such a visa absorbs much of my energies, it has merely instrumental value: it permits escape from present oppression and opens the way to a better life. "Instrument" or "means" here signifies not just that which influences an outcome, but also and especially that which is not part

6. I.e., entails by itself alone, or with an added premise. See the discussion of "necessary means" in the third model, in p. 59's note 9. The added premise specifies that other means are unavailable.

7. Where X is not A, B, C, or D.

of the final outcome.[8] Or, to put it another way: a means is a *step*, like a milepost for a journey; one event or state can be a step to another, and steps are always left behind. If steps or means are needed for realization of the hoped-for outcome, then a person can hope for the outcome only if he also hopes for the needed means. The complex ultimate hope, therefore, includes hope for the needed means.[9]

The point of this model is that there is a way in which an ultimate hope, complex by virtue of complexity in its objective, is complex not simply by virtue of the constitutive elements of what is hoped for (the first model) but also by virtue of that which may have the character of a means towards what is hoped for. She who wills the end wills the means; she who hopes for the end hopes also for the means. Consequently, the complexity of the hope includes hope for the means required; means are not therefore "ordinary" hopes, but, *in one sense, part* of the whole that is hoped for.

The contrast between the step or means model and the "foretaste" model that follows corresponds to a contrast often made in eschatological hopes. In one view, the final outcome will see all that is previous quite left behind; in another, all that is previous is gathered up in the final outcome.[10]

8. Challenge can be brought against the notion of mere means. The best case in its defense in one where the instrumental outcome is negative, and makes possible a positive final outcome, e.g., the deposition of a government to make way for a new form of government. Here the deposition is not desired for its own sake, nor for its share in the final outcome. But the challenge, on the other hand, insists that all means employed, all steps taken, are part of the final outcome. Argument here depends on logical and ontological analysis of part and whole. To the degree that the challenge is upheld, then a contrast between means and end fades, and consequently the contrast between this third model based on means or step and the fourth based on "foretaste" also fades. Perhaps the contrast is a relative one, like John Dewey's contrast between instrumental and consummatory experiences.

9. If means are needed, then means are necessary conditions. The first and second models have their elements as *constitutively* necessary conditions. In this third model, needed means are *instrumentally* necessary conditions. Such a necessary condition may be particular: without precisely *this* step, the outcome hoped for is impossible. Or it may be a type: without *some* step of this sort the outcome is impossible. In this latter case, any one particular instance of a required type is only hypothetically necessary; only when other instances are unavailable does it become a simply necessary condition.

10. Both the left-behind pattern and the gathering-up pattern must be distinguished from one where intervention or interruption is involved. The two patterns express influences of prior on consequent in one process; they do not express influence that comes from outside the process, from, e.g., divine intervention. Yet they need not be incompatible with such.

The fourth model of an ultimate hope's complexity differs from the third as *foretaste* differs from step. A step is left behind; a foretaste or "down-payment" is included in the final outcome. This model accommodates hopes in which part of what is hoped for is something that will remain in and be an aspect of realization of the final objective. A foretaste is, however, not a part in the sense of having full footing as an item in an aggregate. It is inchoative, but also admits of some qualitative difference between itself and that of which it is a foretaste. If a contrast can be made between step and foretaste, then a contrast can be made between the third and this fourth model in sketching complexity in ultimate hope.

A fifth model of the complexity of an ultimate hope, again based on complexity in what is hoped for, can be called the *organic,* and within it obtains a relationship I will call *embodiment*. An example is helpful: let us say that what is hoped for includes the overcoming of alienation. But if we can speak of the overcoming of alienation as the overarching concept involved in what is hoped for, we can designate it as A. This concept, however, governs the acceptability or unacceptability of certain other conceptions, of relationships like the relation of worker to product of work, the relation of teacher to students, and the relation of government to individual initiative. We can call those conceptions of relations which are judged acceptable: B, C, and D. With respect to these, the overcoming of alienation, A, has a *pre-eminence,* since A is the criterion by which B, C, and D are judged acceptable in their formulation. As a consequence, hope for A entails hope for B, C, and D. But A, and B-C-D, are abstract; B and C and D are conceptions of relationships. What is hoped for is the *concrete* realization of a concept, because B and C and D have no particular time, locale, and persons as part of them. Realization of what is hoped for can take place only with individual persons and times and places. So realization of B and C and D requires that they take on a local habitation and a name – in b and c and d. The latter *embody* the former.

What is hoped for is not just A, nor even A with its (conceptual) parts, B and C and D. What is hoped for is the whole, which includes the concrete events and states b and c and d. If the whole is represented by O, then O is A and B-C-D with the particulars b-c-d. Hope for O entails hope for B-C-D and some concrete actualizations. Indeed, real hope for O is possible only when some b and c and d are within the realm of possibility. Hope for concreteness is part of hope for the abstraction, because realization of utopia requires that it cease to be no-place.

This model seems especially applicable to complex ultimate hopes expressed in metaphor, symbol, analogy, or utopian language. It can be argued whether this model reduces to the second model, an ordered aggregate, or whether b and c and d can be mere means or steps (the third model) or include foretastes (the fourth model).[11] The term "embodiment" for the relations between B-C-D and b-c-d is a help in noticing that realization must be concrete, even where expression of the hoped-for is abstract. There is no organism without a body, but the body is not just the spatio-temporal juxtaposition of the elements (as in the second model).

The five models sketched here do not pretend to exhaust the ways in which ultimate hope can be complex, especially according to complexity in its objective. They are offered at this point as some way of organizing perceptions of hope in the philosophers under discussion; they also suggest fruitful questions to direct to them.

Some additional observations are important for this preliminary sketch of ultimate hope. To speak of ultimate hope is not to suggest that any such hope is good. Some may be good; other such hope may be illusory, demonic, contra-human, and stem from self-deception. Ultimate hopes must be evaluated case by case for soundness. Furthermore, there can be analysis of fear in a fashion parallel to that of hope; one can consequently speak of one's *ultimate fear.*[12] There can be, it would seem, both these ultimate dispositions in the same person. What will later be said about fundamental hope can be applied to ultimate fear as readily as to ultimate hope or its lack. Finally, we could for completeness' sake conceivably speak of which of such ultimate dispositions, hope or fear, is, in the last analysis, *dominant.*

This sketch of ultimate hope, its superordination, unity and complexity, and its parallel notion of fear, is finished. We turn now to an aspect of hoping which is not aimed at an objective, and thus approach the notion of fundamental hope.

Context of the fundamental

Of first importance in fundamental hope is presenting the case for speaking of a context of fundamentality at all: within this context, hope will be one of the orientations.

Ultimate hope is an aimed disposition, with a focus, a target, some sort of definiteness in its objective. Ultimate fear is, in similar fashion, aimed. The context of the fundamental, however, is the way in which, the manner with which one "has" or "holds" one's ultimate disposition of fear or hope. In speaking of fundamental hope or its opposite, we speak of that which has no

11. It may be possible to consider B, etc., as *classes* and b, etc., as instantiations. This understanding may fit better those cases where A and B-C-D can be instantiated repeatedly. But if there are cases of once-and-for-all realization, I prefer not to use the class-instantiation terminology.

12. Fear, in the analysis of many, is aversion from the possible. A typology of senses given to terms like fear and hope, confidence, desperation, and so forth, can be found in J.P. Day, "Anatomy of Hope and Fear."

focus, but does have an orientation, toward the future. It is the personal tone of one's ultimate (or non-ultimate) hope or fear, but it can obtain when one neither hopes nor fears. When the fundamental context is that of fundamental hope, it can be one way of explicating the phrase "am hopeful." And fundamental hope has despair, rather than fear, as its opposite; but to contrast hope and despair is to anticipate.

Some argument is needed that it is necessary for hope analysis to speak of the context of fundamental attitude in general and of fundamental hope in particular. Hope-analysis, it is argued, is incomplete if only aimed hopes, non-ultimate and ultimate, are brought into view.

The context of fundamental attitude, the *manner with which* one hopes or fears, can be specified as that which is *not reducible to* an ultimate disposition of hope or fear, nor to its elements of desiring and believing possible, but is *always a concomitant* of such disposition.

One difficulty with this general definition is that it is too broad; it can include two features related to ultimate hopes (but which are *not* the context of the fundamental): how I deal with the outcome of my ultimate hope, and what my reasons, causes and motives are for my ultimate hope. Each of these will be reviewed, as much to show connections and contrasts and to give examples as to indicate, in a preliminary way, what the context of fundamental attitude is not.

Of any given hope at any given time, the outcomes are three: either the hope is realized, or it is disappointed, or it is unresolved. Faced with such outcomes, a person does a number of things; there are a number of sequels.

With realization or fulfillment I may simply be at peace: I have no further hopes, no further desires; I enjoy the actuality of what I was longing for. Or: with my hope satisfied, I turn to a new hope, perhaps even one only now made possible by the realization of the prior hope; there is something new and different that draws my longing. Or: with my hope fulfilled, I want it again; realization brings desire for repetition. Or: fulfillment is followed by desire for not just iteration but increase, more. Obviously, there can be mixture of these patterns, all consequent upon realization of a hope.

Another group of sequels shows up with hope's disappointment. With hope dashed, some turn to hope for something else. Others do not hope, for "hope would be hope for the wrong thing." This is for some a refusal to hope; for others, a holding of oneself in abeyance. Some say "My hope is gone, but *I* am not gone"; "Gone is my hope, but I'm not yet a goner." But others are dejected, depressed, despairing, and these latter attitudes are of differing existential weights.

A third set of sequels attends a hope that is unresolved. With my hope's outcome inconclusive, I may stay with it. Or, I may shift to something else more promising. I may wait, actively or passively. I may work, feverish or relaxed. I may cling desperately: "Without this, I am lost." I may with measure and serenity turn myself in another direction, revising my hopes. Or I may well revise them, but in revising I am just as frantic as I would be had I clung to them. I may just drift off from the hope, unable to, or not knowing how to, wait; recall the rootless waiting of Beckett's Vladimir in *Waiting for Godot:* "let us perserve in what we have resolved, before we forget."

A survey of sequels of hope's outcomes turns up a wide range of activities: critique of hope, abandonment, perseverance, doubt, ratification, re-assessment, waiting, shifting to another hope, and so forth. One could argue that sequels, or sequel-determining, always accompany an ultimate hope and yet are not reducible to it. Some of these sequels are simply the shifting of hope surveyed above. But it is more accurate to say that *what* sequel is determined may be due to *how* the initial hope was held; the manner of one's ultimate hope has consequences for determining which sequel to that hope's outcome is deemed appropriate. Successive dealings with such outcomes let one know that more is involved than a series of hopes. Shall I wait, or shall I abandon hope? The appropriate answer to such a question depends, not only on the hope, but also on *how* it is held. A rough list of such *hows* will be given later.

A look should be taken at reasons, causes, and motives, the *whys* of aimed hopes and fears. Such would seem concomitant with yet irreducible to such dispositions; furthermore, if the sequel, what I do next, depends on the how, does it so depend as on a reason? Reasons, causes, motives, however, have influence as determinants. They push or pull toward hope or fear, toward hope for this rather than that. The manner or *how* of one's ultimate disposition does have a bearing on that disposition, but not simply as a determinant. Therefore it is at best a half-truth to say such are the substance of what this essay calls the context of the fundamental, the manner, the *how*, the personal tone with which one has ultimate hope or fear or neither of these dispositions.

Some of these tones, or *hows,* might be labeled, in Procrustean fashion, as arrogance, despair, openness, presumption, Heideggerian *angst,* readiness, or closed-ness. They are not determinants of a hope's sequel, nor are they the whys of hope, though they are related to both.

Two examples may help. In Sophocles' *Oedipus the King,* Oedipus has his heart set on finding out who killed the king (who happened to be his father). His resolute pursuit seems rash, hubristic. To cleanse his city is an ultimate hope, but a hope – to simplify – pursued in a way similar to what Kierkegaard calls despair-at-being-oneself: defiance.[13] And in quite a different vein, Albee's George and Martha are, at the end of *Who's Afraid of Virginia*

13. *Sickness unto Death*, pp. 200-203.

Woolf?, quite without a recognizable future. But the tone of their talk together at the end has, beneath the knowing bitterness, some resignation, and within that, a wisp of a feeling that what has been need not be all that the days to come will see. George and Martha are not unseeing, but what they have seen of each other, grim as it is, is not the absolutely entire story.[14] These plays show us hope and its lack, but they also suggest *how* such disposition is held: by Oedipus, with a fixedness bordering on arrogance, and by George and Martha, with a bitter weariness that yet does not write *finis* to the relationship.

Here hopes and despairs can be identified, and what becomes of such dispositions is also evident. And we can easily enough gather why. But beneath these factors is what can only be termed tonalities of soul, and it does not surprise us that such is the real heart of the drama. It is such tonalities that govern what shall count as a why, and these in turn affect how one deals with one's ultimate disposition. In fact, some tonalities seem unqualifiedly to support, and others simply to inhibit, sound dealings with dispositions.

Fundamental hope

Of a number of possible fundamental orientations or attitudes, one of these is hope. In this preliminary characterization, some features of fundamental hope are presented as hypothesis, awaiting both sifting against the three philosophers' approaches and resolution in chapter 13. What follows is thus by way of proposal.

Fundamental hope is not aimed hope, with an objective or target. But it does have an orientation, and this is toward the future. (Fundamental hope's actuality requires aspects engaging the present, as well, as we shall see.)

The best preliminary characterization of fundamental hope is as an openness of spirit with respect to the future. This means that, in relation to an ultimate hope or its contrary, one does not deny evidence or mis-calculate it. One faces up to the evidence. But openness also means a sense of the limits of evidence. Opposed to it are probably such closures that move from a judgment that all the evidence is in and accounted for to the stance that therefore "I've got it made," or "Everything's going to be all right"; or, on the contrary, "There's no way out"; "I'm a goner." It knows the difference between "This cause is lost," and "All is lost." The tonality here – to be called hope – is thus distinguishable from optimism and presumption on the one hand and pessimism and despair on the other. Openness is openness of the self, and knows the difference between self and evidence. It is not sloppiness where careful reckoning is required. With respect to the

14. The movie version shades a bit towards optimism; in the play whatever hope there is is clearly hope-in-spite-of.

desiderative side of human existence, openness is not allied to denial of desires, but is on the side of and supports being in touch with them. But it does not entail capitulation to desires, nor is it content to take willful desire as the last and deepest impetus of the person. It is not on the side of the fixated, the cramped. But neither is it on the side of the flaccid. It is not fickleness where fidelity is asked. It does not usually stand alone, but is hemmed about by the tendency of the closures that metastasize, beyond their bearing on the objective ultimately desired, right into the very heart of one's self.

This sketch offers an orientation that some would find very appealing – so much so that they might without further ado declare that fundamental hope is sound.

The term "sound" will play a significant role in this essay; its conditions of applicability to ultimate hope will be set forth later,[15] but initial explanation is appropriate here. "Sound" is a medical metaphor; if hope is sound, it is kin to health. Whatever is sound is on the side of a good condition for people to be in, on the side of the genuinely human and the humanly good. As a health metaphor, "sound" obviously includes the *intra*personal. But it also suggests the *inter*personal, and the public, as in "sound planning," and "a sound economy." Whatever is sound is such that it is a high and fully human achievement, at home in and supportive of both the human mind and heart and the human world.

But *is* fundamental hope sound? If Pandora has only hope as her dowry, is it a blessing, or the final curse? Situations are conceivable where such hope's opposite, fundamental despair, is the appropriate stance.[16] But this large question must await this essay's end.

At this point, however, the essay turns to some philosophers who have formulated understandings of hope. Their contributions to hope analysis will be used as a proving ground for the approach advanced so far. The philosophers are Ernst Bloch, Immanuel Kant, and Gabriel Marcel. To them are directed these questions: Do they have notions of ultimate hope? Do they have a notion of fundamental hope in the sense advanced so far in this essay? Do they offer any clarification or modification of terminology? What do they have to say about the relationships between ultimate hope and fundamental hope?

15. Evaluating hope as *sound* vs. unsound is begun in chapter 13. The term "sound" encompasses positive evaluation of hope's conative and affective aspects as well as its cognitional aspect; features of the cognitional aspect could be evaluated as plausible or true. It is also fruitful to evaluate hopes as *justified* vs. unjustified: this approach of James Muyskens is commented on in chapter 13's note 20.

16. On the reasonableness of despair, see p. 147.

CHAPTER 10

ERNST BLOCH'S FULL HOPE: "EXPLOSIVE, TOTAL, AND INCOGNITO"

No contemporary philosophical study of human hope should ignore the work of Ernst Bloch. This is not just because his chef-d'oeuvre is a massive treatise on hope. Nor is it because his work is startlingly original; much of his approach is drawn from others. His writing, however, may well be the principal contemporary statement of a hope that is, in a thoroughgoing way, linked to social and historical processes. Many of those who analyse hope focus primarily on the individual, and proceed in ways primarily psychological and existential, with little account taken of history. The hopes Bloch analyses are the hopes of societies and cultures, and the axis of fulfillment is thoroughly historical. Because of such emphases, his thought is at least a healthy corrective to individualistic analyses; in many respects it is the more salutary approach.

But for the purposes of this essay, Bloch has another relevance. Atheism is an integral part of his critical exposition of hope, and thus he offers a position prima facie at odds with those who understand hope essentially within a theistic context. His atheism constitutes one pole of the issue to be joined at the end of this essay. But in the present context of ultimate and fundamental hope, Bloch offers another contribution – a kind of ultimate hope that gives depth to what has just been outlined.

What follows will be exposition of those features of Bloch's analysis that bear most directly upon the development of this essay. Critique of his thought, or, more precisely, critical utilization, is deferred to chapter 13, where Bloch and Kant and Marcel can be brought together for dialogical sifting of ultimate hope and fundamental hope. Bloch's thought is taken here as a paradigm or exemplar of the kind of philosophical reflection on hope that takes society and history seriously, and that situates hope in a basically Marxian atheism.[1]

A word should be said about Bloch's principal work, especially since this essay, while relying primarily on *Das Prinzip Hoffnung*, omits its development and jumps *in medias res*.[2] In some fifty-five chapters arranged

1. This essay therefore will not treat explicitly or systematically the unity and development of Bloch's thought, nor whether he is faithful to Marx. The chief themes of Bloch set forward here are central to his thought, and are not contradicted in a major way by other parts of his writings.

2. References are, respectively, to the text of Bloch's *Gesamtausgabe* (Frankfurt a. M.: Suhrkamp, 1959-) and to published English translations. Since some books in

in five parts, the work takes up an encyclopedic range of human dreams, arts, artifacts, and experience – music, furniture, satire, utopias, medicine, death, myths, marriage, and much more. The five parts, however, reveal the order of the work. The first and shortest gives an opening report of images called "Petty Daydreams." The important second part sets forth Bloch's foundational analysis in an exposition titled "Anticipatory Consciousness"; it gathers together reflections on human drives, dreams, and daydreaming, to bring to light what Bloch calls anticipatory consciousness, manifesting itself affectively as expectation-affect and cognitively as consciousness' utopian function. (This function will become our starting point.) Correlative in the world to this utopian function is the really-possible, and to set forth real possibility Bloch contrasts it with other kinds of possible. It is Marx who has grasped the essential structure of the really possible, and therefore a commentary on Marx's "Eleven Theses on Feuerbach" gives an initial degree of concreteness to a "mature" utopian function. The part closes with a sketch

English are translations of German editions which gathered chapters from several of his works, references to such translations indicate both the book's English title and, in parentheses, the title of the chapter. Thus, with the help of the bibliography, the translated chapter can be situated in the context of Bloch's entire corpus.

Where no reference to a published translation is given, the translation is my own.

Bloch's principal works bearing on hope are: *Atheism in Christianity: The Religion of the Exodus and the Kingdom*, trans. J.T. Swann (New York: Herder and Herder, 1972); *Atheismus im Christentum: Zur Religion des Exodus und des Reichs* (Frankfurt a. M.; Suhrkamp, 1968), and *Gesamtausgabe*, Bd. 14; *Man on His Own: Essays in the Philosophy of Religion*, trans. E.B. Ashton (New York: Herder and Herder, 1970), in which appear "Man's Increasing Entry into Religious Mystery," and "Religious Truth"; *On Karl Marx*, trans. John Maxwell (New York: Herder and Herder, 1971), in which appears "Karl Marx and Humanity: The Material of Hope"; *A Philosophy of the Future*, trans. John Cumming (New York: Herder and Herder, 1970); *Das Prinzip Hoffnung* (Frankfurt a. M.: Suhrkamp, 1959 & 1970), and *Gesamtausgabe*, Bd. 5; *Tübinger Einleitung in die Philosophie* (Frankfurt a. M.: Suhrkamp, 1970), and *Gesamtausgabe*, Bd. 13.

References to these are abbreviated as follows:

AC	*Atheismus im Christentum*; *Atheism* (AC 165/122 indicates respectively the German and the English text)
(KMH)	"Karl Marx and Humanity: Material of Hope"
(MIE)	"Man's Increasing Entry into Rel. Mystery"
MO	*Man on His Own*
OKM	*On Karl Marx*
PF	*Philosophy of the Future*
PH	*Das Prinzip Hoffnung*
(RT)	"Religious Truth"
TEP	*Tübinger Einleitung in die Philosophie*

of a few basic symbolic forms of anticipatory daydream.

The third part is transitional: in a survey touching clothes, travel, story, screen, and stage, Bloch depicts the kaleidoscope of human wishing, the variegated visions which, like fun-house mirrors, deform as they reflect. The fourth part explores wishes less illusory and more directed toward world improvement – extensive yet partial utopias based upon medicine, social planning, technology, architecture, discovery and colonization of new worlds, worlds both terrestrial and in the realms of painting, poetry, philosophical wisdom, and human liberation from burdens of work. Bloch labels this part "Construction."

The fifth and final part is "Identity: Wish-images of Fulfilled Moments," set against the separations and oppositions of human existence. In *Faust*, in images opposed to death, in religious mystery, in pursuit of the highest good, in the promise of Marxian humanization, there appear ever fuller and more accurate symbolic expressions of really possible and complete overcoming of all that separates humankind from each other and from nature.

The opus thus has a movement: from initial hints of hope and a laying of foundations, through images first deformed and then well-formed but inadequate, to images that present the core of sound hope. The movement is a pedagogic one: *spes* becomes *docta*, the utopian function becomes mature, *Hoffnung* becomes *begriffene*. What this means and how it comes about emerges in the exposition of Bloch that follows, an exposition selecting from Bloch according to the issues of this essay.[3]

Utopian function

So far in this essay, any ultimate hope has been assumed to be a hope for something definite. It may be diverse culturally and historically, but it must have some shape to it: the objective of any ultimate hope can in principle be differentiated from the objective of another ultimate hope. But the way in which Ernst Bloch conceives what this essay has termed "ultimate hope" suggests a shift in how what is ultimately hoped for – its objective – is conceived as definite.

In searching out the conception Bloch suggests for ultimate hope, we can take as a starting point a few of his formulations: "Every hope implies the highest good, incursive bliss"; "Even the weakest hope... essentially relates to the All"; "...positive expectation-affects [among which is hope] inevitably have the Paradisiacal as the unconditional feature of their intentional

3. A fuller conspectus of *Das Prinzip Hoffnung* is that of Thomas Wren, "The Principle of Hope," *Philosophy Today* 14 (Winter 1970): 250-58. See also Wayne Hudson, *The Marxist Philosophy of Ernst Bloch* (New York: St. Martin's Press, 1982).

object."[4] These formulations, abstract and general as they are, do present a linkage of some sort between every hope – presumably definite – and something prima facie highest or all-encompassing. Knowing the real import of such formulations is best achieved by proceeding through Bloch's understanding of what he calls *the utopian function of consciousness.*[5]

In using the term "utopian" Bloch aims to make room for a sense of utopia that is not necessarily pejorative. The route to such a sense begins with his analysis of daydreams; these are what give the clue to the reality of "anticipatory consciousness."

Day-dreams are not best understood, as Freud understood them, as a preparatory or fragmentary phase of night-dreams.[6] Both night-dreams and day-dreams deal with fulfillment of wishes. Those of night bear on fulfillments which are veiled and related to the past; but those of day are essentially anticipatory and inventive.[7] (This does not of course mean that day-dreams are reliable simply as they stand.) Day-dreams, Bloch maintains, differ from those of night in several significant ways: day-dreams are not subject to determinisms the way night-dreams are; they have present in them the ego or self in a way that night-dreams do not; they aim at improving the world they depict; they are always going somewhere, yet not in a closed sort of way.[8]

What reflection on day-dreams reveals is a second threshold of consciousness. The first and more familiar threshold leads to the preconscious and the unconscious on the side of the past; here are what is forgotten or repressed – what is no-longer-conscious. But Bloch submits that day-dreams indicate a threshold on the other side, leading into the *not-yet-conscious*. The

4. PH 122, 127 (italics omitted).

5. For purposes of this essay, the principal sources for understanding Bloch on utopia in general (not his discussion of particular utopian conceptions) are: PH (chap. 15) 129-203; TEP (chaps. 11-16) 11-153, most of which appears in PF 84-144. Among helpful studies are: Pierre Furter, "Utopia and Marxism according to Bloch," *Philosophy Today* 14 (Winter 1970): 236-49; and Arnold Metzger, "Utopia und Transzendenz" in the festschrift *Ernst Bloch zu ehren*, ed. Siegfried Unseld (Frankfurt a. M.: Suhrkamp, 1965), pp. 69-82.

6. PH 97ff. His citation of Freud is in *Vorlesungen zur Einführung in die Psychoanalyse, Gesammelte Schriften* 11 (London: Imago, 1940), pp. 387-88. (*Introductory Lectures on Psycho-Analysis*, Standard Edition 16, chap. 23, pp. 372-73).

7. PH 85.

8. PH 96-111. It seems that some night-dreams are also anticipatory, and some day-dreams lack the features that Bloch ascribes to them. But Bloch's sketch of day-dreams does, in the main, successfully point toward and bring into relief what he calls anticipatory consciousness.

terrain on this side – where what is new dawns – is relatively unexplored, yet can be recognized especially in youth, in times of change, and in human productivity. Bloch maintains that exploration of such terrain is crucial for understanding the type of cognition involved in hoping.[9]

But there is more to hoping than cognition, even if anticipatory. Another aspect emerges via Bloch's notion of *expectation-affect*. Hoping is, in one sense of these terms, an emotion or affect.[10] Affect is contrasted with both physical processes and organic corporeal states.[11] Hope is not a mood, though it is related to mood.[12] It has its roots in the one or many drives that lie deep in human reality, and, like other affects, hope stems from such drives (*Triebe*) when these are felt (*gefühlt*) as impulses (*Triebgefühle*). Since impulses are in some sense transitive ("Every impulse... is related to something outside itself"[13]), and hope is essentially an affect involving impulse, hope is essentially in some sense transitive.[14]

When Bloch categorizes affects – in order to situate hoping – he departs from more familiar classifications. He divides affects into fulfilled affects and expectation-affects.[15] The former are affects directed to what is present or near at hand, e.g., envy, greed, respect.[16] Expectation-affects look to what is not yet at hand. Among these latter Bloch lists dread, fear, hope, faith. With expectation-affects there is always something as yet uncertain about the outcome. Such uncertainty is rooted in the kind of future intended in expectation-affects. Fulfilled affects have no genuine future; what will be is

9. That hoping involves a type of cognition Bloch maintains throughout, as when he says at the beginning: "In such a manner the anticipatory function is active in the field of hope; the latter is therefore taken up *not only as affect* – as the opposite of fear (for, indeed, fear too can anticipate) – but *essentially as an act of orientation of a cognitive type* – and here the opposite is not fear but memory." PH 328, OKM 99.

10. PH 1.

11. Ph 116ff., 121ff.

12. Ibid.

13. PH 123.

14. Bloch also recognizes an easiness of spirit that ranges from organic condition to an *in*transitive emotion, e.g., a sanguine temperament (cf. PH 78). The more a person has a focused desire and not just an organic condition, the closer one is to having the hope-for-something that is Bloch's principal subject matter. This contrast between the organic and the realm of desiderative hope proper is an important contrast in Marcel. Marcel, however, describes a goal-oriented desire – i.e., transitive – on the *organic* level, while Bloch highlights the organic-*in*transitive.

15. The familiar classification of approach- and aversion-affects Bloch locates *within* the class of expectation-affects. Approach-affects indicate that we want something; aversion-affects, that we do not want it. PH 82.

16. PH 82.

already established. An expectation-affect looks to a genuine future, to what as yet is not.[17] Genuine future is not just a matter of that which we are not yet aware of; rather, included in the basis for that lack of awareness is reality which is itself unfinished.[18]

The distinction between genuine and ungenuine future founds Bloch's contrast between the Novum and the New (*das Neue*).[19] The vague general idea of "new" has been around for a long time, recognized in springtimes and first love and in the religious "I make all things new." But it took Marxism, Bloch maintains, to elucidate the difference between the New and the Novum. The New encompasses something which is essentially nothing more than the automatic emergence of virtualities in nature – a sort of acorn-to-oak image; or, it expresses what is essentially a return to the originating condition – the new is the Primum, Omega is Alpha; the path is a circle. But true Novum is not cyclic return; nor is it product of developmental process to which humanity is related only contemplatively. Novum – genuine future – is dependent on human will, and is a bringing together of material- or world-possibilities with human labor.[20]

While expectation-affect does have this distinctive sense of future connected with it, our present focus is on its relation to desiring.[21] Hope is

17. "All affects are related in time to the essential feature of time, i.e., to the mode of *future*; but, while fulfilled affects have only a non-genuine future, i.e., one in which objectively speaking nothing new happens, expectation-affects essentially imply a genuine future: a future of the Not-Yet, of that which objectively speaking has not yet come into being." PH 83.

18. What Bloch speaks of as *Noch-nicht-sein* (not-yet-being) is bipolar: subjectively it is *Noch-nicht-bewusst* (not-yet-consciously-known) and objectively it is *Noch-nicht-gewesen* (not-yet-having-been).

19. PH 230-35.

20. Ibid.

21. "Genuine future" is closely tied to Bloch's conception of the "really possible." It should be pointed out here, however, that a distinction should be made between (1) Bloch's presentation of hoping as expectation-affect with stress on the *affective-desiderative aspect*, and (2) his presentation of expectation-affect with stress on the "genuine future" connected with this notion. The latter connection is based upon a particular metaphysics of process and time. It channels interpretation of genuine hoping's fulfillment away from the model of repetition or return, and toward a model of superabundance, as these categories were developed earlier (chapters 2 and 8). In Bloch, the connection between hoping as expectation-affect and genuine future is such that a hope-for-return, because it lacks genuine future in its objective, is not really an expectation-affect at all, and therefore isn't really hope. But if Bloch's metaphysics is separated from the notion of expectation-affect – and I think it can be – the analysis of hope as an expectation-affect with roots in drive and orientation toward the not-at-hand can stand in its own right, and be recognized as parallel to the analysis of hoping

one of the expectation-affects. It is a positive expectation-affect, with fear as its negative counterpart.[22] If we bring together the elements of Bloch's analysis of hope as affect or emotion, we take it as one that is transitive, ordered to what is not at hand, and positive. Bloch's analysis is therefore basically the same as that carried out in Part I, where hoping is examined as emotion and as desiring.

We can now bring together the cognitive aspect that shows up as anticipatory consciousness and the affective aspect wherein hoping includes desiring. Bloch does just this when he maintains that when hoping appears not just as emotion, but as conscious with respect to its act and known with respect to its content, it becomes what he refers to as the utopian function of consciousness.

> And thus we've reached the point where hope, the expectation-affect proper to forward-oriented dreaming, no longer presents itself as simply an emotional state of the self... but shows up *conscious* and *known* as utopian function.[23]

Become at least inchoately self-aware and aware of one's objective, the person who hopes is the person who has a thrust toward utopia. (It should also be noted that utopian function is as well a thrust *against*: against all that is wretched in the present situation, against all forms of alienation; it arises in the face of "the darkness of the lived moment."[24]

But such awareness does not ipso facto make hoping sound.

Before turning to Bloch's treatment of *how* utopian hoping becomes sound, brief reference should be made to how consciousness' utopian function differs from other modalities that resemble it. Though utopian function seems closely related to, among other things, individual interests, ideology, pursuing an ideal, Bloch holds that utopian function can and should be distinguished from these. Utopian function cannot be reduced to or simply identified with imagining pursuit of one's individual interests or private desires, yet it is in touch with these, inasmuch as what is aimed at is a *social* good that affects all individuals.[25] And though this utopian function looks like ideology, because both envision what is not, nevertheless the utopian function, if true to itself, is a spur to action beyond the unmasking of ideologies.[26] Furthermore, the utopian function of consciousness should not be confused

as desiderative and as emotion in chapters 3 and 6.

22. Bloch also relates hope to anxiety, confidence, and despair. PH 121-28.
23. PH 163.
24. PH 167-68, 338ff.
25. PH 171-74.
26. PH 174-80.

with that function by which people hold ideals, especially insofar as the latter inspire, admonish, and guide, but fall short of actualization. The utopian function is a function attuned to the real, and is aimed not at approximation, but actualization.[27]

Utopian function is not universally sound, even when distinguished from its look-alikes. To have desire, to reach in consciousness forward towards Novum, to be aware of yearning and of yearning's direction, and even to do so in ways not reducible to self-interest, ideology, and ideal-holding, is still not enough. All this can still be wishful thinking.

> Mere wishful thinking has been discrediting utopias since history began, both in the realm of practical politics and in all the rest of the announcements of velleities – as though every utopia were abstract. Doubtlessly the utopian function in abstract utopianizing is only immaturely present, i.e., still predominantly lacking a solid subject, and lacking relation to the really possible.[28]

Bloch thus introduces the manner in which utopian function can be brought from the abstract and immature to the concrete – through definite personal agency in touch with the really-possible.

"Really-possible" is not a casual phrase for Bloch. He distinguishes and contrasts the really-possible that enters into mature utopianism from three other types of possible, and his intent can be seen by surveying these four senses or levels of "possible."[29] The first he calls the "formally possible."[30] This is the realm of whatever can in some respect be thought.[31] Different from this abstract possible is the possible according to knowledge, the epistemic possible or the possible which is "objective after the manner of things."[32] This sense of possible is gradated according to the relative incompleteness of our *knowledge* of factual conditions. Differing from this what-we-know-as-possible is a third: the objectively or factually possible.[33] The objectively possible is gradated, not according to incompleteness in our knowledge of

27. PH 189-99.
28. PH 164.
29. PH 258-88: Kapitel 18, "Die Schichten der Kategorie Möglichkeit."
30. "Das formal Mögliche." In understanding and labeling Bloch's senses of "possible" I am indebted to Pierre Furter's "Utopia and Marxism According to Bloch," pp. 240-41.
31. "Something which is 'possible-for-thought,' a *formal* capability; for 'possible-for-thought' comprises everything that in general can be thought as standing in relation." PH 259.
32. "Das sachlich-objektiv Mögliche."
33. "Das sachhaft-objektgemäss Mögliche."

factual conditions, but according to incompleteness in the factual conditions themselves.[34] The inadequacy of even this notion of the objectively or factually possible is that it derives solely from the side of "object." The subject merely recognizes it, and counts on it, but does not influence it. We can put these three senses of "possible" in other words. The formally possible is that which is not precluded by thought alone. The epistemically possible is that which is not precluded by what we know. The factually possible is that which is not precluded by the way things are. "The way things are" means conditions obtaining among objects, in relation to which persons – insofar as persons are contrasted with objects – stand only as spectators.

What Bloch points out as the sense of "possible" germane to mature utopian consciousness is the "objectively-really-possible."[35] This conception does not assume – as the third sense of objectively or factually possible does assume – a single face or pole or cutting edge to process. The notion derives from a grounding in Bloch's Marx-inspired understanding of matter along the lines of left-wing Aristotelianism – matter as active, not just passive. But, dialectically understood, matter as capability has *two* faces or poles: the partial conditionality of objects in nature, and the partial conditionality or lack of conclusiveness of humanity working in history.[36] The lack of fully determining conditions for either nature or humanity considered separately yields a notion of possibility that derives from the *interaction* of these two faces of process.[37] Mature utopian consciousness does not just contemplate the indeterminacy of natural and historical process; it participates, collaborates.[38] It collaborates; it does not uniquely determine. Bloch considers inadequate any notion of possibility which either stresses agencies in the world of objects (where these are contrasted with but are unaffected by an agent-subject) or stresses agencies of subject(s) alone. His model is interagency of subject and object. In stressing interaction rather than any monopolar factually possible, Bloch follows a lead he has seen in Marx.

34. "But the *factually* possible that now emerges is constituted differently from this known-as-fact possible. The difference obtains insofar is it's a matter, not of our knowledge of something, but of the something itself as capable of being this or that. The factually possible stems not from insufficient *knowledge*, but from the insufficiently developed grounds of condition. It therefore designates not a more or less adequate *knowledge* of conditions, but rather it designates the more or less adequately conditioning in the *objects themselves and in their situations*." PH 264.

35. "Das objektiv-real Mögliche."

36. PH 271ff.

37. Thomas Wren has perceptively observed that Bloch's notion of partial conditionality only postpones – I'd say relocates – issues of determinism. Wren, "The Principle of Hope," p. 251.

38. PH 166.

> At this point [his third thesis on Feuerbach] Marx is waging war on two fronts: against mechanistic environmental theory, which tends ultimately to fatalism, with regard to existence, and against the idealistic subject theory, which culminates in ''putschism,'' or at least in excessive optimism with regard to activity.[39]

The dialectically really-possible is as much worked out as it is recognized; it is in fact recognized in the working out. But a notional beginning, a conceptual orientation toward the really possible is available, Bloch maintains, through the writings of Marx. Therefore *Das Prinzip Hoffnung* can have a movement to it, even on the level of theory. In this work Bloch takes Marx's ''Eleven Theses on Feuerbach'' as his initial ground, and then moves into and through a survey of utopias misleading and partial, into those forms of hope and utopian consciousness where genuine overcoming of human alienations is heralded.[40] But such overcoming is only heralded. Movement toward its actualization takes place not in thought but in the concrete; hence its presentation even as sound hope is as direction and intimation, not as floor plan.[41]

This general way in which the really-possible is grasped is the clue to understanding Bloch's phrase *docta spes* (learned hope). When he expands this phrase, he does so as *docta spes, begriffene Hoffnung, or dialektisch-materialistisch begriffene Hoffnung*.[42] Hope is not learned just theoretically, and *begriffene* is best rendered close to its root sense, ''to grasp.'' The import then of Bloch's label is: hope that has learned, hope that is *engagé* in terms of dialectical materialism. His thrust is against a hoping that is complacent and naive, and is on the side of one that is active and comes to grips with world process in mutual involvement understood in Marxian terms.

39. PH 301, OKM 71. The idealistic subject theory sounds much like Fichte; we shall look at him in our treatment of Kant.

40. See pp. 67-69 for a conspectus of *Das Prinzip Hoffnung*'s movement. The final stage, ''Identity,'' will receive attention in the following pages' discussion of Full Hope: Explosive, Total, Incognito.

41. ''Bloch believes that Marxism, which he sees as a critique of pure reason, must be supplemented with a critique of practical reason. Now in fact, the critique of practical reason of Marxism has not yet been written, it will never be *written*, at any rate not with ink and paper. Our critique of practical reason is the praxis of Socialism.'' Thus Manfred Buhr rebukes Bloch for wanting more theory when praxis is needed. But others have thought Bloch himself deficient even in theory, especially in areas of pedagogical and political applications. See Furter, ''Utopia and Marxism,'' pp. 246-47, for such criticism, and for references to criticism by Ludz and Habermas. Buhr's ''A Critique of Ernst Bloch's Philosophy of Hope'' appears in English in *Philosophy Today* 14 (Winter 1970): 259-71; citation is from p. 270.

42. PH 5, 8.

Full hope: "explosive, total, incognito"

The shape of hope that has become *docta* is a full hope. The last chapters of *Das Prinzip Hoffnung* offer a silhouette of comprehensive hope that suggests some changes in the conception of ultimate hope employed so far in this essay, i.e., superordinate but yet definite, distinguishable from other hopes.

Access to Bloch's notion of ultimate hope comes through his evaluation of religion. He goes beyond usual interpretations of Marx in deriving from Marx the view that religion is not just the opium of the people, but also the way they cry out.[43] The outcry is against their present condition, and for a blessed future; and what is expressed here is a hope that is total.[44] Granted that it must be "inherited" through Marxism,[45] it is still the same vision – explosive, total, and incognito.

Explosive

"Eye hath not seen, nor ear heard, neither have entered into the heart of man, the things which God hath prepared for them that love him" (1 Cor 2:9). No ordinary future is the one pledged by God. Its scope does not fall short of "You shall be as God."[46] In these shapes of the message Bloch finds a longed-for future that shames the bourgeois vision of Feuerbach. Feuerbach was right in holding religion to be really about humanity's achieving its essence, but he made that essence too small.

> From heaven, Feuerbach returned the religious contents to man, in the sense that man is not created in God's image but God in man's, or rather in that of man's current ideal prototype. This makes God vanish completely as the world's creator, but it gains a vast creative region in man, a region of fantastic riches and fantastic illusions, in which the divine amounts to the hypostasized human wish picture of the highest rank. Feuerbach equates this "wish theory of religion" with "anthropologization of religion," or with abolishing the "celestial duplication of man." Feuerbach, of course, knows man, the subject duplicated in religion, only as he has so far appeared and is now given, and he knows this form only as the abstractly stable one of the so-called human species. Lacking from his view is the historical-social ensemble of the human "type" of

43. PH 1520, MO (MIE) 212. See also, in MO, Bloch's essay "Religious Truth" (extracted from TEP 180ff.).

44. Total hope is in its genesis biblical: "The total expansion of hope that we find in humanism came into the world only in one form – that of the Bible." TEP 184, MO (RT) 116.

45. PH 1414, MO (MIE) 163.

46. Genesis 3:5. Bloch uses this expression often, e.g., PH 1504, MO (MIE) 202; TEP 183, MO (RT) 114-15; PH 1556.

> the moment; lacking above all is its inconclusiveness. The flatness of the "homo bourgeois," which Feuerbach absolutized, can definitely not accommodate the contents of religion, no more than the bourgeois has ever been the subject from which the wealth of divine images would come forth. Least of all can Feuerbach's statically extant subject accommodate the religious images that explode the status, the chiliastic ones of "Behold, I make all things new," and of the kingdom.[47]

Against Feuerbach's flatness Bloch sets not only the *dis*continuities and elevations in humanity's religiously imaged future – the new, the leap, the Kingdom[48] – but, with and beyond Feuerbach, the very attributes of God. "Totally Other," therefore – now that theology is recognized as anthropology – becomes the adequate measure of humanity's hope. "The crux remains that '*total Otherness' applies to the eventual human projections of religion also*. It takes total Otherness to give the appropriate measure of depth to everything that has been longed for in deifying man."[49] And *Ens perfectissimum* no longer denominates God, but points towards the goal of human longing.[50] Religion recognized and mature is, Bloch maintains, a messianism without God, "*not a static and thus apologetic mythus, but a human-eschatological and thus explosively posited messianism*. Therein alone... lives the *sole hereditary substrate religion can signify*: to be a *total hope*, and an explosive one."[51]

What the religious vision has offered, and Marxism corrected, is a hope not limited to vulgar domesticated anticipations, but one which ever shows the marks of "going beyond the limited."[52] Such going beyond is not according to an unfolding of virtualities contained in the process from the beginning – the acorn-to-oak model;[53] *dis*continuity is the hallmark of the hope that is genuine.

Total

Religion brings to light total hope, "the *totum of a hope that relates the whole world to a whole perfection*."[54] Marxism inherits this total hope as

47. PH 1517, MO (MIE) 209-10.
48. PH 1407, 1408, 1411, 1413, 1493, 1502-04, respectively in MO (MIE) 156, 157, 159-60, 161, 191, 200-202; PH 1411; AC 86/57.
49. PH 1407, MO (MIE) 155.
50. PH 1413-14, MO (MIE) 161-63.
51. PH 1404, MO (MIE) 152.
52. "Grenzüberschreitung" ("going beyond – overstepping – limits") is a favorite classification for those hopes Bloch sees as more truly prophetic.
53. See PH 1626, OKM (KMH) 41-42.
54. Ph 1403, MO (MIE) 151; and cf. PH 1415-16, MO (MIE) 163-64.

hope for the "*humanum*."[55] The *humanum* is often expressed negatively – to overcome alienation, "to abrogate all relationships in which man is degraded, enslaved, abandoned, and wretched."[56] Our present focus is not on the negative expression, but on "all": full hope is all-encompassing; it looks toward what is, to employ Bloch's colorful phrase, "not limited to such trains of purposes as are already surveyable and, so to speak, locally patriotic."[57]

Incognito

The problem is to discern *content* for such a total hope. One of its classic formulations is "the highest good," and Bloch devotes a chapter to exploring what this phrase means.[58] He takes notice of the diversity of ideals, often adopted without question from the social context. But he maintains that these would not serve as models if they were not understood to be related to a need for the best life, and directed toward the most perfect form of that life. Prior to adoption of any of the ideologically and historically shaped goals, there is a "fundamental act" (*Grundakt*) of orientation to a final total goal, the highest good.[59] Bloch discovers in history, and more or less accepts, a threefold formal characterization of the highest good: permanence, unity, and ultimate purpose.[60] But such is still only formal; content is not yet at hand.

We do have, as a sort of content, *images*. Bloch finds two images that are most powerful. The Buddha presents the highest good in the form of complete and restful peace. The kingdom of God proffers the highest good in the form of life, life at its fullest.[61] Such images Bloch terms "witnesses," "ciphers," and "symbols."[62] Even the Marxist vision is not more than a cipher.[63] There

55. PH 1608, OKM (KMH) 22-23; PH 152lf., MO (MIE) 213f.

56. PH 1604, OKM (KMH) 18, quoting from the Introduction to Marx's *Contribution to the Critique of Hegel's Philosophy of Right*.

57. PH 1408, MO (MIE) 157.

58. PH, Kapitel 54: "Der letzte Wunschinhalt und das höchste Gut."

59. PH 1556.

60. Ph 1559. Bloch must then wrestle with problems of how a processive view of reality can be reconciled with the finality of the highest good, and how nature and human will are related in the highest good – a discussion of Kant which we shall join presently. Bloch's concern with problems arising from the Marxist view of man as *homo faber* is less central for our essay. The final or terminal character of the hoped-for, with the Kantian issue of nature and will, re-appear in later discussion of the historical-transhistorical and the subject-object frameworks of hope.

61. PH 1600.

62. Ph 1586, 1591f. "Cipher" suggests not only mystery, but also, in the last analysis, dispensability. "Witness" connotes something substantial in its own right, albeit pointing or leading beyond.

63. This seems a fair conclusion from PH's last chapter; yet this cipher is not

are, of course, ciphers or witnesses which mislead, and others which do not. But there is as well a kind of cipher or symbol which is "real." A real-cipher or real-symbol is one which not only points in a direction but also *participates* in the realizing of a goal. It is a function of words to express, well or poorly, the real-symbol; this latter, however, real in itself, has also a latent dimension: it holds hidden something yet to be.[64] Attaining real-symbols does bring satisfaction, but also opens up a broader quest.[65] Real-symbols participate in a goal which is explosive and total inasmuch as they both have substance of their own and yet inaugurate and promote actualization of a goal yet hidden.

The goal is not clear; all we have are images. What it is that full hope has aimed at has not shown itself. *Deus absconditus* is now *homo* but no less *absconditus*: "It does not yet appear what we shall be" (1 John 3:2). Bloch's word for our total but veiled future is Incognito. It is a future undecided: it can be Nothingness, or All.[66] The All has many faces: "Happiness, freedom, non-alienation, the golden age, the land flowing with milk and honey, the eternal feminine, the trumpet call in Fidelio, and the Christ pattern of the resurrection day afterwards – there are so many and diverse witnesses and pictures, yet all have but one focus, which speaks to us eloquently, notwithstanding its silence."[67] This ever inchoate character, veiled and not yet decided, Bloch recognizes "...where the best remains only a fragment, and where every end again and again only becomes a means to serve the as yet completely invisible, final, and ultimate goal, which is as yet unavailable in and for itself."[68]

This sketch of Bloch's conception of ultimate hope is enough to convey that he takes such hope to have, beyond hope's diversity of expression and even of "real-symbol," a basic unity. At various points throughout *Das Prinzip Hoffnung* he explored the shapes that unity might take – as fulfillment of humanity's principal drive for self-preservation and self-expansion,[69] or as what is recognized as the humanization of nature and the naturalization of man.[70] In the context of his contrast between the New and the Novum, he took the latter as plural, and saw them ordered to one Ultimum.[71] We noted

therefore other than leading in the right direction. Cf. for example PH 1628, OKM (KMH) 44.

64. PH 1592.
65. PH 1600.
66. PH 1550, MO (MIE) 240; see also PH 1533, MO (MIE) 225.
67. PH 1627, OKM (KMH) 43.
68. PH 1628, OKM (KMH) 44.
69. PH 10, 72ff., 84ff.
70. E.g., PH 277.
71. PH 232-35.

earlier his assertion that every hope implies the highest good, incursive bliss, that it is essentially related to the All, and that it has the Paradisiacal as the unconditional feature of its intentional object.[72] Basically, different shapes of hope are aimed at from a stance that has only one single orientation; there is a fundamental act oriented toward the best as a totality, an act that is prior to desiring any objective, however broad or narrow. Bloch goes so far as to say that the best is in the last analysis the only thing willed.[73]

This sounds like a commonplace, but its special sense in Bloch can be fleshed out if we add to it what we have seen so far. This basic movement toward the best does not of itself appear, but it is the condition for hope for any objective. Any objective is hoped for as a realization of what is held to be the best possible. What is held to be the best possible has many shapes, some which mislead and some which lead aright. Approach to those that lead aright has become manifest through religion, insofar as religion has presented shapes of hope which are explosive and total albeit incognito. Marxism has given to such shapes their true human scope. But because the shapes are also veils, even in Marxism, achievement of such is not only an actualization of something good but also a beginning of something better.[74] In this way such shapes are symbols or ciphers which participate in what they point to – a goal which is all-encompassing yet still hidden. These real-symbols, despite their diversity, all lead Odyssey-like to the one discovery of both homeland and self.[75]

The voice which Bloch adds to dialogue on ultimate hope expresses the following concerns. Ultimate hope is best approached as aimed at a social objective, located in history, rather than as an individual's objective realizable only outside history. Such hope is better advised if it is in some way total, that is, its objective is all-encompassing. That totality is not however readily circumscribable; its dimensions are not the pedestrian ones of current experience. Its dimensions are in a way open-ended, in a progression thoroughly historical. We find in Bloch an exposition that is pedagogical, unfolding symbols of the future and analyses of utopian consciousness, and implying that anything less than full hope is a deficient hope (though such

72. See pp. 69-70.

73. PH 1552.

74. This suggests comparison with the notions of embodiment or foretaste described in chapter 9. Bloch's equivalent concept joins mysticism and revolutionary praxis. On the former, see PH 1534-40, MO (MIE) 226-32.

75. Cf. "But even the cosmic-*plurality* of real-symbols taken together point to that Ithaca where the Incognito of the traveller comes to an end, as does that of the destination as well." PH 1593.

lesser forms do have weight insofar as they bear upon the highest good). Moreover, a deficient objective vitiates the very act of hoping: one does not do sound hoping if what one aims at is unsound. Bloch's conviction is that the subjective and the objective are not estranged: the really-possible and (veiled) highest good meshes with human cognition, anticipation, affectivity, and desiring at their best.

CHAPTER 11

IMMANUEL KANT AND THE HIGHEST GOOD

Introduction

We now turn to Immanuel Kant, with the same intent as governed our examination of Bloch. What does Kant offer as an understanding of ultimate hope and fundamental hope? Of the three questions enunciated in the *Critique of Pure Reason*, it is the third, "What may I hope?" that frames our subject.[1] Not all of Kant's writings are under review. Our investigation proceeds in three phases, roughly corresponding to three of Kant's works, and yielding three somewhat different presentations of the objective of hope. His treatise *Perpetual Peace* presents as a sound hope civil peace; the *Critique of Practical Reason* presents the individual's highest good; and *Religion Within the Limits of Reason Alone* suggests that ultimate hope is for the ethical commonwealth and kingdom of God.[2] In each case we are dealing with only that hope which is *sound*. To ask "What may I hope?" is to ask neither the de facto question "For what do I hope," nor the question of moral obligation, "What ought I to hope for." What I *may* hope for is that which I am entitled to or justified in desiring because it is possible. Indeed, much of Kant's efforts in dealing with hoping's objective is devoted to explaining

1. A 805-806/B 833-834. Elsewhere Kant sums up the three questions "What can I know?" "What ought I to do?" and "What may I hope?" in a fourth: "What is man?" *Kants gesammelte Schriften* 9:25.

2. References to Kant are given to the Prussian Academy edition *Kants gesammelte Schriften* (Berlin: Georg Reimer, 1902 –). *Zum ewigen Frieden* is in vol. 8; *Kritik der praktischen Vernunft* is in vol. 5; *Religion innerhalb der Grenzen der blossen Vernunft* is in vol. 6.

References are given as well to English translations: *Perpetual Peace* is cited from Lewis White Beck's translation in the Library of Liberal Arts edition (New York: Bobbs-Merrill, 1957). *The Critique of Practical Reason* is Beck's translation, Library of Liberal Arts edition (New York: Bobbs-Merrill, 1956). *Religion Within the Limits of Reason Alone*, translated by Theodore M. Greene and Hoyt H. Hudson, is cited from the Harper Torchbooks edition (New York: Harper & Row, 1960).

References to these are abbreviated as follows:

CPrR	*Critique of Practical Reason*
KpV	*Kritik der praktischen Vernunft*
PP	*Perpetual Peace*
RGV	*Religion innerhalb der Grenzen der blossen Vernunft*
RLR	*Religion Within the Limits of Reason Alone*
ZeF	*Zum ewigen Frieden*

how it is that what is proposed is not illusory. Explaining what makes such hope not impossible, by pointing to what it is that is capable of effecting what is hoped for, and how we can recognize this, is one of Kant's principal cares.

Hope for perpetual peace

The first phase of our inquiry into Kant's sense of ultimate hope takes up his 1795 treatise on *Perpetual Peace*. The peace of which he speaks is not interior and psychological, nor is it ethical. It can obtain within and between states, and is essentially legal and political; its opposite is war. Hope for such peace is a hope termed in this essay "societal"; it obtains not just in people's hearts nor just in face-to-face relationships, but between groups ordered in civil societies.

Kant holds that such civil peace is possible, and, indeed, that it is in a way destined to be. But this conviction does not stem from some Pollyannaish view of human nature. Kant fully acknowledges civil and moral evil in people: the natural state of human beings is war;[3] and perpetual peace is to be secured without the moral improvement of human beings and indeed despite their hostility.[4]

Kant must establish that civil peace, as something more than just a truce between wars (that is, "perpetual"), is as a matter of fact possible, even in the face of human disposition toward evil. If man is to recognize an obligation to enact the articles Kant formulates in the corpus of his treatise, the goal must be shown to be not chimerical. And the goal is not chimerical because *nature guarantees perpetual peace*.

> The guarantee of perpetual peace is nothing less than that great artist, nature (*natura daedala rerum*). In her mechanical course we see that her aim is to produce a harmony among men, against their will and indeed through their discord.[5]

"Nature" here is not contrasted with human beings, but includes personal agents.[6] Furthermore, it is "nature" that yields the best understanding of peace's guarantor, rather than "divine providence"; the latter Kant avoids because it goes beyond the limits of human reason.[7]

The manner in which nature effects civil peace is basically through

3. ZeF 348-49, PP 10.
4. ZeF 360-61, 365-66, PP 24, 29-30.
5. ZeF 360, PP 24.
6. See ZeF 361, note, PP 24, note 1.
7. "The use of the word 'nature' is more fitting to the limits of human reason and more modest than an expression indicating a providence unknown to us." ZeF 362, PP 26.

arrangements of equilibrium between selfish competing interests within and between nations. What is required of human beings is that which arranges the balance – "the good organization of the state (which does lie in man's power)."[8] The substance of Kant's essay proposes articles of law that would secure such organization. Nature herself will maintain such separation of nations as is prerequisite to international balance. And the expanding "spirit of commerce" will secure the world against outbreaks of violence in war. The outline and sample processes Kant mentions permit him to conclude: "In this manner nature guarantees perpetual peace by the mechanism of human passions."[9] The process may be long or short, but civil peace is inevitable.[10] The practice of virtue, while not necessary to the process – and not likely – does contribute to the process and does secure the goal of perpetual peace.[11]

The way we can know the grounds for peace's possibility is not observation or inference, but "from a practical standpoint... the concept is dogmatic and its reality is well established."[12] This practical standpoint consists of two elements: analogical application to nature of human purposiveness, and confirmation and some empirical establishment of such sense of direction through illustrations of how nature moves us willy-nilly toward perpetual peace.[13]

In the context of Kant's larger concerns, we can note that human beings have a *duty* to make real the social order of public law that would secure perpetual peace.[14] Obligation, however, comes from the moral law; it is not derived from the goal of such peace.[15] The goal is not chimerical (even though its attainment may be in the form of endless approximation) because there are processes of nature by which even evil intent – even the intent of devils! – can be turned to establishing civil peace. Inasmuch as a person can have practical certainty[16] of the advent of perpetual peace (and assuming he counts it desirable), he may *hope* for civil perpetual peace, whether he does his duty by enacting requisite civil law, or not.

Kant's treatment of civil perpetual peace yields the following conclusions pertinent to this essay: the goal of perpetual peace may be hoped for because

8. ZeF 366, PP 30.

9. ZeF 368, PP 32. See ZeF 365-68, PP 29-32, for Kant's exposition of the factors effecting peace.

10. ZeF 365, 367, PP 29, 31. Kant also suggests inevitable triumph of *moral* good over moral evil, albeit only through a slow process (ZeF 379, PP 45).

11. ZeF 378, PP 43.

12. ZeF 362, PP 26.

13. ZeF 362ff., 365-68, PP 25f., 29-32.

14. ZeF 386, PP 53. See also ZeF 349, note, PP 10, note 1.

15. ZeF 377, PP 42.

16. Not predictive theoretical certainty. Cf. ZeF 368, PP 32.

it is not chimerical; its eventuality in history is guaranteed by processes of nature (perhaps assisted by human ordering) not subject to frustration by human evil intent. Such processes are practically certain, based upon insight into nature's purposiveness and observation of some patterns in history. What is required of human beings by the moral law, however, is the legal ordering; achieving the goal is not the morally acceptable motive.

This sketch of Kant's presentation on civil peace, besides suggesting questions and comparisons for later sifting, suggests immediately: Is such peace an *ultimate* hope? In one sense of course it is: there is no obvious reason why a person could not have, as a hope superordinate to all others, hope for civil perpetual peace. To ask about any hope's being ultimate is to ask whether it *can* be ultimate, or whether it *is* de facto held by some or all as ultimate hope; it is another question whether it is proposed as a legitimate or sound ultimate hope (*May* I hope for this?). In the context of *Perpetual Peace*, i.e., that of civil strife and historical progress, Kant assumes that civil peace is desirable and proposes what human beings should do to work for it – a "should" stemming from the moral law – and he allays fears that the desired outcome is not possible. Because such peace is possible, it is legitimate to hope for it. Therefore *Perpetual Peace* allows us to say that hope for civil peace, *if* actually ultimate, is also *sound* because it is guaranteed by nature.

Hope for the highest good as the individual's deserved happiness

"Meaning in history is to be found not only in the reaching of a goal, but also in the preservation of a form: the human form of man qua moral being."[17] This remark of Michel Despland introduces the second phase of our survey of Kant on hope, and presents a further principle for consideration in any doctrine of hope: something other than the goal alone is important. This other element is the moral character of a person. A person may reach her or his goal; a person may be moral. But does one element guarantee the other, so that a moral person succeeds, or a successful person is by that very fact moral?

Though others might equate being moral and reaching a goal, Kant held for their mutual irreducibility; in his terms, virtue is one thing and happiness another, and the advent of one does not necessarily mean the presence of the other. But the concept of the conjunction of the two is the idea of the highest good, and the actual advent of deserved happiness to one who is virtuous is the actualization of the highest good. Kant's treatment of the highest good makes it a prime candidate for that human hope which is ultimate, and to an

17. Michel S. Despland, *Kant on History and Religion, with a Translation of Kant's "On the Failure of all Attempted Philosophical Theodicies"* (Montreal and London; McGill-Queen's University Press, 1973), p. 281.

examination of his doctrine we now turn, taking as the principal text his *Critique of Practical Reason*.

Virtue

The highest good is a concept that is a synthesis of two concepts, virtue and happiness. But at the outset, let us take a detour; let us suppose that *virtue alone* constitutes the highest good. In doing so we depart from Kant's explicit position, but we intend to follow out Kant's analysis in other respects, and we shall thereby see some key issues in his approach. From the point of view of this essay, the principal reason for this detour is that hope requires a sense that its objective is possible, and because Kant steadfastly maintains that virtue is *within the power* of the moral agent (while happiness is not), it is plausible to entertain the notion that ultimate hope (along *some* Kantian lines) is *hope-for-virtue*. The detour will prove to be a dead end, yet one not without significant vistas.

Some distinctions must be made with regard to virtue. To choose in accordance with and out of respect for the moral law is to be moral. But morality is of two types. Holiness is moral choice in its perfection; it is not to be found as actual among finite rational beings in the world. The morality appropriate to finite rational beings is *virtue*, which is "moral disposition in conflict" between the poles of sensuous inclination and pure rational principle.[18] Yet complete accord with and perfect respect for the moral law remain ever obligatory for finite beings, and, given the human condition, the obligation to perfection becomes in the concrete the obligation to *endless progress* in virtue.[19]

Because persons are obliged to endless progress in virtue, that which such obligation requires is as actual as the obligation itself; hence we arrive at *endless duration* – immortality – as a postulate of pure practical reason, required for the obligation to be what it is.[20] To recognize endless progress

18. KpV 84, CPrR 87.

19. KpV 122, 128-29, CPrR 126-27, 133.

20. KpV 122ff., CPrR 126ff. It is worth making an observation about immortality and body and the arena of human virtue. There is a problem that arises from the notion of endless duration or immortality – the problem of the relation between such duration and death. If duration is the arena for virtue, and moral choice as virtue is under conditions of conflict between sensuous inclination and rational principle, then it seems difficult to conceive of such duration, and choice of principle over inclination, except in terms of space and time and body. Virtue therefore seems to require body. But death seems to affect body. Though it is unfair to press one context with another context's questions, it does seem in Kant that death not only has no sting, it doesn't even constitute enough threshold to stub one's toe on. But perhaps it suffices – if not to solve this problem, at least to situate it – to recall that Kant distinguishes between

in virtue as obligatory is to assume the requisite endless duration, and if one acknowledges such an assumption, one may hope for endless progress in virtue. Past progress in virtue gives another basis for the hope,[21] and with hope for endless progress goes hope for immortality.[22] But all of this depends on a context of understanding that one's own powers are sufficient to make such progress actual.

Is it all that unambiguous in Kant that virtue lies within a human being's own powers? Certainly it is his essential position that finite rational beings are capable of self-determination in accord with and out of respect for the moral law, and that therefore they are of course capable in themselves of being virtuous. But in *Religion Within the Limits of Reason Alone*, under the pressure of taking seriously people's bent toward evil and the difficulty of change of heart, plus their existence as social beings, Kant offers remarks that have some small but nonetheless countervailing thrust against the autonomy at the heart of his foundations for ethics. There are two contexts involved here, that of God's grace, and that of people helping each other in society – "vertical" and "horizontal" qualifications on autonomy. The second context will be taken up in the third phase of this discussion of Kant. Regarding God's help (grace) and human virtue, Kant has a principal position and it is clear enough: God's help is possible but unknowable,[23] and rational human beings are responsible for what is in their own power, their own efforts towards virtue and their own moral dispositions.[24] But there is a hint at a kind of trust – in Kant's preference for the man "who trusts without knowing how that for which he hopes will come to pass" over the man "who absolutely insists on knowing the way in which man is released from evil."[25] Such trust is not a *knowledge*, that is, an estimation based on past events. Furthermore, there is his speaking obliquely of God's help, stressing that after first making himself

anthropomorphisms that are dogmatic-constitutive and those that are symbolic-regulative; immortality involves anthropomorphisms of the symbolic-regulative type (Cf. A 697-701/B 725-729, and RGV 168-69, RLR 156-57). But there is also a hint that practical reason overcomes this contrast (KpV 135, CPrR 140).

21. KpV 123, CPrR 128; RGV 68-69, RLR 62.
22. KpV 128, CPrR 133.
23. RGV 174, RLR 162.
24. RGV 44-45, RLR 40-41.
25. RGV 172, RLR 159-60. The last chapter of Allen W. Wood's fine study, *Kant's Moral Religion* (London and Ithaca: Cornell University Press, 1970), argues strongly that Kant not only does have a place for trust in God's forgiving grace, but even that "The doctrine of divine grace is necessary to Kant's resolution of the first antinomy of practical reason, and it must therefore be accorded, along with freedom, immortality, and God's moral governance of the world, the status of a *postulate of practical reason*" (p. 248).

worthy to receive it, a person must "lay hold of this aid"; aid here may be either removal of hindrances or positive assistance.[26] Such remarks are exceptions to the strict moral autonomy that governs Kant's approach to virtue. But they are nevertheless hints, even in the context of virtue, of a kind of assistance or trust that qualifies what effects virtue, and therefore would also qualify what serves as basis for hope for virtue.

Deserved happiness

The detour just concluded supposed the plausibility of taking just hope for virtue as ultimate hope in a Kantian context, on the strength of Kant's essential position that it is virtue that is possible through man's own power. Now we return to his explicit position, and examine his doctrine of the highest good as happiness accorded to virtue. Our goal is to grasp what is implied in taking hope for the highest good as the sound ultimate hope in Kant.

The highest good is in the first instance an idea; it is the outcome of pure finite reason in its practical or moral use seeking unconditional totality.[27] The highest good is the name for the unconditional totality of the *object* of pure practical reason.[28] It expresses the horizon toward which practical reason pushes. Direction of such reason is determined by the moral law. But practical reason cannot be indifferent to the goal of such direction, and its effort not to be so yields the concept of the highest good.

How this is so can be seen through taking Kant's treatment of happiness as starting point (since in other contexts happiness often steps forward as candidate for the goal of reason used practically). By happiness Kant means the satisfaction of all desires, the condition where everything goes according to wish and will.[29] Characteristic of this condition is consciousness of such satisfaction, or pleasure.[30] Happiness as an idea is a totality, "the satisfaction of all inclinations as a sum."[31] The happiness of which Kant speaks is one's own individual happiness, not some general weal. Because happiness encompasses satisfaction of all an individual's desires, and desires differ from individual to individual,[32] any conceptual shift from happiness in the abstract

26. RGV 44, RLR 40.

27. KpV 113, CPrR 117.

28. KpV 108, CPrR 112. It is not the unconditional ground of the will; the moral law is such a ground.

29. A 806/B 834; KpV 124, CPrR 129.

30. KpV 22, CPrR 20.

31. *Grundlegung zur Metaphysik der Sitten*, *Kants gesammelte Schriften* 4:399. In the translation *Groundwork of the Metaphysic of Morals* by H.J. Paton (New York: Harper & Row, 1964) (hereafter, referred to as Paton), p. 67.

32. Desires also exist on different levels within the same individual (KpV 22ff., CPrR 21ff.).

to the happiness of one concrete individual requires a shift from pure reason to conceptions empirically determined.[33]

One's own happiness, taken by itself, is inadequate as the totality of a goal for reason employed practically, because by itself happiness is not moral,[34] and it is counter to the requirements of an intelligible moral world that happiness be accorded to one without virtue. The appropriate totality is one where happiness is joined to virtue, or more precisely, to commensurate virtue. The highest good is happiness in exact proportion to virtue, or deserved happiness.[35] One is obliged, as Kant understands it, to act in accord with the moral law and out of respect for it. One is obliged as well to promote the highest good.[36] And one is obliged also – contrary to many impressions of Kant – to promote, albeit indirectly, one's own happiness.[37]

Kant's texts on obligation to promote happiness are clear enough, but his argument wants some clarification if practical reason is not to be understood as slipping into heteronomy.[38] Such clarification stems from the form of the moral law: "Act in such a way that you always treat humanity, whether in your own person or in the person of another, never simply as a means, but always at the same time as an end."[39] But to treat oneself and others as ends is to order events to serve as means to ends of rational beings. Now ends of rational beings include both given needs and inclinations, and chosen aims or goals. Hence, to act out of respect for the moral law as requiring oneself and others to be treated as ends is to be ready to aim at, in applied moral reasoning, satisfaction of at least *some* needs and wishes of rational beings, not excluding oneself.[40] This does not mean that such objectives even partially *determine* the will; it does mean that indifference to persons' needs and desires is indifference to rational beings as ends, and is thus indifference to, rather

33. KpV 25f., CPrR 24f.

34. KpV 113, CPrR 118.

35. For discussion of the possibility of two interpretations of the concept of the highest good, see note 47 below.

36. Kant uses several locutions to speak of effecting the individual highest good: "realize," "promote," "bring forth," "make real," and "contribute to the realization of" (see KpV 109, 113, 119, 143-44, note, CPrR 113, 117, 123-24, 149, note 6). Similar locutions are used with respect to effecting the ethical commonwealth.

37. *Grundlegung*, p. 399, Paton, p. 67; KpV 93, CPrR 96.

38. Wood in *Kant's Moral Religion*, pp. 58-59, explains and defends Kant's inclusion of happiness within the form of the moral law, and gathers Kant's texts (including KpV 34-35, CPrR 35) to support his explanation.

39. *Grundlegung*, p. 429, Paton, p. 96.

40. Wood (*Kant's Moral Religion*, pp. 58-59) cites *Tugendlehre* to the effect that benevolence to all save myself would be benevolence lacking the form of universality. *Kants gesammelte Schriften* 6:450.

than respect for, the moral law.[41] Promotion of happiness is thus part of what the moral law requires. In this way happiness is included in the object of pure practical reason, and its promotion is obligatory.

But now, for the finite rational individual self morally engaged, a gap opens. One's own virtue is more or less in one's own power. But happiness is not; at least there is not a reliable link between one's moral intent and what eventuates in the realm where satisfaction of one's own desires is worked out. The happiness exactly proportionate to one's own virtue is not, it seems, in one's own power to effect. Doing so would require both an ability to know and an ability to effect. It supposes that we can know needs and how to meet them; it supposes that one's moral will can bring it about that one's choices become causes for effects in nature.[42] But theoretically we cannot know cause as agency of effect, but only as antecedent with respect to consequent; and practically we cannot, of ourselves, systematically shape the world to our

41. The moral law not only requires that persons be treated as ends, but that they operate as legislating members of a *kingdom* of ends (*Grundlegung*, pp. 433-34, Paton, pp. 100-102). This latter notion adds, to the notion of persons, an order *between* persons, and is the way in which Kant lays a foundation for dealing with conflicts between one person's needs and wishes and those of another in a way which precludes treatment of anyone solely as a means.

42. One might well ask, "Isn't the issue whether one's choices can become *causes of happiness* (rather than causes for effects in nature)?" A word should therefore be said about relations between effects in nature and happiness – the satisfaction of desires. Both are on the same side of the gap, the side of consequences. On the other side, that of intent, we have, if one is moral, choices to treat persons as ends, or choices as if one's maxim were becoming a universal law of nature. Keeping this in mind as we return to the side of consequences, we see an apparent difference between the consequences of persons-as-ends-being-served and those of desires-being-satisfied (happiness). But the difference only obtains if these ends are understood after the manner of teleology in nature, so that optimal outcomes are some sort of accord or harmony with nature. But this is not the outcome envisioned (cf. Despland, *Kant on History*, pp. 162-63). Man in Kant sets his own ends; his freedom leaves him at the threshold leading from nature to culture (cf. *Critique of Judgment*, § 83). Hence his ends are – to borrow a phrase from John Dewey – ends-in-view. Considering his ends after the pattern of nature is only a *type* for seeing the universal character of decision of freedom; nature is a pattern only "as if" (KpV 67-71, CPrR 70-74). Because human ends are personally chosen, there is ideally no gap between serving persons as ends and satisfaction of desires.

But the emphasis in formulating the consequence-side of the gap as "effects in nature" is for the sake of reflecting Kant's thrust against the stoics, one which shows up also in the iteration of "in the world" when he speaks of action, happiness, and the highest good. Happiness occurs "in the world," in the realm of nature. (See KpV 124 and also 129, 119, CPrR 129 and also 134, 124).

intent.[43] We cannot control processes in nature so that persons as ends may be served.[44] The gap therefore emerges as one for finite reason employed both theoretically and practically. Because one is obliged not to be indifferent to consequences of moral decision, one is obliged to promote the highest good – in effect, to bridge the gap on the level of practice. But for moral intent to be reasonable, it must not be impossible to bridge the gap on the level of theory. A two-fold synthesis is therefore necessary: one which allows moral choice to be reasonable, that is, to be engaged in the world and not be pointless therein, and one which allows theoretical reason to live with the gap that obtains theoretically between agency and outcomes in the world. The synthesis bridges the gap; it does not close it, but does allow commerce across it.[45]

Synthesis on the practical level – the joining of proportionate happiness to virtue – is not in our power to effect. Yet we are obliged to work for it as the highest good. But Kant holds we cannot work for what we think to be impossible. Therefore, because the moral law commands with moral necessity, what is required to preclude practical fruitlessness must be available. Happiness, as that element both essential to the highest good and yet not thoroughly in one's power to effect, is therefore on the part of practical reason a hope, and what is required that it be possible is, on the level of theoretical reason, a postulate.

It is well known that the synthesis known as the highest good is understood by Kant to require two postulates, immortality and God. Immortality is required to ensure the possibility of the synthesis in the subject; closing the gap between will and outcome seems impossible short of a condition in which termination of life does not obtain. And God is required to be the cause of the synthesis, that is, cause of the advent of individual happiness according to a person's virtue. The principal issues concerning postulation – what postulation is, its relation to the moral law, its necessity, its term and the reality or belief-status of that term, and the specification of that term as God

43. KpV 113f., CPrR 118.

44. Teleology is therefore "regulative." Cf. *Critique of Judgment*, §§ 76, 84.

45. The gap is more clearly visible if we compare Kant with the approach of J.G. Fichte in his essay, "On the Foundation of Our Belief in a Divine Government of the Universe." Fichte recognizes no gap: "The moral deed succeeds infallibly and the immoral deed fails just as certainly"; and "That there is a moral world order,... that every good deed succeeds while every evil one fails and that everything must go well with those who love only the good – all this is not doubtful at all but the most certain thing in the world and the basis of all other certainty, in fact the only truth that is objectively absolutely valid." This essay is available in English in *Nineteenth-Century Philosophy*, ed. Patrick L. Gardiner (New York: Free Press, 1969). Citations here are from pp. 23 and 26.

– are the subject-matter of the treatment of Kant in Part III.

Suffice it here to delineate what Kant offers from the *Critique of Practical Reason* for an understanding of ultimate hope. The moral law includes, in the totality of its object (the highest good), happiness. Kant's answer to the question "What may I hope?" is "I may hope for happiness proportionate to virtue, inasmuch as this is the highest good." Hope for happiness is sound hope; it is sound because its possibility is implied by what the moral law obliges, and the moral law is an apodictically certain starting point. Here some clarification should be provided for the notion of possible (and with it, an anticipatory sketch of postulation of God).

There are operative in the second Critique two general senses of possible, and the possibility of the highest good is located within the second.[46] The first is the logically possible: that which can be thought without contradiction. The second is that which is possible by virtue of being necessarily related to some fact the actuality of which is indisputably given. For example, the fact of actual moral obligation requires personal freedom in the sense of capability of self-determination. Freedom as possible self-determination is a necessary condition for the obligatory character of moral law. If a person is as a matter of fact obliged by the moral law, then it is possible for that person to exercise self-determination.

We can term such possibility "factual possibility," since it can be inferred from what is factual. The possibility of the highest good is of this same type. It is related to the moral obligation to promote the highest good. True moral obligation requires that the objective be possible.[47] For the objective to be actual, proportionate happiness must be accorded to the virtuous individual.

46. The two general senses are formulated by Lewis White Beck in his *Commentary on Kant's Critique of Practical Reason* (Chicago: University of Chicago Press, 1960), pp. 272-73, note 32.

47. There is a suggestion that the objective might be twofold (and then there would be two possibilities under discussion). Beck (*Commentary*, pp. 268-70) has raised the question whether there are not *two* concepts of the highest good to be found in the *Critique of Practical Reason*. One encompasses happiness exactly proportionate to *whatever* degree of virtue is attained; Beck terms this the "juridical conception." The other depends on the ineluctable character of obligation to holiness, although holiness is only asymptotically attainable; the highest good retains the notion of proportionate happiness, but here happiness is measured to *maximum* virtue; Beck terms it the "maximal conception." He holds that Kant began with the juridical conception, but employed the maximal conception in postulating immortality. I think for purposes of this essay the following is sufficiently established in the *Critique of Practical Reason*: a person cannot do other than strive to obey and respect the moral law to the greatest extent possible (maximal virtue), since to settle knowingly for less would require heteronomy and thus be departure from the moral law and not virtue at all. Hence the

But, given the finite character of the person and the gap between intent and outcomes, actual proportionate happiness requires actual immortality and the agency of God as fairminded and rational cause of both the moral law and nature. Lack of immortality, or lack of God as author of nature, means not only the non-actuality of proportionate happiness, but also its impossibility. Conversely, if the person is immortal, and if God exists, then proportionate happiness is possible, and therefore the highest good is possible. And if the highest good is possible, a person can be truly obliged to promote it.

We can put these two senses of the factually possible in somewhat different language. Freedom as capability of self-determination is a necessary condition for the fact of moral obligation. The reality of God[48] is one conjunct of the sufficient condition for the possibility of the highest good; joined with the finite individual's immortality, the reality of God ensures the highest good's possibility, and only the individual's virtue is further required for actualization. Immortality and the reality of God are consequently necessary conditions for the actualization of the highest good.[49] But they are necessary conditions in different ways: immortality (and virtue) are each conditions sine

formulation of the highest good as *exact* proportion between happiness and any level of virtue is not soundly construed as allowing into moral reasoning a ground for mediocrity. Indeed, Kant seems to use "exact" to refer to what fairness requires, in contrast to what "benevolence" might give, *un*deserved happiness (KpV 131, CPrR 135). Exactitude (the juridical conception) thus contrasts with what is undeserved. The obligation to pursue the highest good, as corollary to the obligation to highest possible virtue (holiness), is not weakened by defining the highest good as an *exact* proportion between virtue and happiness. Kant seems to argue that *whatever* the level of terms of the proportion, human agency is inadequate to secure, in necessary connection, exactitude, and that therefore more than human agency is required, if the obligation regarding the highest good is not evacuated on grounds of impossibility.

48. The meaning of "God" in "God exists" or "the reality of God" is: a reality not only *capable* of according happiness, but also *willing* to do so – two aspects found together in the notion "agency" when agency is personal.

49. Argument can be made that not both are necessary conditions: either God is not necessary, or immortality (of at least one sort) is not necessary. Only immortality is required if, as one grows in virtue, inclinations contrary to moral principle fade away. Thus, if happiness is the state of all going according to one's wish and will, as one's wish and will come into accord with the moral law, happiness would result. This would render God, as postulated cause of harmony between the realms of nature and moral choice, unnecessary. But this approach would approximate the stoicism from which Kant chose to differentiate himself. Indeed, Kant takes pains to argue that happiness is *not* virtue. Only if "wish and will" remains on the level of choice only – and does not move to that of act in the world, in the realm of nature – does the reduction have force. On occasion Kant explicitly contrasts moral happiness and physical happiness

qua non; God is necessary condition as causal agent, *bringing about* happiness exactly proportionate to virtue.

What Kant is doing is starting from the standpoint of the finite rational self morally engaged; i.e., trying to be virtuous; he proceeds to spell out the requirements of that engagement if it is not to be pointless. Kant is convinced that moral intent is not in the last analysis without suitable consequences, though he sees suitable consequences following in no necessary fashion in this world. Yet in the larger picture, if moral intent is not to be pointless – if proportionate happiness is to be possible – there must be available that which is required to effect what one must pursue but cannot ensure. The spelling out of what is required is called a *postulate*.

Before going further, it is worthwhile to note some conclusions from the second Critique bearing on ultimate hope and fundamental hope. (1) Kant's ultimate hope is hope for the highest good as inclusive of proportionate happiness. (2) This hope is implicit in what the moral law obliges, and the moral law obliges all rational beings. (3) This hope is sound insofar as it is logically linked to moral obligation and to reason; it is as sound as the moral law and reason are. (4) Spelling out the conditions of this soundness, especially how it is possible, is postulation. (5) Postulation of God provides some basis for a notion of trust: one who obeys and respects the moral law implicitly trusts the Author of both the moral law and nature. This notion of trust will have some connection with understanding fundamental hope. Conclusions three and four will receive closer scrutiny in Part III.

Hope for the ethical commonwealth and the kingdom of God

A third phase of exploration of Kant's contribution to understanding ultimate hope reviews his notions of the kingdom of God and the ethical commonwealth. In the second Critique, the kingdom of God is for the most part synonymous with the highest good, and therefore what is said of the former is said of the latter: if one tries to be moral and has the rational faith of practical reason, one may hope for the kingdom of God.

But in the treatise that establishes the focus of this phase, *Religion Within*

(RGV 67, 74-75, note, RLR 61, 69, note); the highest good always includes physical happiness.

Or: only God is required if God can regard an unending progress as a series already complete, comprehending as a totality what in finite beings is a progression (KpV 123, note, CPrR 128, note 1). God can "make permanent the disposition to this unceasing approximation" (RGV 171, RLR 159). Thus, endless duration would not be required as arena for endless progress. God's regard, or God's making the disposition permanent, is sufficient to shift immortality from being an endless duration under conditions of obligation to virtue to at least duration of another sort.

the Limits of Reason Alone, Kant's doctrine is at once more complex and less clear-cut. The treatise comes to grips with evil in a major way. Kant recognizes in human beings a propensity to evil,[50] and this recognition signals the emergence of several factors heretofore only secondary in his ethical analysis. The propensity to *evil* is recognized in experience, and thus there is greater weight given in ethical theory to the experiential.[51] Furthermore, the notion of *propensity* to evil – as well as that of disposition to good – leads to a distinction between two levels of imputable acts. One is that in which the supreme maxim of accord or discord with the moral law is freely adopted. The other is that in which actions themselves are freely chosen.[52] Distinguishing between two levels of act brings to light, in general, the level of basic disposition (the locale of *virtus noumenon* or its opposite) and the level of observable behavior (the locale of *virtus phenomenon* or its opposite).[53] Recognition of propensity to evil grounds Kant's view of calls human beings as evil by nature in at least two senses. People corrupt each other's moral dispositions, and they are in a continual state of war with one another. The bias toward mutual corruption Kant calls humanity's ethical state of nature, and the warring status of humanity – a pattern seen in *Perpetual Peace*, written shortly after – is humanity's juridical state of nature.[54]

But human beings have an obligation to leave their ethical state of nature where within them principles of virtue and immorality are in open conflict, and join an *ethical commonwealth*. Kant's expression encompasses the key features of this obligation and its implications.

> Now here we have a duty which is *sui generis*, not of men toward men, but of the human race toward itself. For the species of rational beings is objectively, in the idea of reason, destined for a social goal, namely, the promotion of the highest as a social good. But because the highest moral good cannot be achieved merely by the exertions of the single individual toward his own moral perfection, but requires rather a union of such individuals into a whole toward the same goal – into a system of well-disposed men, in which and through whose

50. RGV 28ff., RLR 23ff.

51. RGV 32f., RLR 27f. "Experiential" means that which does not belong to the concept of man – which would be necessary – but rather that which is observed in human behavior nonetheless. The Critiques of pure speculative and pure practical reason prescind from such experiential considerations, from "human nature," and from "all the hindrances to morality (the desires)." KpV 8, CPrR 8f.; A 809/B 837.

52. RGV 31f., RLR 26f. This distinction helps Kant to situate problems in understanding moral conversion: how a good man can do a bad act, how a person can become virtuous without being already virtuous.

53. RGV 47 and also 14, 31, RLR 42f., and also 12f., 26f.

54. RGV 96-97, RLR 88f.

> unity alone the highest moral good can come to pass – the idea of such a whole, as a universal republic based on laws of virtue, is an idea completely distinguished from all moral laws (which concern what we know to lie in our own power); since it involves working toward a whole regarding which we do not know whether, as such, it lies in our power or not. Hence this duty is distinguished from all others both in kind and in principle. We can already foresee that this duty will require the presupposition of another idea, namely, that of a higher moral Being through whose universal dispensation the forces of separate individuals, insufficient in themselves, are united for a common end.[55]

Here Kant asserts that the goal of the human race is a social goal, the promotion of the highest as a *social* good.[56] Such social good is not to be reduced to the aggregate of individual highest goods, that is, the collection of cases where commensurate happiness is accorded to the virtuous. Since it is each other that people corrupt and attack in states of nature, the ethical commonwealth envisions interaction by which such negative influence would at least be abated – a union or system of well-disposed persons. Furthermore, the duty involved in such pursuit goes beyond that of the second Critique, in which it bears first upon obedience to and respect for the moral law and then, if this condition is met, upon promotion of the highest good. It is *sui generis* inasmuch as in the second Critique duty is taken to bear only upon what is in one's power – to obey and respect the moral law is in one's power, while regularly to effect the individual highest good is not – while in *Religion* duty to join an ethical commonwealth "involves working toward a whole regarding which we do not know whether, as such, it lies in our power or not."[57] Such possible inefficacy of human will leads Kant to "foresee that this duty will require the presupposition of another idea, namely, that of a higher moral Being through whose universal dispensation the forces of separate individuals, insufficient in themselves, are united for a common end."

Understanding the conditions of possibility for realization of this common

55. RGV 97-98, RLR 89.

56. The notion of the highest good in *Religion* generally presumes, as it goes beyond, the notion of the highest good as found in the second Critique. See, for example, RGV 139, RLR 130.

57. The duty to join an ethical commonwealth is also unlike other duties because it is an obligation "not of men toward men, but of the human race toward itself." How it could be a duty for the latter and not for the former is puzzling. Perhaps "men [Menschen]" is here taken as "individuals"; if so, it seems that in this treatise the *moral* individuality of rational beings is being qualified by social imperatives. This interpretation is supported by Kant's contrast between one's "own private duty [jeder seiner Privatpflicht]" and the *sui generis* duty of uniting in an ethical commonwealth (RGV 151, RLR 139).

end brings us to considering several interrelated notions – the ethical commonwealth and the kingdom of God, and the historical or transhistorical situation of possible realization of this common end. The background for this is of course a fuller formulation of the highest good and the factors bearing on its attainment. In general, working towards an ethical commonwealth is *humanity's* contribution to the highest good. The advent of the kingdom of God in its fullness is *God's* doing, unknowable to us. The locale for such possible attainment is not clearly historical or transhistorical, although Kant's speaking of a kingdom of God *on earth*[58] suggests continuity with what we term "historical."[59]

Reviewing Kant's presentation of ethical commonwealth and kingdom of God, we find repetition of some old themes and introduction of some new ones. There is stress on duty, and on the necessity of a higher moral Being to complete the possibility of what one is obliged to work for. New emphases include (1) the recognition of imputable evil, (2) the shift to the *social* duty to work for an ethical commonwealth and the parallel amplification of the highest good as social, (3) the application of the noumenon/phenomenon distinction to recognizing the difference between disposition and observable

58. The phrase is part of the title of RLR's Book III, and occurs throughout this part. See for example RGV 93, 95, 122, 124, RLR 85, 87, 113, 115. Bloch notices this phrase, and speaks of Kant's highest good as *diesseitiger* (PH 1561).

59. More can be said about these matters. The highest good is taken in RLR as encompassing not only deserved happiness but also necessarily involving "union of men"; this amplified highest good is not in man's power (RGV 139, RLR 130). Its social component, the ethical commonwealth, is uncertainly in man's power (RGV 98, cf. 94-95, RLR 89, cf. 86). The kingdom of God is occasionally seen to be the same as the ethical commonwealth (RGV 151, RLR 139), but more often seen as different from it and coming to full reality only by God's doing but in a manner unknown to us (RGV 151f., RLR 139f.). The ethical commonwealth is a people of God, and a people of God is humanly realizable only in a church (RGV 98-101, 151f., RLR 90ff., 139). But distinction between church *invisible* and church *visible* (ethical commonwealth) permits some further nuances to the contrast between what is not and what is in man's power, what is not and what is the full kingdom of God (RGV 100f., and cf. 192, RLR 92, and cf. 180). Whether the advent of the kingdom is in history or is transhistorical is likewise unclear. The contrast between "here on earth," "in the world," and "after-ages" seems merely regulative or representative (RGV 134ff., RLR 125f.). The same is true of notions of what is beyond one's individual death – eternity, and so forth (RGV 68, 69-71, note, RLR 62, 63-65, note). The inevitability of the kingdom's advent, and concomitant emergence of the universal religion of reason, are likewise veiled. Kant tempers anticipation of positive outcome with the caution that statements in this area are not literal (RGV 122ff., 131, 134, 135, 161f., note, RLR 113f., 122, 124, 126, 149, note).

behavior, (4) the blurring of the line between what is and what is not in our power in securing the highest good (as ethical commonwealth preparing the kingdom of God), (5) a similar blurring of the locale, historical or transhistorical, for the actualization of the highest good, (6) the emphasis that the kingdom of God is God's founding, not humanity's, though how this is done is unknowable, plus (7) the point – this was noted earlier – that there may be, in the matter of virtue, a "God's doing" called "grace" which not only is unknowable but also deserves no consideration in a person's facing up to duty.

Review

We can now survey the three phases of Kant's contribution to conceptions of ultimate hope and fundamental hope. Our intent is not so much to summarize as it is to single out those aspects most germane to further discussion.

Several suppositions underlie most of Kant's approach. The first is that of rationality – rationality in the sense of order. Order pervades not just the realm of the conceptual, but also that of "world." It characterizes even those areas that pure reason cannot pierce theoretically; where reason cannot reveal what is "constitutive," it is not left merely with the irrational, but can formulate the "regulative." Second, this order is moral, in the sense of fair or even-handed. The highest good is an exact proportion because such a proportion is what is deserved. Nothing is gratuitous, at least not in any significant way. Third, there is a contrast between the pure (a priori) and the experiential (non-necessary). Obligation initially obtains in the realm of the former, and here it is categorical for the person as individual. It is only when the context encompasses humanity as social, in warring states and as mutually corrupting, that obligation enjoins social cohesion, either simply civil for perpetual peace, or civil-ethical for the ethical commonwealth preparing the kingdom of God. Moral evil is found in the realm of the experiential; it does not show up a priori. But when it does show up, it operates as a negative basis for qualifying the autonomy that characterizes Kant's truly moral person. Fourth, there is the issue of standpoints: the finite rational agent morally engaged is the principal figure of Kant's moral and religious thought. (There is also the minor figure of one merely desirous of civil peace – such a person will have his or her reward.) Reflection arising out of this morally committed perspective can point to possibilities approachable to the morally detached only as paralogism. Fifth, Kant concerns himself with *sound* hopes. His question "What may I hope?" begins with hope for happiness[60] but focuses, in the moral context, on whether such hope is justified, and on what grounds.

60. A 805-806/B 833-834.

The principal issues that should be kept in mind regarding ultimate hope include the conception of what is properly the highest good, personal autonomy, the gap between human will and outcomes, and the agencies that nonetheless can make such highest good possible. Of the three hopes we have focused on – for perpetual peace, for the individual highest good, and for the ethical commonwealth/kingdom of God – only the last is the full highest good as concretely desirable and possible. Only such a hope is in Kant not only sound but also truly ultimate, because only the notion of the ethical commonwealth gathers the unqualified good of the will (virtue) and the unrestricted good of desires (happiness) *together with* the conditions of social existence and personal and interpersonal propensities to evil – the full picture of Kantian anthropology.[61] But here, in an inchoate fashion, the ideal of moral autonomy is at least put in a context that is open to mutuality, to persons aiding persons, and even to (unknowable) divine grace. And hope for the ethical commonwealth/kingdom of God leaves blurred the locale of its possible fulfillment – historical or transhistorical – as well as the demarcation between its effecting agencies.

We noted the various expressions dealing with effecting the highest good.[62] The same shifting language besets the notion of effecting the ethical commonwealth/kingdom of God. "To intend" is not enough; "to ensure" is too strong; "to promote" the ethical commonwealth ("in so far as it is in our power" is Kant's frequent caution) is as good as any locution he does use. His meaning is clear to this extent: choice passes into action with effects in nature (and, in *Religion*, in society), but inasmuch as nature and society are not uniformly docile to personal intent, a gap arises between human good will and outcomes. In the second Critique, the gap is between individual human will and effects in nature. In *Religion*, the gap obtains, we can infer, among persons and between persons and social institutions. In this context the distinction between what is and what is not in our power recurs, but now it may be between "the human race"[63] and, if not the ethical commonwealth, at least the kingdom of God. The tenor of *Religion* permits extending the notion of inadequate agency operative in the second Critique from the single individual to humankind generally. In the second Critique, individual finite rational moral agency was found inadequate, and required, via postulation, adequate agency to ensure moral world order and thus give grounding to hope. In *Religion*, collective finite moral agency is sensed as inadequate and

61. Omitted here is reference to Kant's brief treatment of "the original predisposition to good in human nature" (RGV 26-28, RLR 21-23).

62. In note 36 above.

63. See RGV 97, RLR 89, and note 57 above.

is said to require a higher moral Being to order the forces of separate individuals.[64] It would appear that there are two kinds of agency involved in such discussion, finite rational agency, individual or collective but inadequate, and adequate agency.

The question of adequate grounding for hope for the full social highest good in Kant turns up *three* agencies – human, divine, and nature. Sorting out these three agencies is matter for Part III, but Kant has raised the question here.

The contribution of Kant to understanding ultimate hope – sound ultimate hope – is now sufficiently clear. What he might offer for understanding fundamental hope is not so clear, or at least not at all as extensive. He does speak of trust, and contrasts this with the manner of the man "who absolutely insists on knowing."[65] More centrally, his "rational faith" bespeaks a readiness to obey and respect moral imperatives without being able to grasp short or long-term outcomes, and without having speculative hold on what grounds such choice's reasonableness. Such a readiness seems compatible with fundamental hope taken as attitude of openness. Openness and trust will be central topics in reflection on fundamental hope in Part III.

64. Kant's wording is of course "require the presupposition of another *idea* [my emphasis], namely, that of a higher moral Being..." (RGV 98, RLR 89). Germane to "idea" is Beck's observation of Kant: "Often, throughout his works, he uses such constructions as 'the concept of x' when the argument permits or even requires simply 'x'" (*Commentary*, pp. 267-68). Following Beck's lead, we can formulate Kant's position as follows: the ordering of separate individuals requires a higher Being, and human recognition that such order is a categorical imperative requires postulation of such a Being.

65. RGV 172, RLR 160.

CHAPTER 12

GABRIEL MARCEL: I HOPE IN THEE FOR US

Introduction

In 1942 Gabriel Marcel found the best formulation of hope to be "I hope in thee for us"; his choice of expression was still the same in 1964. His approach to hope, as to all philosophical issues, is that of – to use the label he preferred – a neo-socratic; if we use the label of others, we call him a Christian existentialist.

With Marcel our intent is the same as that governing exploration of Bloch and Kant, to lift out and set forth those aspects of his thought bearing on hope. This chapter is long, but such length seems needed both in order to respect the exceptionally close connections between Marcel's analyses, the experiences that give rise to them, and the general framework of his thought, and in order to sift out and distinguish, for this essay's purposes, reflections bearing on ultimate hope and especially on fundamental hope. The chapter contains hints of the ontological models operative in Marcel, but, in general, issues of ontology and of theism are held over to Part III.

Marcel's thought on hope has a substantial consistency. It has been one of his central themes from the 1930s to the 1960s. His two most important treatments of the topic are the essays "Sketch of a Phenomenology and a Metaphysic of Hope" (1942), and "Desire and Hope" (1963), though hope is discussed in many of his works.[1]

It is crucial at the outset to recall one of Marcel's cardinal principles: human experiences are not simply hetero- or homogeneous, not simply capable of being grouped into certain families or areas; they have *depth,* or, in his terms, they can be found in diluted form and in forms more highly purified or saturated.[2] In a similar vein, he finds for philosophy an important difference between the *full* and the *empty,* between that which is what it ought to be and that which is devoid of both meaning and value.[3] In this essay's study of Marcel, "full hope" will be, in general, that hope which is more truly

1. The principal writings of Marcel important for philosophical analysis of hope, and the abbreviations this essay uses to refer to these, are listed in p. 37's note 2.

2. HV 29.

3. "I have written on another occasion that, provided it is taken in its metaphysical and not its physical sense, the distinction between the *full* and the *empty* seems to me more fundamental than that between the *one* and the *many*.... Life in a world centered on function is liable to despair because in reality this world is *empty*, it rings hollow." PE 12.

what hope is at its best; further sophistication of this notion appears as the study proceeds.

Captivity, despair, desire, and hope

The situation of those held prisoner in World War I not only engaged Marcel's efforts at that time, but became a seminal experience for his reflection. He came to hold that the experience of the prisoner is paradigm for the human condition.[4] The structure of captivity is found also in human illness. Indeed, captivity and illness form two of the central human experiences that demand philosophical reflection, and illness that is terminal is the subject of some of Marcel's most acute reflections.

There are many forms of captivity, of being in some kind of bondage or trap, but the structure of any time of trial is the same, whether it be one's own interior trial or one like that of the prisoner of war. There is impossibility: I cannot get free; I am unable to think, to write; I cannot be with my loved ones; I am unable to walk. What we have here are not just constraints in some sense external to my personal core; "in addition, that which characterizes all the situations we are evoking at the moment, is that they invariably imply the impossibility, not necessarily of moving or even of acting in a manner which is relatively free, but *of rising to a certain fullness of life, which may be in the realms of sensation or even of thought in the strict sense of the word.*"[5] Another chief characteristic of such captivity is my own involvement: we have to do here with matters where much that involves myself is at stake, where the outcome is truly taken to heart. In contrast to such involvement are those issues in which I take no risk, in which I am essentially a spectator, in which I do not share the struggle. My hope for release from captivity of any sort is quite different from my hoping for a team to win while I congratulate myself that I have nothing wagered on the outcome.[6] The hopes which are Marcel's concern are those which may arise out of an experience of captivity. The less one's life is experienced as involving trial and captivity, the less room there is for either hope or despair.[7]

In fact, there can be hope only where there can also be despair: "The truth is that there can strictly speaking be no hope except where the temptation to despair exists. Hope is the act by which this temptation is actively or victoriously overcome."[8] Captivity tempts to despair. And since hope is the

4. DH 281; see also MB 2, 178f.

5. HV 30. Emphasis is Marcel's.

6. HV 29-30, 40.

7. Alienation, in a number of its senses, is equivalent to some of the kinds of captivity Marcel speaks of. HV 30f., 59; PE 40ff., and, regarding possessing, BH 162ff.

8. HV 36; and cf. DH 278 and PE 28.

act by which the temptation to despair is overcome, to trace the visage of despair is to conceive the features of hope, since hope is the opposite of despair.

Marcel begins an analysis of despair by taking up the case of a person incurably ill.[9] Let us suppose I develop an incurable illness, and the disease proceeds apace. Suppose it is I who decide that my illness is incurable. In such a case my decision may contribute to my decline, and even ensure that my judgment is correct. Or: suppose that it is the doctors, and not I, who communicate to me that my condition is irremediable – and this I do not accept. In such a case my non-acceptance may be not just denial of my situation; it may become a factor in proving the prediction wrong. What is important here is my own involvement in prediction; "a certain margin is left to me, a certain possibility of contradiction, precisely because it was someone else and not I who declared my recovery to be impossible."[10] My attitude makes a difference for the outcome.

Despair, however, in terms of this example, is not "acceptance of the facts." Marcel sees something quite different: the essence of the act of despair "seems as though it were always capitulation before a certain *fatum* laid down by our judgment."[11] Granting the role of our own judging – as we just saw – we must inquire further: what is involved in *capitulating before* a fate we have declared? To capitulate, Marcel says, is not just to recognize the inevitable as inevitable, but "it is to go to pieces under this sentence, to disarm," or better, "to renounce the idea of remaining oneself."[12] It is to be so fascinated by the predicted destruction that one begins to anticipate this destruction. There is an "acceptance of the facts" that not only contributes to their actuality but hastens their coming by being as well an abdication of one's own person. Counter to this capitulation – for this is the essence of despair – is the path of finding some way of retaining one's integrity, some way of interior consolidation, of rising above one's fatum.[13] Hope is this path; but before tracing it, we must inspect other features of despair.

Despair is attended by a particular sense of *time*.[14] To despair is to take time as "plugged up," as "closed." One cannot "take one's time" in the matter because there is not time; or rather, time, I am sure, will inevitably bring only

9. HV 37ff.
10. HV 37.
11. Ibid.
12. Ibid.
13. The stoic exhibits one manner of such consolidation. Marcel admires the grandeur of such an attitude, but he ultimately faults the stoic's attitude for being the highest form of self-concern, lacking responsibility towards others. HV 38.
14. DH 280ff.; HV 52f., 39; MB 2, 181.

repetition of the factors that effect my captivity.[15] To despair then is, among other things, to anticipate that time will bring no new factor. It involves anticipating the dreaded outcome. Despair's sense of time is therefore closely connected with impatience. Despair cannot wait. But here we must distinguish a spectrum of kinds of waiting, for hoping's waiting is an active waiting. There can be a waiting which is a readiness to act, an alertness to what may come; and there can be a devitalized waiting that is close to torpor and indifference.[16] This is not to suggest that despair includes a waiting characterized only by torpor. Despair does involve an enchantment with, a fascination with, an obsession with the dreaded outcome.[17] But this can, it seems, engender strenuous activity as well as lassitude. Despair and hope are opposites in their sense of time; hope is able to wait. And waiting, at least the active waiting of hoping, reveals something about the crucial difference Marcel maintains between desire and hope.

Desire, Marcel maintains, is quite different from hope. Whereas others contrast hope and fear, it is *desire* and fear that are strict opposites.[18] Characteristic of desire is that it is impatient; it brooks no delay, for this defers satisfaction; it hears no objection, for objection means delay. Hence desire as such has a relation to time that involves rejection of time: there is "no question of waiting."[19] Also characteristic of desire is that it is covetous, egocentric. Its movement is on behalf of the I-myself. It is on the side of "having" rather than "being"; its mode of realization is possession. What is desired (in desire as such) is desired essentially for me.[20] Characteristic of desire also is its sharp focus. Desire, Marcel maintains, is always desire of something.[21] The key to understanding this last remark, however, lies not simply in the definiteness of the something, but in the type of fixed adherence existing between the one who desires and the object desired.

Marcel's phenomenology of despair opens up onto his analysis of despair's sense of time, and this in turn links up with impatience and waiting. Being unable to wait characterizes what Marcel takes as the essence of desire (which is not only imperious but covetous). Hence we will not be surprised to find that hoping is characterized by a sense of time as open, by an ability to wait actively, by a willing or wishing that is not desiderative in Marcel's sense of desire. Before fleshing out this sketch of hoping by contrasting it with features

15. HV 42, 52, 60.
16. DH 280ff.
17. HV 41, 42; DH 282.
18. MB 2, 176-77; DH 279.
19. DH 280.
20. DH 279; PI 231-32; BH 162, 166f.
21. MB 2, 181.

that characterize despair, we should take account of the functions of imagination.

Imagination is the representing to oneself of the objective desired or feared. The type of such representing is what is at issue here. We have already alluded to the way in which despair involves becoming enchanted or fascinated by the *dreaded* outcome, until one lives by anticipating and advancing its onset. Does hoping conversely involve being enchanted or fascinated by the *wished-for* outcome? Do I hope more the more I vividly imagine the fulfillment of my hope? Is hope the better for being more specific? Marcel recognizes a problem, and poses the objection: does not distinct representation, together with firm belief that the outcome will actually take place, give us precisely that manner in which hope is illusory? In response, Marcel formulates the principle:

> The more hope tends to reduce itself to a matter of dwelling on, or of becoming hypnotised over, something one has represented to oneself, the more the objection we have just formulated will be irrefutable. On the contrary, the more hope transcends imagination, so that I do not allow myself to imagine what I hope for, the more this objection seems to disappear.[22]

But Marcel himself wonders aloud whether this is not an evasion. While I may or may not give precise representation to the manner of my hoped-for deliverance from trial or captivity, still I fasten onto the hoped-for outcome, and bend all my powers toward it. Does not this re-constitute the force of the objection – that here we have the mechanism of illusion?

Marcel's response returns us to the point where we began. Operative here are *two* mechanisms, not one. The first is the focusing of wishing upon the favorable outcome; but the other is what was discussed earlier, focusing on the dreaded outcome, as part of the temptation to despair. Between the two is human liberty, the power to decide whether the case shall be declared closed, or declared held open.[23] If imagining means fixing upon, then both despair and hope *can* imagine thus. But hope slides toward the illusory the more it insists upon just one specific form of liberation.[24]

We can now gather together the elements characterizing hope, elements largely identified through contrast with elements of despair. Hope has time as open-ended; hope can wait, actively. Hope is not desiderative insofar as

22. HV 45.
23. Ibid.
24. This blunts but does not wholly turn aside the objection. It surfaces in the next section as: Can hope have focus, can it be definite, or must it cease to want anything if it is to survive?

this term means impatient or covetous. Hope imagines without fixation. Hope is non-capitulation in face of even the inevitable, yet is compatible with recognizing the inevitable as precisely just that. A closer look, however, should be taken at such an act that does not accept a fate yet does accept the factual situation. What sort of a non-acceptance is this?

Hoping's non-acceptance is not the same as resistance; it is not a psychic stiffening, a rigid clinging to one's own self, ideas, or projects. It involves relaxation.[25] How this can be so returns us to the notion of patience. There is a learning to be patient with oneself, analogous to what is going on when we are patient with another person and are in touch with the reasons why we are so. ''Hope means first accepting the trial as an integral part of the self, but while so doing it considers it as destined to be absorbed and transmuted by the inner workings of a certain creative process.''[26] This certain creative process is most central to Marcel's understanding of hope; it forms the principal subject-matter of the next section, one keynoted by the question: What becomes of hope when it faces disappointment?

Hope for salvation, hope for us

The case of a person's illness provides context for Marcel's distillation of hope's essence.[27] The invalid hopes to recover by a certain date. He may despair if he is not well when the period is up. The invalid's own judgment has a key role here; it can maintain that there is still room for hope when the alloted period has elapsed. ''Here hope appears to be bound up with the use of a method of surmounting, by which thought rises above the imaginings and formulations upon which it had at first been tempted to depend.''[28] Here is a fragment of the ''certain creative process'' just mentioned. But Marcel continues:

> In this example, it depends no doubt on more than a question of dates. The very idea of recovery is capable, at any rate in a certain spiritual register, of being purified and transformed. ''Everything is lost for me if I do not get well,'' the invalid is first tempted to exclaim, naively identifying recovery with salvation. From the moment when he will have not only recognized in an abstract manner, but understood in the depths of his being, that is to say *seen,* that everything is not necessarily lost if there is no cure, it is more than likely that his inner attitude towards recovery or non-recovery will be radically changed; he will have regained the liberty, the faculty of relaxing.[29]

25. HV 38-39f.; see also PE 23, 34.
26. HV 39.
27. HV 45ff.
28. HV 46.
29. Ibid.

Here we have the positive, relaxed non-acceptance of, or rather non-capitulation before the likely outcome, which we took note of earlier, a non-capitulation characteristic of hope. But here we note a shifting in hoping's objective: hope for recovery can fade, because recovery is not "everything." "Hope, by a *nisus* which is peculiar to it, tends inevitably to transcend the particular objects to which it at first seems to be attached."[30]

To set one's hope on a particular object and to hold to that objective seems to involve setting limits or conditions on one's hoping. In doing so "I myself put up limits to the process by which I could triumph over all successive disappointments... Indeed, I own implicitly that if my expectations are not fulfilled in some particular point, I shall have no possibility of escaping from the despair into which I must inevitably sink."[31]

> We can, on the other hand, conceive, at least theoretically, of the inner disposition of one who, setting no condition or limit and abandoning himself in absolute confidence, would thus transcend all possible disappointment and would experience a security of his being, or in his being, which is contrary to the radical insecurity of *Having*.
>
> This is what determines the ontological position of hope – absolute hope, inseparable from a faith which is likewise absolute, transcending all laying down of conditions, and for this very reason every kind of representation whatever it might be.[32]

We have, on the one hand, a hope persistently aimed at a particular object, and thus limited in such a way that the hope is subject to disappointment; and on the other hand, we have a hope which sets no conditions or limits, transcends any imaginative presentation of hope's fulfillment, and proceeds with absolute confidence. Does this mean that one whose hope is absolute avoids disappointment by hoping for nothing in particular?

No; Marcel's absolute hope does not exempt itself from disappointment. Indeed, he warns *against* construing such hope as some sort of perhaps divine guarantee that certain terrible happenings will not overtake us.[33] Such construal would then mean re-introduction of conditions: absolute hope would mean that I will undergo (and surmount) *these* trials but not those others. Such "absolute hope" implicitly maintains that if those other trials came my way, I would have no alternative but to despair. Marcel's point, rather, is that one who hopes absolutely is not *overcome* by disappointment, not that he or she does not risk disappointment and meet with it.

30. HV 32.
31. HV 46.
32. Ibid.
33. HV 47.

But the question is not so easily dispatched. It seems that being particular in one's hope means *holding on* to its anticipated fulfillment; this does risk disappointment. But if absolute hope can meet disappointment without being overcome by it, does it not do so by *letting go* of what was hoped for, so that in the end one hopes absolutely by ceasing to hope for anything particular? There is here a sort of dilemma: hoping for something in particular risks disappointment and seems to set conditions; hoping absolutely seems to be unconditional, and seems to overcome disappointment by, in the end, backing off from desiring what was hoped for, deciding one really doesn't want it. The dilemma catches a person between hopes that court tragedy and hopes that best be trimmed – unless, of course, everything is going to turn out all right! Resolving this dilemma will clarify the meaning of "conditional", and offer further distinctions in the notion of that which is hoped for, through exposition of *how* one may not be overcome by disappointment.

Let us look again at the prisoner-patriot.[34] He refuses to despair of his country's liberation. He may realize that he himself will never see this liberation. His hope – to be very precise – is for his country's liberation; it is not primarily for his own release, nor is it primarily that *he* will see the day of his land's freedom. Here we do have hope for something definite. The lines along which Marcel moves to resolve the dilemma posed do not involve diluting the ardor and definite focus of the patriot's hope. But further reflection reveals that in a sense the patriot has judged that he has no right to give up hoping; to despair would be disloyal. His judgment rests on the implicit affirmation that to hope is to prepare the way for, and to give up hope is to lessen the chances of, his land's liberation. It is not a matter of simple causal efficacy; rather, it is a case where to hope is to strengthen and to give up hope is to loosen a bond between the patriot and his country's future.

There may be more than the bond with his country; there may be one with his fellow prisoners. "If a real bond is established between me and my companions in captivity, a bond of love, I will then be able to think more or less explicitly that, after all, even if I may not see our country again, you at least, my comrade, will undoubtedly have that joy, and up to a certain point I feel sympathetically this joy which will be yours."[35]

The impact of the dilemma is softened because nuances are introduced beyond the simple either-or of holding to the particular hope versus giving up particular hope. The hope of the patriot is one that does really want something. But the manner of his wanting is *not for himself*. He hopes to see the day of his country's liberation; but, faced with the prospect that he himself will not survive till that day, he does not sullenly leave off hoping

34. HV 48.
35. DH 282.

when it appears that he will not make it. There is to his hope a steadfast focus, but the final outcome he wants is not essentially for his own sake alone. His is a hope based on a bond with his country and with his fellow prisoners. There is therefore a definiteness or focus to the hope, but the hope is nonetheless one that accepts and is not overcome by at least one kind of disappointment, his own dying before the day of liberation. This suggests a way in which hope can have definiteness to it *and* overcome disappointment. The key features of such hope are that the outcome is not essentially wanted for my sake alone, and that the hope rests on a bond uniting him who hopes with others involved in what is hoped for. Conditionality is tied up with outcomes wanted for oneself (so that non-fulfillment means I am lost); a hope's merely having a focus does not qualify it as one laying down conditions. There is thus an avenue opened for absolute hope having some definiteness.

But what of hope in the face of one's own death? The patriot can accept his death and hope for his country. But the invalid – how can a dying invalid have a definite hope that is not wanted essentially for himself? When one's own death is the prospect, can one hope unconditionally, absolutely?

At a philosophy congress in 1937, Leon Brunschvicg had an exchange with Marcel that the latter often refers to.[36] Brunschvicg reproached Marcel for attaching more importance to his own death than Brunschvicg did to his. The central feature of Marcel's response was his putting the entire issue on the plane of love. "My death is important to me in relation to the other and the grief it is likely to cause him."[37] A person may be rather indifferent to his impending death when he sees himself isolated from all others. This is not to say that there is not operative, on another plane, a drive for self-preservation, an organic vitality.[38] But hope proper is located on the spiritual plane, and on this plane one's relation to oneself is mediated by relation to another.[39] Here returns the theme first sounded regarding prisoner-patriots: hoping involves a bond. It may be with one's country's future, with one's fellow captives, with another person. In addition, Marcel recognizes such a bond even between me and my own self in the face of my own death, a bond mediated, however, by the presence of another. The lack of such a bond obtains when, on the plane other than that of organic self-preservation, my living or dying is of little importance to me. How, on the other hand, it may well be quite important to me was pointed out in Marcel's response to Brunschvicg. Marcel later gave a more particular description of the

36. DH 284; PI 230f.; MB 2, 169.
37. DH 284.
38. HV 49, 36.
39. HV 49.

intersubjective context of one's own hope in the face of death, and it merits full quotation.

> It seems to me that we have to put ourselves exclusively on a concrete intersubjective plane. By that I mean that in the case we are considering [framed by the question, Does it depend on me to hope or not to hope, when everything urges me to despair] I have to treat the despairing person as my neighbor and ask myself what I can answer if he questions me. Assume that he asks the question: "Do you pretend that it is in my power to hope, although all the exits seem to me closed?" Doubtless I will reply: "The simple fact that you ask me the question already constitutes a sort of first breach in your prison. In reality it is not simply a question you ask me; it is an appeal you address to me, and to which I can only respond by urging you not only to depend on me but also not to give up, not to let go, and, if only very humbly and feebly, to act as if this Hope lived in you and that means before anything else to turn toward another – I will say, whoever he is – and thus to escape from that obsession which is destroying you."

Marcel continues,

> What it is important to understand thoroughly is that if it is shifted to the level of intersubjectivity, the problem changes its nature: the despairing person ceases to be an object about which one asks; he is re-established in his condition as a subject, and at the same time, he is reintegrated into a living relation with the world of men, from which he had cut himself off.[40]

The question of the possibility of hope in the face of my own death is wrongly posed, therefore, solely from the stance of I-myself (alone). Furthermore, the matter is not helped if to I-myself I add an observer/commentator, as if he could, from another viewpoint, tell me something about my future I don't already know. The context must be intersubjective, and this is not effected simply by adding an observer (or by myself taking this observer-role). It is effected by someone being a neighbor. And this means that I am *enabled* to ask a question of *someone else.* The form of hope in the face of one's own death is a turning toward and being received by another. The key is not in words, but in being a neighbor. The event of the exchange – it need not, it seems to me, be verbal – makes possible a movement in the invalid's own disposition toward himself. The exchange has, as its essential ingredient, love. It is love that permits a person to effect a new relationship – in this case, to himself. Marcel has formulated the general principle:

40. DH 285.

> To love anybody is to expect something from him, something which can neither be defined nor foreseen; it is at the same time in some way to make it possible for him to fulfill this expectation. Yes, paradoxical as it may seem, to expect is in some way to give: but the opposite is none the less true; no longer to expect is to strike with sterility the being from whom no more is expected, it is then in some way to deprive or take from him in advance what is surely a certain possibility of inventing or creating. Everything looks as though we can only speak of hope where the interaction exists between him who gives and him who receives, where there is that exchange which is the mark of all spiritual life.[41]

Such exchange can enable a person incurably ill to accept the inevitable yet not go to pieces before it. The possibility of hope in the face of one's own death, therefore, depends on a relation of love with an other. And the possibility of unconditional hope – of absolute confidence – is not cut off simply because it is my death that is at issue, that is, because it would seem that any definite outcome must be wanted "for my own sake." The door is left open for an attitude which does not capitulate before the prospect of death. Such a relaxed non-capitulating acceptance (which we explored earlier) rests concretely on a bond of love. Such bond is with an other; yet relationship to an other permits establishing a bond with oneself: self-consolidation in face of one's own death is a bond mediated by the loving presence of an other. Such a bond, and the relaxation it permits, does not admit to characterization as a self-centered hope, wanted "for my own sake."

It seems, therefore, that even with the prospect of my own death, unconditional hope, absolute hope, is not precluded. One need not choose solely between definite disappointable and conditional hope, and focus-less indefeasible absolute hope. There can be some sort of definiteness or focus, but not one that requires my despair when I meet disappointment, yet on the other hand not one that is simply given up to shield me from disappointment. The basis of this focus is some kind of bond of love, variously constituted, as with one's country, with a friend, with oneself. What then can be said about this focus?

All hope, Marcel maintains, is hope for salvation.[42] That is to say, all hope in its fuller, not diluted, forms, is for salvation. There is an understandable temptation to take "salvation" as one's own individual salvation, "for my own sake." But what has emerged in our dissolution of the dilemma between definite hope and absolute hope shows that hope for salvation in Marcel is unlikely to be fleshed out in an individualism. Just the opposite is the case. While quite reticent in delineating salvation, Marcel does put plainly the one

41. HV 49-50.
42. BH 75, 80; DH 283; HV 30; PE 28.

characteristic: "it is precisely only in the light of intersubjectivity that one can speak of salvation."[43] Hope at its best is not hope for me. It is hope for us. Indeed, hope at its best holds both myself and you as equiponderant, not for separate outcomes, but for an outcome – not thoroughly known – which joins us together. Such joining is not to be understood in terms of competition or of purely functional interplay. It means a sharing of life – a "communion" – of which the bond between patriot and country, between invalid and friend, between me and my self – between him who gives and him who receives – is the basis. But such a bond – between an "us" – is also hope's *focus.* The forms of "us" may be manifold. But hope for salvation, from whatever captivity, is hope essentially for us.

Hoping's ontological import

One theme of Marcel has been so far deferred. It was hinted at through mention that the captive patriot implicitly affirmed that to hope is to prepare for, and to give up hope is to lessen the chances of liberation. The issue is hoping's *ontological import*: just what is it that hope aims at, and what effect does the hoping have on that outcome? Is it enough to say – is *this* all that Marcel is saying – that hoping at its fullest joins people together? Another way of raising the same issue is to ask whether full hoping is "only subjective," that is, it admittedly makes a difference for the one who hopes, it is a useful stimulus, but it is otherwise without effect; it neither sheds light on meanings, nor does it guarantee realization.[44]

What difference does hoping make? Possible difference has a two-fold range: first, does hoping make a difference regarding what it is that is hoped for, so that by hoping I contribute to the actualization of what I hope for; second, does hoping influence something other than what I hope for, issuing in a by-product or consequence distinguishable from that at which hoping aims.

A general, and background, principle of Marcel is that hope bears upon that which does not lie within my power. Indeed, he ventures a quasi-definition along these lines: "Could not hope therefore be defined as the will when it is made to bear upon what does not depend on itself?"[45] More germane to the questions posed: "Everything goes to show that hope does not bear upon what is in me, upon the region of my interior life, but much more on what arises independently of my possible action, and particularly of my action on myself: I hope – for the return of someone who is absent, for the

43. DH 285.
44. HV 57.
45. PE 33.

defeat of the enemy, for peace."[46] Response to the questions posed is thus framed in terms of that which is *other* than myself – possible difference is difference in what "arises independently of my possible action." (This is not to say that hoping has *no* effect upon the one who hopes. There is effect, but indirect: if hope is "an inner action of defence by which I should be able to safeguard my integrity when it is threatened by an obsession," it is not *simply* this; in fact, "it is not the actual safeguard which we are aiming at; if this is secured by hope, it can only be indirectly.")[47]

So hoping is supposed to bear upon events, not just states of myself – how? Marcel puts the issue: "If it is permissible to say, as I already implied above, that hope has the power of making things fluid, it remains to be seen exactly how and upon what this power is exercised."[48]

There is prima facie implausibility to the notion that by hoping I can make a difference in the outcome. There may be suasive power in this suggestion if it is taken as meaning that hoping is an autosuggestive technique.[49] But it seems that just such an interpretation is rejected as the whole story when Marcel sets out to assert that hoping is more than a useful stimulus. Gathering his explanation of how hoping makes a difference is hindered by the fact that his own response is diffusely presented. But there is a distinction he makes which is the key to his explanation.

It is one thing to bend to the task of hollowing out a tunnel, or building a pyramid. It is quite another to be engaged in genuine creation. For the former it seems that the outcome could be effected "by pitiless masters driving a multitude of terrorized slaves with whips."[50] Where only material results are at issue, "the inner disposition of the agent – or it would be better to say the instrument – can and should be regarded as a contingent fact in relation to the result to be produced."[51] Here we might have hope as no more than a useful stimulus. Results do not essentially depend on hope in the agents. It is another matter when results are not "only material." In genuine creation, there must be love of what is created.

46. HV 41.

47. Ibid.

48. Ibid. In a similar way, William James argues in "The Will To Believe" that faith in a fact helps create the fact.

49. Naming it auto-suggestive technique, however, does not answer the question. MB 2, 180f.

50. HV 57.

51. HV 57. In any particular case, care is needed in claiming that the results are "only material," though there is a clear enough contrast between, say, successfully vending subway tokens and successfully writing a symphony or book.

> Now it is precisely where such love exists, and only where it exists, that we can speak of hope, this love taking shape in a reality *which without it would not be what it is.* When this has come about it is untrue to claim that hope is merely a subjective stimulant, it is, on the contrary, a vital aspect of the very process by which an act of creation is accomplished.[52]

In sum: hoping directly makes an essential difference in the outcome where outcome is not simply material, where outcome involves love of what is created. If as complements to this position we bring forward two other key notions we have already seen, the difference that hoping makes emerges more clearly. The first is the notion that hoping is not the same as desiring if the latter is primarily covetous, for me. This obviously is incompatible with love of what is created. The second is the notion that hoping at its best is hope-for-us, that is what is aimed at – the result intended – is some kind of human community, and is, furthermore, not a hoping which clings to one representation of what the favorable outcome must be.

Hoping therefore makes a difference by influencing the outcome when that outcome is not purely material, but involves love of what is created. Such love is not a covetous attitude. Such love is one which intends a joining together of those who hope and are hoped for, a sort of true human community. Hoping makes a difference when it is hope-for-us.

Social hope

Marcel is often chided for focusing on face-to-face relationships to the neglect of broader social and political contexts. In light of this essay, we can now raise the question whether he has an adequate theory of social hope, something echoing the societal thrust of Ernst Bloch, or the ethical commonwealth of Immanuel Kant.

It is precisely Marcel's sense of the type of results with respect to which full hoping makes an essential difference that provides the correct approach to Marcel's grasp of social hope. If social hope is directed toward engineered relationships, where what is wanted is desired primarily *for me,* and where the frame of reference is that of individuals in competition to the detriment of the formation of "we," then this hope is no different from that attending the building of a pyramid: only material results are desired, and, for such, hoping is at most a useful stimulus. But if the society conceived is more than an essentially material result, then full hoping itself makes a key difference to its possibility. For Marcel, the kind of society hoped for and the hoping itself are intimately linked. Degraded hoping contributes to social decline, and some social visions (as counter-utopias) require only covetous "hoping" as

52. HV 57-58.

stimulus. Conversely, proferring other social visions ("for us") contributes to the possibility of overcoming the temptation to despair, and fully to hope (both as absolute and as having a definite focus for social living) is actually to contribute to social amelioration, especially insofar as such hope is active.[53]

While his social thought hardly constitutes a social *philosophy,* he does have a *basis* for such, a basis which, in its stress on the difference between essentially material results and those that engender true human community, is very central for a social philosophy and for a philosophy of social hope.

Hope in Thee

The best expression of the form of full hope Marcel finds to be "I hope in thee for us."[54] The character of this "thee" needs to be explored, together with what is involved in hoping-in.

The obvious approach to this "thee" derives from the paradigm situations Marcel reflects upon. The invalid is able to allow the possibility that his impending death does not require going to pieces at the prospect if he has someone as neighbor, as friend, before whom he can place his anxiety. The prisoner-patriot is able to refrain from declaring that all is forever lost for his country if he is not radically alone, but is joined with fellow patriots. In the second case, "thee" points to the others with whom one shares a life and a desire for liberation. In the first case, "thee" points to the person who mediates the invalid's disposition toward himself.

What is important to understand is that the thou is not a he or a she: the

53. It is beyond the scope of this essay to gather and present Marcel's social philosophy. Certain observations can be made, however, and certain bibliographical directions indicated. A guide to the development of Marcel's social thought can be found in Conversation 5 between Marcel and Paul Ricoeur, in *Tragic Wisdom and Beyond*. His initial hostility to technology is abated. His core conviction is concern for the integrity of man as sacred, and this establishes the point of view from which he reflects on social issues and events. His reflections are often negative, criticizing intolerance, the treatment of man as pure function, and the waging of war through "the spirit of abstaction." He recognizes a difference Ricoeur suggests between an ethics of the possible and reasonable and an "ethics of conviction," the latter continually exerting pressure on the political and social order, and he accepts characterization in the latter role, as the "vigilant philosopher." Some of his earlier social thought appears in *Man Against Mass Society* (1951), Gateway Edition (Chicago: Henry Regnery, 1962). His own social role is delineated in "The Philosopher and Peace" (1964), in *Philosophical Fragments* (Notre Dame, Ind.: University of Notre Dame Press, 1965), and reflections touching *inter alia* atomic war, Vietnam, and human survival can be found in essays in *Tragic Wisdom and Beyond* (1968).

54. HV 60 (1942); "The Philosopher and Peace" (1964), in *Philosophical Fragments*, p. 19.

relation is not one where the other person is available as object – as him or her – but is in some way *present,* turned toward, actively involved with, addressed. Between I and thou there is a bond of love, not just of such causal interaction as that in which either person could indifferently be replaced by another. Positively, the relationship is one of both conferral and evocation: it is not quite accurate to say that the thou *gives* me (that is, transfers to me) the power to withstand the temptation to despair, nor that the thou simply occasions the activation of my own inner resources (in such a way that any other person would equally "trigger" such activation). This relationship is close to being the core of hoping-in. But the relationship, seen positively as based on love, is subject to diminishment both in its living and in its verbal expression.

> I should however add that here, as everywhere for that matter, a certain slipping or degradation inevitably tends to come about. "To hope in" becomes "to expect from" then "to have due to me," that is to say "to count on" and finally "to claim" or "to demand."[55]

We have thus a picture of the emergence of what hope-in is *not,* namely, a relationship analogous to those of rights and obligations, of commerce.

What has been said so far inclines us to "locate" the thou outside the I who hopes. To a large degree this is helpful, especially insofar as the hoping at issue involves two persons face to face. We have adverted to the limitations upon understanding relationship between I and thou in simply causal terms. At this point another nuance must be added, the relation of thou to the "us" of "I hope in thee for us." To begin with, the "us" is pluriform: it involves union of "myself to myself, or the one to the other, or these beings to those other beings."[56] The range of the "us" may be – to employ rough categories – intra-personal, interpersonal, or inter-societal. Marcel admits there are difficulties conceiving how I can be a community with myself; the face-to-face community and the social community are more obvious.[57] There is a thou

55. HV 56. Marcel continues: "The perpetually recurring difficulties which a philosophy of hope encounters are for the most part due to the fact that we have a tendency to substitute for an initial relationship, which is both pure and mysterious, subsequent relationships no doubt more intelligible, but at the same time more and more deficient as regards their ontological content."

56. HV 60.

57. "Avowedly, it is conceivable that there is some difficulty in admitting that I form with myself a real community, an *us*: it is, however, only on this condition that I have my active share as a centre of intelligence, of love, and of creation." HV 61. The community of myself may be what is implied in having a sound love of oneself. Marcel speaks of "the city which I form with myself," a city made up of diverse

with whom I aim to form an "us"; this thou may be an aspect of myself, or may be another person, or other beings.

But more is involved, in hope that finds expression in the locution "I hope in thee for us," than the intra-personal, interpersonal, or inter-societal thou with which I aim to form an us. Between this "thou" and this "us" Marcel asks (and answers) "What is the vital link? Must we not reply that 'Thou' is in some way the guarantee of the union which holds us together, myself to myself, or the one to the other, or these beings to those other beings?"[58] What can be said about Marcel's understanding of this Thou is discussed later.[59] But what he has to say in the present context seems to apply to full hope, absolute or less than absolute.

But of specifically absolute hope he has more to say. Such hope transcends all laying down of conditions, every kind of representation, and involves abandoning oneself in absolute confidence; attending this is a security in one's being and a transcending of all possible disappointments.[60] The question now upon us is: what is the relation between the "thee" of "I hope in thee" and the *unconditionality* that characterizes absolute hope? It cannot be presumed that the "thee" of absolute hope and the "Thou" that guarantees the union are the same, but Marcel is explicit on the source of absolute hope:

> The only possible source from which this absolute hope springs must once more be stressed. It appears as a response of the creature to the infinite Being to whom it is conscious of owing everything that it has and upon whom it cannot impose any condition whatsoever without scandal.[61]

Such infinite Being is God, "absolute Thou."[62] What we have here is the presentation of the position that the source of absolute hope is the infinite Being.[63] Laying down conditions would be a declaration, not quite that the resources or philanthropy of the infinite Being are lacking in some respect (this would be hoping as *calculating* or as *claiming*), but rather a declaration of something deeper – "that God has withdrawn himself from me," that is,

elements and relatively unified, but hardly *separable* from the surrounding nourishing and challenging countryside.

58. HV 60.

59. Part III, chapter 18.

60. HV 46.

61. HV 46-47.

62. HV 47.

63. I say "presentation"; the degree to which such a position rests, and rests soundly, upon an *argument* or other form of intelligible support is examined in this essay's Conclusion.

has severed a bond of love.[64] Given the intersubjective nature of hoping, absolute hoping as transcending all laying down of conditions is grounded or finds source in reality conceived as thou. And if hoping of the form "I hope in thee for us" is absolute, then its condition of possibility is a Thou of love unlimited (not just of resources unlimited or philanthropy unlimited), and this Marcel recognizes as God.

What has been said about the relationship between I and thou – a relationship of love and, with regard to hoping, of conferral and evocation – provides context for Marcel's approach to the question of whether one hopes *freely*. (Recall that hoping involves a "decision" that all that makes despair obvious is, in the last analysis, not to be taken as final.) Answering the question in general is as impossible as answering in general whether an individual does anything freely.[65] Less abstractly, Marcel maintains that while "it is both true and false to say that it depends on us whether we hope or not," it can also be said that hoping involves an interior force, a faithfulness; yet exercise of this interior resource depends on "a co-operation, whose principle will always remain a mystery, between the goodwill which is after all the only positive contribution of which we are capable and certain promptings whose centre remains beyond our reach, in those realms where values are divine gifts."[66] Hoping remains an act that is one's own, yet in response to an other; it is in their Kantian senses, neither autonomous nor heteronomous.[67]

But not only does hoping stem from freedom; it leads to freedom. Here Marcel's argument supports the more general principle that hoping – full hoping – is a good and salutary thing for humans to do. The argument turns on the understanding of freedom as a freedom for, and is opposed to the freedom of the dilettante.

> To say that the freest man is the one who has the most hope is perhaps above all to indicate that he is the man who has been able to give his existence the richest significance, or stake the most on it. But this is enough to exclude absolutely the pure dilettante, that is, the one who, living only for himself, seeks solely to collect such experiences as will awaken in him, each time with different shades and nuances, a feeling of exaltation which fulfills him for that moment. But from such a flame, can anything remain in the end but ashes?[68]

64. HV 47. Actually, Marcel's exposition includes another step. He says that *despair* is declaration that God has withdrawn himself from me. *Laying down conditions* (not just as wanting something, but as insisting on or clinging to that objective) means that I am *prepared to despair*, that I consider I have no alternative but to despair, if what I want is not forthcoming.
65. DH 285.
66. HV 63.
67. See BH 172-74 for some remarks of Marcel on these notions.
68. EBHD 147.

With this we have come circle, to restatement that that hoping is best which stakes most; yet not *full* circle, for while this text pronounces hoping's worthwhileness, still outside this circle lies *challenge* to hope, inspection of the relations that can and do sometimes obtain between reasons – good reasons or bad – and hoping. May one hope if one has insufficient reasons for doing so, Marcel asks.

Reasons and hoping

To follow Marcel's exploration of relationships between reasons and hoping, we must make explicit at the outset two understandings he assumes. The first is that the hoping at issue is one that has some *definiteness* to its objective, such that even if it has the form of hope-for-us, this is equivalent to hope-that-we-will-meet-with-a-recognizable-outcome. Should hoping be taken as an act or disposition without any definiteness or focus to its objective, then reasons would have no purchase on the reasonableness of what is hoped for. Reasons would then bear solely on hoping as subjective, as a stimulus more or less useful. The second understanding he assumes is that "reasons" has initially only the vague sense of whatever can be reckoned, assessed, figured out. Marcel's presentation does yield, at the end, more precise senses of both reasons and hoping.

This said, we can turn to Marcel's presentation.[69] He begins with the question: "Can one hope when the reasons for so doing are insufficient or even completely lacking?" The question needs a distinction. If I as an observer ask the question, the answer is yes: *she* can hope when *I* judge the reasons inadequate. But if the one who is doing the hoping asks, the answer is no: one who judges that she has inadequate basis for hoping shows by that very fact that any hope she may evince is at most a simulation.

But Marcel maintains that one who both hopes and assesses the basis of her hope performs a reckoning only by *detaching* herself in a way from her hope. Such detachment appears most readily when I who hope am trying to persuade another to share my hope. The point Marcel makes is this: such a question occurs in a different register from that of hope; it "springs from a calculating faculty of the reason."[70] There are thus two levels or registers, that of hoping and that of calculating. To question hoping is to suspend hoping for the sake of giving place to the process of calculating likelihood. Were this all in one and the same register, then calculation of likelihood would be related to hoping in a way similar to that in which premises are related to a conclusion. There would be an argument: X is probable entails I hope for X.[71]

69. HV 63-67.
70. HV 64.

If such be the case, then of course one cannot hope if reasons (as probabilities one knows) are insufficient.

But suppose the issue of reasons and hoping is posed in *this* way: Is it permissible to hope when reasons are insufficient or lacking? *May* I hope in such a case? Here is raised the question of hoping's legitimacy, admissibility, soundness, not only in the case where reasons are sufficient, but *even when they are not.* (This question becomes Ariadne's thread for the complexity of the term "sufficient.") Again: if hoping and reasons (as calculating probabilities) are in the same register, then it is not so much that with insufficient reasons one *cannot* hope; one *ought* not to hope, one *may not:* one has no right to hope. But: if hoping and assessing reasons are in *different* registers, then is hoping purely irrational or fideistic? Is one therefore entitled to hope under any and every circumstance?

Marcel doesn't want to say that one is. He puts a case.

> Take for instance a mother who persists in hoping that she will see her son again although his death has been certified in the most definite manner by witnesses who found his body, buried it, etc. Is not the observer justified in saying that there are no reasons for hoping that this son is still alive?[72]

He essays a reply by offering a subtle distinction. "Insofar as the hope of the mother is expressed as an objective judgment, 'It is possible that John will come back,' we have the right to say: 'No, objectively speaking, the return must be considered impossible.'" But beneath the objective judgment, as such unacceptable, "she has within her a loving thought which repudiates or transcends the facts." It is absurd, Marcel maintains, to dispute "her right to hope, that is to say to love, against all hope. More exactly, what is absurd is the very idea of a right which we can recognize or dispute."[73] What is indisputable is the loving thought; but shall the *affirmation* "It is possible that he will come back" be permitted? Granting the distinction between the loving thought and the affirmation, the rightness, that is, the soundness or acceptability of the affirmation depends on what it means. The closer it is to a judgment of prevision or to a judgment based on probabilities, the more tellingly does absence of reasons bear critically upon it. And the more the loving thought is that of an egoistical love, the more its affirmation should be suspected of being predictive. But "the nearer it approaches to true charity, the more the meaning of its declaration is inflected and tends to become full

71. "It is as though to hope were to argue in a certain way and as though there were a possibility of enquiring into the validity of the arguments." HV 65.

72. HV 65.

73. Ibid.

of an unconditional quality which is the very sign of a presence." "This presence," Marcel explains, "is incarnated in the 'us' for whom 'I hope in Thee,' that is to say in a communion of which I proclaim the indestructibility."[74]

This exposition of Marcel requires comment. The mother's hoping includes two elements, a loving thought, and an affirmation or declaration. If the affirmation is intended as predictive – well, she has no title to make such prediction. But what else could the affirmation "[It is possible that] he will come back" be? Marcel maintains that the predictive force of such an affirmation is rooted in a love which is really desire; fulfillment of the prediction is an outcome wanted for the sake of the one who predicts. But if the love is non-desiderative, if it is "true charity," then the mother who loves, while genuinely wanting her son's return, is not clinging to its prospect for her own sake, is not making its fulfillment the condition necessary if she is not to despair. Such is the unconditional quality in her loving thought. Yet it does not cease, as loving, to have a focus. This focus is on "us," herself and her son. To this extent it is definite. But it does not insist on or imagine particular outcomes, other than that they further the communion in which the "we" are joined.[75]

Is there some sort of contradiction between Marcel's maintaining that I *cannot* hope (I have ipso facto ceased to hope) if I judge the reasons insufficient, and his maintaining that I *may* hope though I judge the reasons insufficient? There is no contradiction if at stake are *two different kinds of hope* (perhaps opposed as poles of a continuum rather than discretely). If my hoping is purely the sum of calculation plus desire, and if calculation is of objects or facts as thoroughly constituted, and if desire is essentially self-centered or covetous, then one cannot (and a fortiori may not) hope when reasons as results of calculation are insufficient. But if my hoping is operative in a register different from that of calculation of probabilities, and is not covetous or self-centered, then one may hope (not must hope) even when reasons are insufficient. "Insufficient" here means that the facts are not

74. HV 66.

75. If Marcel is correct in distinguishing two registers (objective calculation or judgment, and nondesiderative love), then objections stemming from one register are not ipso facto conclusive, although they do stand against affirmations made in the same register. But some form of the question remains "*Is* there a thou after death such that, with an I, there can be formed an us?" Pursuing such a question lies beyond this essay's scope; ultimately for Marcel an answer depends on an absolute Thou that makes an us beyond death possible. But Marcel's notion of different registers suggests comparisons with this essay's different ontological models, especially as they frame different ways of posing the question of existence – as object, as subject, and as in interpersonal relation. See chapter 14.

thorough warrant for the likelihood of the outcome I desire; I do not have enough for prediction. This latter hoping is what Marcel has in mind when he says that hoping involves challenge to the evidence upon which others would challenge it.[76] To challenge evidence is not necessarily to deny or ignore it; it is to question whether and how it bears on the future. It is the decision to hold the case open, though in expectation of what, one cannot say. The two kinds of hoping also involve two relatively different kinds of content, of that which is wanted. On the one extreme, there is hope-for-X, where X is an outcome not only definite but adhered to in such a way that disappointment leaves no recourse but despair. The actualization of X may even be predicted, as if announcing its imminence would assure the outcome. On the other extreme there is hope-for-us, where us has a personal definiteness, but not in such a way that one's not going to pieces is conditional upon a particularly imagined fulfillment. There is an unrestricted quality to hope for us.

As complement to this contrast between two kinds of hoping, we have Marcel's contrast between purely material results and essentially spiritual or personal outcomes. It seems that hoping-for-X in the sense just delineated is congruent with hoping for purely material results. But where hoping is for some kind of genuinely human community, we are closer to hoping-for-us; not only does the hoping itself make a difference for the outcome, but one has, to a greater degree, some title to hope even when past performance is insufficient reason – provided one does not so insist on specific outcomes that disappointment requires despair.[77]

A final comment on "reasons." Marcel takes "reasons" as the results of objective reckoning. But it is consistent with his thought to recognize quite a different basis for hoping, when hoping is full hope. Such a basis is the thou in whom I hope. But presumably thou can as well be judged insufficient – that love is lacking which would enable one to resist despair and anticipate communion.

By way of definitions

Most of what Marcel has to say about hope can be gathered and reviewed in terms of the formulations he offers that approximate definitions.

But before looking as such formulations, we should survey the several senses of hope in Marcel. To begin with, there are those forms that are trivial (I hope to catch an early bus), where not much of oneself is at stake. There are those forms where hoping is simply desiring (in Marcel's sense) plus

76. What characterizes hope is "*the very movement by which it challenges the evidence upon which men claim to challenge it itself.*" HV 67.

77. It is illuminating that Marcel tentatively finds despair and solitude identical – the reverse image of hope for *us*. HV 58.

calculation. There are those which are linked with hope-in but contrasted with this in its purity, as when "to hope in" means "to have due to me." These diffuse and overlapping forms are all contrasted with that which is the form of full hope: I hope in thee for us. It is taken as "full" for many reasons, but they all sum up in this: such hope is most consonant with the human condition, where "human condition" points both to how human kind is constituted and to that "certain vital and spiritual order which we cannot violate without exposing ourselves to the loss not only of our equilibrium, but even of our integrity";[78] full hope is both that of which we are capable and that which is worthwhile. Full hope may be an ordinary aspect of our lives, but of this full hope there are – to alter the metaphor – levels of saturation, the highest of which is called absolute hope.

Most of what Marcel has to say about hope pertains to hope that is *more or less full* (his delineation of absolute hope will be recapitulated later.) What he says, therefore, pertains in a more-or-less fashion to many of the quasi-definitions we can glean from his works.

Several of these we have seen before. First, at the core of hope is a movement by which is challenged the very evidence alleged against it. Second, hope is a particular thrust of the will; perhaps hope can be defined as the will when it bears on what does not depend on itself. This formulation captures hope's resistance to being called "merely subjective." Third, hope is defined vis-à-vis despair; it is the act by which the temptation to despair is overcome.[79]

Among those quasi-definitions not yet cited, we have a fourth, and this is Marcel's most elaborate statement.

> Hope is essentially the availability [disponibilité] of a soul which has entered [engagée] intimately enough into the experience of communion to accomplish in the teeth of will and knowledge [à l'opposition du vouloir et du connaître] the transcendent act – the act establishing the vital regeneration [par lequel elle affirme la perennité vivante] of which this experience affords both the pledge and the first fruits.[80]

The bedrock on which hope rests is relationship of love ("experience of communion"). Such experience has made possible "the transcendent act," an act that is not limited to what we reckon and what our desires are ("will and knowledge"), an act in which I assert[81] an alive continuance – of what? – of that of which the relationship of love is both an experience already ours

78. HV 54.

79. The three are, respectively, from HV 67, PE 33, and HV 36, and are noted above on pp. 124, 114, and 104.

80. HV: English, p. 67; French, pp. 90-91.

81. It seems better to translate "*affirm*" by "assert" rather than by "establish."

(''first-fruits'') and also an intimation or pledge of what might yet be. Hope is the soul's disposition of readiness or responsiveness – perhaps we can contrast this with stolidity or frantic need – a responsiveness that has its manifestation in a process of surmounting the conditions calculation and desiring would put on our outlook.

A less obscure statement gives us a fifth approximation to hope.

> Hope consists in asserting that there is at the heart of being, beyond all data, beyond all inventories and calculations, a mysterious principle which is in connivance with me, which cannot but will what I will, if what I will deserves to be willed and is, in fact, willed by the whole of my being.[82]

Familiar here is the notion of going beyond calculations. Also recognizable is the un-self-centered character of my willing: my will is consonant with another will, is at the same time directed toward what is worthwhile, and is as well expressive of all that I am. New in this quasi-definition, however, is ''connivance,'' or rather ''assertion that there is a mysterious principle in connivance with me.'' The tone is conspiratorial – in the root sense of this term. Principle-in-connivance seems to be a less personal way of alluding to the same thing indicated by hope-in-thee-for-us.

There is, finally, a sixth quasi-definition: perhaps hope means first of all the act by which a clear line of demarcation between what consciousness knows for a fact on the one hand and what it wishes or desires on the other is obliterated or denied.[83] Here again is the stress on hope's surmounting calculation and desire or wish, but here it is assumed that consciousness tends to assign them a clear and common border. The facts are what is; my wish aims at what is not but ''ought'' to be. Hoping, Marcel suggests, sets aside such a border.[84] Akin to this setting aside is Marcel's notion that hoping has the power of making things fluid – especially where what is at stake are results not purely material.

A few of these quasi-definitions employ ''assert,'' ''affirm,'' or ''deny'' in their expression. It seems obvious that such assertion need not be verbal. Indeed, it seems that such assertion is to hoping as a precipitate is to a

82. PE 28.

83. ''There is only room for hope when the soul manages to get free from the categories in which consciousness confines itself as soon as it makes a clear line of demarcation between what it knows for a fact [ce qu'elle constate] on the one hand and what it wishes or desires [ce qu'elle veut ou ce qu'elle voudrait] on the other. Perhaps hope means first of all the act by which this line of demarcation is obliterated or denied.'' HV: English, p. 10; French, p. 9.

84. See also MB 2, 178. Here opens a vista on an overcoming of contrasts between fact and value, ''is'' and ''ought.''

solution, becoming evident when another factor intervenes. In another terminology, such assertion is the conviction or belief that can be distilled from the hoping. This sheds light on the relation of hoping-in to hoping-for expressed in the formula "I hope in thee for us." Hoping-in is basically non-egoistical love; hoping-for (us) is anticipating an open but salutary future on the part of both the one who hopes and the one hoped-in, together. Hoping-in is the basis or ground of hoping-for; it makes the latter possible. And out of hoping-in can be precipitated that in whom or in which one hopes, yielding "There exists. . ." This is a sense that can be given to "Hope consists in *asserting that there is...* a mysterious principle which is in connivance with me." It seems more precise to say that hoping *requires* asserting that there is a principle, rather than *consists* in asserting. To withhold such assertion is incompatible with hoping-in, but making such assertion – having such a conviction, without necessarily verbalizing it – is not the heart of hoping. Assertion is derivative from hoping-in. The basis for the assertion is the bond of love, the experience of communion, or the connivance of a principle.

So far we have been attending to hope more or less full. According to this qualitative differentiation, there varies the degree or strength of hope's characteristic willing, challenging, and *disponibilité*. But now we turn to absolute hope. Marcel maintains that it is a *theoretical possibility.*[85] He does not claim that everyone actually hopes absolutely, or even that at least one person does. (This is also the case with full hope; let each one look to his own life to see whether he or she hopes, and with what sort of hope.) But he does maintain it is possible, possible that there be one who sets no condition or limits, abandons himself or herself in absolute confidence, and thus transcends all possible disappointment and experiences radical security in his or her being. Setting no conditions does not mean being indefinite in hoping, having no focus to one's hope. It does not mean running no risks. The hope has this sort of definite focus: for us. And it can imagine specific wished-for outcomes, yet not in such a way as to render despair inevitable in default of specific outcomes. What makes such unconditional hoping possible, or rather what is the core of such hoping, is the relation of love with absolute Thou, or the connivance of a mysterious (unlimited) principle.

Contributions to notions of ultimate hope and fundamental hope

Ultimate hope

This section gathers and orders those elements of Marcel's understanding of hope that bear upon this essay's notions of ultimate hope, fundamental hope, and the relationships between them. With regard to ultimate hope, it is of course possible within the realm of Marcel's thought to conceive of *any*

85. HV 46.

hope being de facto ultimate, that is, actually superordinate to all other hopes.

But Marcel's prime emphasis is on a hope that can be *rightly* ultimate, soundly preferred to all other hopes. What he *commends* is our theme at present; fuller substantiation of what he proposes awaits later parts of this essay (although some reasons for its soundness emerge with Marcel's exposition).

Sound or right ultimate hope lies in the general direction of hope for salvation. (It is also hope for eternity,[86] an objective echoing hope's outlook in the face of death, affirming a *perennité vivante*.) But, as we have seen, hope for salvation is *not* to be construed as just the individual's rescue and exaltation out of captivity purely individual. Hope for salvation, as full or non-deficient hope, is *hope for us*. This is not an individualism *à deux*; the "we" of hope-for-us has a kind of generalization to it – one evident in the hope of the captive patriot for his country, and for and with his fellow prisoners. Even in the case of the invalid's hope, there is an us hoped for – a community of the sick person with himself – though the nature of this community is not without its puzzling aspects. At any rate, the us of hoping-for is not to be limited to face-to-face encounters. Hope-for-us is hope for communion, for life shared in such a way that neither egoism, as preference of my interests over yours, nor altruism, as preference of your interests over mine, is adequate to describe what is willed by either party. Marcel sees in Christian theology's notion of the mystical body of Christ a hint of what this might mean, and he sees approximations to this in Marxism.[87]

Despite the open-endedness, the unconditionality of what is hoped for in our regard, there are *some general features* to what is anticipated. There is return or restoration or homecoming. There is surprise, the new. And there is, besides the new, the better. "This aspiration can be approximately expressed in the simple but contradictory words: *as before, but differently, and better than before*"; it is also renewal, promotion, "a transfiguration."[88] Furthermore, what is anticipated in full hope has its own proper language form. Full hope requires modification of "standard" expression from "I hope that P" to "I hope that *we*...," and from "I hope for X" to "I hope for us to . . ." The first-person-plural pronoun is essential to the language of full hope.

A word should be said about Marcel's judgment on the usefulness of the notion of totality, since it bears upon the degree to which his ultimate hope-for-us might be considered as a complex whole having parts. Hewing as

86. DH 278.

87. Marcel uses the context of this remark to speak of Ernst Bloch and his *Das Prinzip Hoffnung*. DH 285.

88. HV 67.

closely as possible to his concrete approach to ontology, Marcel contrasts plurality of individuals as things with plurality of persons as active centers. Things can be collected into wholes; persons do not lend themselves to being treated as elements of aggregates – unless they are taken as things.[89] It is sufficient for this section of the essay to note Marcel's judgment that "the category itself of totality is strictly inapplicable to what is spiritual."[90] He does not conceive of the content of hope-for-us as a circumscribable *summum,* but only as a "highest." He does, however, suggest something that meshes with this essay's sketch of ultimate hope as an *organic* totality. Marcel speaks of the experience of communion as "the pledge and the first-fruits," and as "the foreshadowing or the outcome" of hope.[91] This experience precedes and makes hope possible; it completes and makes hope fulfilled. It is concrete to the particular persons involved. As concrete, such experience gives hope-for-us a local habitation and a name, and thus embodies hope-for-us. In addition, as first-fruits or as outcome which is also foreshadowing [*pressentiment*], it is congruent with what this essay described as foretaste.

Fundamental hope

Several aspects of Marcel's exploration of hope illumine this essay's tentative notion of fundamental hope. Most of them have emerged through the quasi-definitions. There is first of all *disponibilité*, spiritual availability, a person's readiness or openness, a person's being really present to someone or something.[92] From one definition, such openness is hope: "Hope is essentially the availability of the soul . . ." On the other hand, perhaps it is not so much that such openness is hope, but that it prepares for hope, *makes hope possible.* Marcel asks at one point, for example, whether openness toward the other, disengagement with regard to oneself, can be identified with hope. He thinks not. Rather, "it opens to the soul what one might call a free field where Hope can spread itself or where (which amounts to the same thing) the word 'salvation' takes on its full significance."[93] Another aspect relevant to fundamental hope is the experience of communion, the bond of love. This is what gives rise to hope; this is as well that which is full hope's fulfillment.

89. MB 2, 63-64. For example, "therein lies the difficulty of reconciling the feelings, not patient of a common measure, which are aroused in us by beings which we love simultaneously – our wives, children, mistresses."

90. MB 2, 174. See also the Author's Foreword to his *Royce's Metaphysics* (Chicago: Henry Regnery, 1956), p. xi.

91. HV: English, pp. 67 and 60; French, pp. 91 and 81.

92. On *disponibilité*, see, for example, PE 39f.; HV 23-26. On presence, see PE 36-39; HV 15.

93. DH 284.

Marcel also maintains that this experience of communion gives rise to, or makes possible, openness (*disponibilité*).

Bringing some order to these notions as they bear on fundamental hope seems to require saying the following. (1) The experience of communion is the ground for full hope (experience of communion is also the objective or aim of such hope). (2) Hope-as-openness is hope-in. (3) There is a double ambiguity in relating hope and openness: is openness the same as hope? or is it that openness makes hope possible? And, is such openness an orientation toward the future, or an attitude in the present? A systematic treatment of hope employing the notion of openness should clarify these relationships as far as possible; such is attempted in this essay's later treatment of trust. Such clarification distinguishes, however, what Marcel is at pains to keep together in his formula "I hope in thee for us."

We do find here brought together themes of openness and mutuality (experience of communion, bond of love); these themes become pivotal in Part III. The notion of mutuality, of course, cannot escape being plumbed in intersubjective terms. Openness, however, might on some readings be taken as essentially an attribute of a subject. While Marcel readily agrees that openness is an attitude characterizing a subject, he does not want to take it as simply an attribute if by doing so he must proceed to consider it in isolation from that to which the subject is open. His intent appears in an observation on his general concerns.

> Perhaps I can best explain my continual and central metaphysical preoccupation by saying that my aim was to discover how a subject, in his actual capacity as subject, is related to a reality which cannot in this context be regarded as objective, yet which is persistently required and recognized as real. Such inquiries could not be carried out without going beyond the kind of psychology which limits itself to defining attitudes without taking their bearing and concrete intention into account.[94]

Subject-situated openness is therefore not soundly analysed apart from that which is the term of its relatedness, and this latter is not to be presumed to be merely "object."

An important aspect of Marcel's analysis is the way hope consists in asserting, affirming, and denying. His exploration for the most part locates such assertion in the context of what this essay calls fundamental hope. But his analysis is germane also to beliefs implied in ultimate hope. His analysis provides a beginning for what this essay carries forward as implications of both ultimate hope and fundamental hope.

94. PE 127. Marcel's ontology is intersubjective; see chapter 18, Implication, Ontology, and Indication.

Absolute hope

Important also for this essay's development is Marcel's notion of absolute hope. Such hope is that disposition of a person who in hoping sets no conditions or limits, is not ready to despair in the face of possible disappointment, and concomitantly experiences absolute confidence and security. As we have seen, hope that can overcome disappointment must have the form of hope-for-us; therefore, if, according to Marcel's interpretation, one has an ultimate hope that is unconditional (absolute), one of its necessary conditions is that its objective be experience of communion, "for-us."

With these Marcellian perspectives on ultimate hope, fundamental hope, and absolute hope, we turn to final formulation of this essay's two principal concepts of hope.

CHAPTER 13

ULTIMATE HOPE AND FUNDAMENTAL HOPE: CONCLUDING POSITION

Types of ultimate hope qua objectives

The notion of ultimate hope employed so far in this essay has a major difficulty: it permits a radical pluralism in what it can refer to. Ultimate hope is aimed hope, and includes whatever de facto is most desired and believed possible. This is not to claim that everyone has such hope, nor even that some do; the notion does single out whatever hope "outranks," predominates, or is accorded priority when hopes can be in conflict. It is now time to recognize how such hopes can be grouped, in order to take systematic account of the contributions of Bloch, Kant, and Marcel, and to forward the reflection of this essay. Initially, the focus is on types of ultimate hope according to their objectives, and of these the two most central for understanding ultimate hope are the notions of reciprocal benefit and relational benefit.

Types of ultimate hope's objectives can be grouped through differences in the notion of benefit, assuming that any hope is aimed at what is worthwhile or beneficial. An opening contrast should be made between individual benefit, in the sense of benefit to *one* individual person or to *one* group, and benefit accruing to *more than one*, to more than one person or group. The notion of individual benefit has both singular and plural forms, the latter being important for highlighting benefit of one group abstracting from, or at the expense of, the interests of another group. This is important for raising the issues of group conflict, of *our* benefit versus *theirs*, when what is at issue is the benefit of another generation in the future at the expense of one's own in the present.

Within the realm of benefit pertaining to more than one person or group, there are several possibly different benefits: general benefit, that is, an aggregate of separable individual benefits; mass benefit, pertaining to an entire group when no useful distinguishing – let alone separation – of individual benefits is possible; paired benefit, that is, benefit of more than one unobtainable by just one, but recognizable in one individual (e.g., a good game of tennis, a meal prepared only for two); reciprocal benefit; and relational benefit, where what is crucial is a relationship *between* individuals that is not reducible to benefits, even reciprocal, pertaining to each.

Relational benefit and reciprocal benefit need clarification. Reciprocal benefit is fulfillment of a brace of separable intentions each aiming at individual benefit, with another's benefit a necessary condition for but not a cause of one's own: "Scratch my back and I'll scratch yours." Such benefit may be symbiosis or alliance; but it differs from what "relational benefit," which I also call "shared life," points to, namely the overcoming of boundaries between one's own and another's benefit (yet without loss of individuality), a constituting of human community. Relational benefit or shared life is not conceptually reducible either to egoism (the de facto or normative priority of my own benefit over another's) or to altruism (the priority of another's over my benefit). The intent of relational benefit is *unitive*. The most obvious context of relational benefit or shared life is face-to-face relationships, of lovers and friends. Indeed, a helpful way of understanding what it means is to take it as relationship where some form of love can come to be. This does not limit shared life to those situations where love does exist, but to those where it is not precluded. Shared life, then, can encompass a broad range of positive relationships and bonds – personal intimacy, friendship, familial bonds, and *some* forms of social, national, and international relations. It obtains wherever using and being used, possession and being possessed, consuming and being consumed, are subordinate to unitive intent.[1]

The elementary types of ultimate hope this essay will henceforward work with are those aimed at *one's own* (individual or group) *benefit, benefit of another* (individual or group), and relational benefit or *shared life*. We can, for a shorthand's sake, label these *hope-for-me*, *hope-for-another*, and *hope-for-us*. These elementary forms have one compound form important for this essay: hope for one's own benefit and hope for another's benefit can be joined in a hope for *reciprocal* benefit, in which each party is ready to serve the other's needs and wants.

It seems to me that the elementary types correspond, respectively and roughly, to Kant's hope for one's own deserved happiness, Bloch's hope for at least others' attaining the kingdom, and Marcel's shared communion. And the compound form, reciprocal benefit, fits Kant's hope for the ethical commonwealth and also Bloch's kingdom, inasmuch as both Kant and Bloch seem to envision a system of fairminded reciprocal utility.

It remains to draw on this essay's understanding of complex forms of ultimate hope's objectives, and ask how the elementary types of benefit, the compound type reciprocal benefit, and relational benefit or shared life, might be related as *part of* one complex ultimate hope's objective. This will shed light on, among other things, the issue of sacrificial "altruistic" ultimate hope.

1. It should be obvious that relational benefit must be wanted for its own sake. Insofar as it is wanted as an instrument for one's own benefit, the persons or realities involved are so many trophies to be exhibited, and with this attitude there can be no shared life, but only its counterfeit.

Some complex forms of hope's objectives

In surveying complex forms of ultimate hoping's objectives, we should look at one situation where benefits are not in conflict and one in which they are.

Where benefits are prima facie *not* in conflict, we can look at relationships between my own benefit and relational benefit or shared life, in order to illuminate issues of hope-for-me and hope-for-us as ultimate hopes. We suppose that, where there is no conflict between objectives, there need be no conflict between hopes, and therefore each and both can prima facie be "part of" an ultimate hope.[2] I have a hope for a distinguished career; I have hope as well for my family. Each of these, insofar as the aims do not conflict, can be part of one ultimate hope: they might be juxtaposed, or they might each contribute to the other. But a particular feature comes into relief when, supposing the objectives' compatibility, we consider how one objective might serve as *instrument* for the other. In our simply-drawn example, career – or at least "my job" – can be an instrument at the service of my family, and vice versa: family life can be taken as a plus factor for one's career. The first aims at one's own benefit in order to participate in shared life or relational benefit; the latter takes up shared life for the sake of one's own benefit. But when the latter ordering obtains, shared life itself collapses – a family cannot simply be a means to further one's career. The point can be generalized as it is made precise: when hope-for-me can be a *purely instrumental part* of ultimate hope-for-us; but hope-for-us cannot be a purely instrumental part of ultimate hope-for-me. The reason why this is so is that taking shared life or relational benefit purely as a means to one's own benefit renders shared life impossible. What Kant said about subordination of motives can be said here about subordination of objectives. He examined the subordination of incentives – motives – in moral choice. They are of two types: desire for happiness, and intent to obey and respect the moral law. Both are natural, and each is sufficient by itself fully to determine the will. A man is not to be denominated good or evil simply for having both motives. But he is good if the desire for happiness is subordinate to the intent to obey and respect the law; he is good if the latter is the condition of the former.[3] Analogously in our example, both hope-for-me and hope-for-us are possible forms of ultimate hope. But if one objective is to be at the service of the other as they co-exist in the one ultimate hope, it is the objective of for-us or relational benefit that has the objective of for-me or one's own benefit as its means; to reverse the order is to evacuate hope-for-us, is to preclude relational benefit.

2. On "parts of" a complex ultimate hope, see chapter 9.

3. RGV 35-39, RLR 31-33. If virtue in Kant could be an object of hope, then since virtue could never be a means to happiness, so hope for virtue could never play an instrumental role for hope for happiness.

When on the other hand objectives *are* prima facie in conflict, the notion of benefit must be expanded from benefit pure and simple to benefit at another's expense. Where I win, you lose; when one neighborhood is demolished to build an expressway, another is spared. Such situations obtain when benefits or losses are in short supply. And, when it comes to *ultimate* hope for benefits, the pattern implied by superordination with respect to ultimate hope applies: hope for the one, if ultimate, does not admit hope for the other as a part of the ultimate hope. This is not to say that concretely I might not be torn between two hopes, vacillating in taking either as the most ardently hoped for; it formulates the truism that you cannot consistently set your heart on objectives that are opposed to each other. In tight times, if my most ardent hope is for my family's financial security, I will have to drop my hope to become, say, an actor.

But we must keep in mind a point made by Gabriel Marcel that substantially qualifies the win-lose situations now under examination, and qualifies, in particular, the notion of *at another's (or at my) expense*. Every teacher and parent knows how to hope for another's benefit, even at his or her own expense. Sacrifices of time, wealth, and psychic energy are made in the hope of another's future well-being. Hope for another's benefit excludes some hopes for one's own, because not both are possible. But Marcel brings to bear a contrast between results which are only material and results which involve genuine creations and love of what is created. Such is the contrast between vending subway tokens and composing a symphony, or between dispensing information and being a teacher; machines can vend and dispense information, but something else is going on where there is genuine creation and love. What Marcel's point suggests is that hope for another's benefit may indeed preclude hope for my own, and vice versa, but this may not be the whole story, even when benefits are in conflict, because one person's benefit at another's expense may be part of a higher hope – where love and creation are involved. If higher hope is for relational benefit or shared life, then hope for another's benefit at my expense – or hope for my benefit at another's expense – may be part of hope-for-us. Conflict of benefits on one level is admitted, but the conflict does not necessarily rule out hope for individual benefit even at another's expense from being part of hope-for-us. Sacrifices, offered or required, can make sense as part of shared life or relational benefit, but only insofar as this latter implies creation of what is loved. Therefore, hope-for-us, as ultimate, *can* have hope-for-me, *even at another's expense,* as part, though the other must of course be included in the us.

Furthermore, there can be no conflict between hope-for-me and ultimate hope-for-us inasmuch as the latter involves love. This sounds a lot like saying that there can be no conflict between individual fulfillment and communal fulfillment if communal fulfillment is given its form by love, and if individual fulfillment is an aspect of communal fulfillment. Indeed, the thesis just enunciated about hopes implies exactly this.[4]

It remains to reflect on the possible conflict between the benefit of shared life and the compound objective of a reciprocally beneficial system. In theory, there can be no conflict if the system is a fair one: fairminded reciprocal a utilization does not preclude shared life, nor does shared life preclude the parties' serving as means for one another. Indeed, either can be part of the hope for the other by being a foretaste: shared life can inaugurate service, and utility can prepare for shared life.

That one be purely an instrumental part of the other, merely a step or milepost in a movement toward the other, seems implausible. Such a relationship would leave shared life behind, rendering it a device and therefore depriving it of life; while this sequence might de facto obtain, to hope for it would be to denature shared life. And that such a relationship leave reciprocal utilization behind – that one might hope to leave it behind – seems to assume that parties cease to have needs and wants of a utilizing sort.

The types of benefit charted so far in this essay are conceptually possible. Whether they are actually possible depends of course on experience, but, on the theoretical level, depends also on a person's basic beliefs or principles of philosophical anthropology and ontology, such as: (a) There cannot be benefit which is purely individual, that is, which has no communal or ripple effect; or (b) No one benefits but at another's expense; or (c) Fulfillment is always fulfillment of individual persons, and anything more complex is only superstructure or shorthand for what reduces to individual benefit; or (d) Human existence is so radically relational that individual benefit is adequately understood only as a precipitate out of what is essentially *between* persons and realities, and this is especially true where higher human activities such as love and creativity are involved. Each of these principles has been formulated in universal terms – "no one," "always"; but the principles may have as well less-than-universal scope, of "some" and "often." Each of these principles has a philosophical anthropology and ontology behind it. Further discussion of such convictions occurs in Part III, but notice is served here that typologies of ultimate hope dependent on *concrete* types of benefit are not without philosophical presuppositions (and experiential confirmations).

4. In apparent conflict between hope-for-me and hope-for-us, is it correct to understand that it is a matter of (religious?) *faith* that there will be no conflict, finally? Or is it a matter of hope? Or a matter of *experience*? If it is a matter of religious faith, then it can be affirmed only in consequence of such faith; for example, Kant's rational faith is that God will apportion happiness to virtue; or, in a different framework, it may be a faith that world history bring you happiness even when you've sacrificed yourself, or been sacrificed, for the sake of a future society.

Tension: modesty and transcendence

Abstractly considered, ultimate hopes' objectives may be complex. In concrete situations, hopes show contrast in their range, and they face obstacles to their fulfillment. Such concrete features yield further characterizations of ultimate hopes' objectives.

Ernst Bloch, for example, emphasized that the objective of good human hopes goes beyond pedestrian limits; it is "explosive." But other hopes are modest and quite definite; they may aim just for repetition of what already is. There seems to be in this matter an ever-renewed tension between staying with and perhaps settling for one's familiar hopes, and moving out and off toward outcomes verging on pipedreams. In one direction, the bias is toward what is at hand; what is, ought to be. The other is toward the New; what ought to be, is already available. The one shapes hopes essentially for repetition; the other, for reversal and superabundance. Each bias needs the other, however. A stress on experience and embodiment and foretaste in hopes counters utopianism, betrayal into the beyond. And emphasis on the Novum, going-beyond, allows for how we sometimes come to know what we wanted only after attaining it. In hoping, both modesty and transcendence have sound and corrupt forms. We can conceive of two forms of ideology: one inhibits change by proclaiming the value of the present; the other innoculates against concrete improvement by declaring the imminence of the Beyond. To both forms of ideology sound hope is opposed. Hope is often imaged as an anchor; we might complement this image with hope as a sail; but sound hope – to play with metaphors further – must also navigate, and do so between two forms of ideology.

Hope-analysis becomes more concrete and closer to the human situation when that situation is recognized as one fraught with obstacles. Some obstacles may be the lack of human physical power; some may stem from ill will either directly or through its consequences. Kant's fuller analysis of human existence led him to situate hope in the context of man's propensity to evil. And most serious reflection about hope finds it embattled by disappointment, death, tragedy. This situation of hope gives characterization to hope's objectives. Hope aims at restoration, at objectives which are remedial, rescuing, healing, recovering, escaping from, redressing, releasing, renewing, liberating, reconciling, returning. On the other hand, hope in the concrete often aims at the more, the better, the higher; it aims at objectives which are growth-enhancing, progressive, transcending, advancing, ascending, genuinely new. Not all ultimate hopes show these two faces of reversal and superabundance, but many do.

The principal hopes of Bloch, Kant, and Marcel fit this twofold schematization. Marcel's full hope is for "restoration and revolution."[5]

5. HV 67.

Bloch's full hope arises in "the darkness of the lived moment" and aims at overcoming of alienation and ushering in a form of life better than even our limited concepts can grasp. Kant's thought, too, meshes with such description insofar as the ethical and juridical states of nature are overcome and happiness, individual and aggregate, is brought from haphazard and partial experience to constant deserved possession.

Alienation

Insofar as the "shape" of full-bodied hope is understood to involve restoration (liberating, redressing, healing, and so forth), it seems necessarily linked to definite kinds of present situations: they are experienced as situations of imprisonment, sickness, estrangement, exile, obstacle, entrapment, and so forth. Similarly, saying that hoping means holding or declaring or finding the future open makes sense only if it is frequently held or declared or found to be closed. To understand hope as aimed at future restoration is therefore to position it in a present context of – to use one term for the many adduced – *alienation*. Hope aiming at restoration is hope experiencing the present as alienating.

Experience of alienation, however, raises some substantial problems for metaphysics. Assuming the present experience of one who hopes is appropriately characterized as alienated, what does this imply about how *reality* is conceived? Metaphysics has been taken as the study of whatever is the case, of what is real qua real (being), or of what can be real (possibility), or of what cannot be otherwise (what is real of necessity). But if we try to speak metaphysically of what is experienced as alienated, we speak of *what is but ought not to be*. Insofar as hope involves alienation, its metaphysics includes not only facts but traps. A metaphysics of alienation would speak not just of realities neutrally interrelated but of realities at odds with each other, mis-using and abusing each other, hostile, indifferent, impotent, lacking integrity and ease. A metaphysics of restoration, then, would speak of realities in mutual support, harmony, integrity. Without pursuing this reflection much further presently, the main point should be stressed: if aimed hoping involves restoration, then metaphysical reflection on its implications cannot do without a metaphysics of alienation (and reconciliation). Metaphysical reflection on hope requires that metaphysics have room for more than just what is, can be, and must be.

In this context it should be observed that alienation is not necessarily the same as finitude: what-is-but-ought-not-to-be is not necessarily the same as what-is-in-a-limited-way.[6]

6. This contrast is derived in part from those of Raymond Aron and William Lynch, to the effect that dissatisfaction with imperfection is not alienation. Lynch quotes

Finitude and alienation

The term "finitude" points to limits; when applied to human existence it indicates, first, the limitations that simply *are*, and, second, the limitations to what human existence *can be* – the limits of the actual and the possible. As employed in reflection on hope, finitude pertains both to the events or states that can come to be (and therefore *may* be hoped for), and to the capabilities of the agencies that constitute grounds for an outcome's possibilities (and that therefore can be trusted in the sense of counted-on). One range of this notion's application is humankind, taken individually or together. Another is the extent and depth of obstacles to hope's fulfillment. Are certain hopes cases of Prometheus versus Zeus? Ernst Bloch, for example, more or less judges humankind capable of overcoming present alienation; Kant judges mankind by itself incapable.

Some may equate finitude and alienation in the concrete, though it seems prima facie unsound to equate what-is-in-a-limited-way with what-is-but-ought-not-to-be. Others may locate finitude as a type of alienation. It would be an interesting exercise to ring changes on alienation and finitude; suffice it here to single out a few ways these notions come together and bear on the subject matter of this essay.

Immanuel Kant, for example, places primary stress in his second Critique on man as a rational self that is finite. In *Religion*, however, the theme this essay calls alienation appears as the division in man between propensity to evil and disposition to good (ground of both are obscure), and as divisions between men in their ethical and juridicial states of nature.[7]

In Bloch, we find a conceptual polarization between subject and object, a present alienation of man from man and of man from nature, but also an overcoming such divisions in a future that goes beyond suppositions of human finitude. Ye Shall Be As Gods (*Eritis Sicut Deus*) is the maxim Bloch uses to express what Marxism inherits from religion.[8]

A rather subtle issue is one occasioned by the thought of Gabriel Marcel. Put more in the terms of this essay than of his, it goes like this. Shall a *lack* of shared life, of life given its tenor in non-covetous love, be understood as finitude or as alienation? Is such a lack simply actual limits that cannot be otherwise, so that to aim for such – at least in certain realms of human life – is to pursue a mirage? Or is de facto lack of such life – what Marcel calls communion – a lack of what *ought* to be, and therefore a situation of

Aron's *Progress and Disillusion* (New York: Praeger, 1968), p. 128, in his *Christ and Prometheus: A New Image of the Secular* (Notre Dame, Ind.: University of Notre Dame Press, 1970), p. 104.

7. In *Perpetual Peace* a similar juridical bellicose state is the starting point for Kant's doctrine of hope.

8. PH 1504, MO (MIE) 202; MO (RT) 114f.

alienation?[9] The issue is not just one for social life or ethics; it has to do also with *ontology*. Marcel's is an intersubjective ontology, as we shall note again, and thus whether communion *is* within the limits of human possibility as something that is not but ought to be and *is possible* – such questions become, in Part III, questions of the concrete applicability of this essay's intersubjective ontological model. If communion does so often not obtain, of what ontological weight is it to say it is possible and ought to obtain?

Types of ultimate hope qua types of desiring

At various points in this essay, various notions of desiring have been brought forward and examined. First, desirings were differentiated according to their objects, and this brought to light, among other things, different modes of desirings' satisfaction or fulfillment – in consumption, in possession, in utilization, and in union. Second, drawn from William Lynch, notions of desiring were developed with respect to the will of another, yielding a contrast between simple absolute desiring and willful desiring. Third, Gabriel Marcel brought forward a notion of desiring as essentially covetous, and one argument of this essay is that there can be a kind of desiring which is not covetous.[10] It is now time to order these types of desiring, clarify them as needed, and relate them to types of ultimate hope.

The first important distinction is between simple absolute desiring and willful desiring. Specification of the latter desiring's object comes from the will of another: I want this because you want me to want it; or I want it because you want me to want something else. It is desiring essentially either rebellious or submissive. Its opposite is simple absolute desiring, and such

9. Marcel's comments on the notion of condition are most helpful here:

"The term 'condition' is one which needs very careful definition. Perhaps we should see in the human condition a certain vital and spiritual order which we cannot violate without exposing ourselves to the loss not only of our equilibrium, but even of our integrity. As, however, the term condition may also be taken sometimes in a slightly different sense which is very nearly that of nature, we must recognize that it is a characteristic of man's condition in the second sense that he is able to fall short of his condition in the first sense." (HV 54).

Not becoming what one can become (the context is *not* one of *achievements*) is not simply a case of settling for different limits but is to become in some way estranged from oneself, alienated. Kant says the same thing: to aim at less than highest virtue is to accept heteronomy as one's principle and therefore to refuse virtue entirely. This should not, however, at least in Marcel's context, support moral Prometheanism, because virtue is not, in Marcel, due to autonomous willing. Perhaps it is not in Kant as well, as Allen Wood has argued: see chapter 11's note 25.

10. This essay's analysis and argument is in chapter 7; Marcel's is in chapter 12, "Captivity, Despair, Desire, and Hope."

desiring takes its specification according to the merits of the objective. The objective it wants, it wants for its own sake.

But this last phrase, "for its own sake," contains an ambiguity. To want something, not in reference to another's will, but for its own merits or excellence, can be to want it either for itself alone, or as a means to something else – because it is an effective instrument.[11] Hence, within the notion of simple absolute desiring, a further distinction needs to be made. Desiring can be differentiated according to its modes of satisfaction: on the one hand, instrumental satisfaction via consumption and possession – utilization – and, on the other, satisfaction via union or mode of being. This is our second distinction, between simple absolute desiring for utilization and simple absolute desiring for union.

But utilization too exhibits a bipolar meaning, at least in differing contexts: utilizing can be utilizing *well*, appropriately, or it can be utilizing done inappropriately, in misuse, abuse, manipulation. "Misuse" is used for instrumentally inappropriate, i.e., ineffective utilization; "abuse" indicates use of whatever should not be treated merely as a means, e.g., persons. Thus arises our third distinction, within utilization and between use and its inappropriate forms.

The best way to draw connections between types of desiring and types of ultimate hopes' objectives – connections important for this essay – is to return to the three types of objectives.

If one's objective is one's own benefit, one can desire such in diverse ways. If one's goal is self-defense or enhancement in the eyes of another, if one is at heart rebellious or defiant, then one's desiring is willful. But if one's goal is fulfillment of one's needs, then the wanting is simple absolute desiring of

11. Senses of something's being desired "for itself alone," "for its own sake," "on its own merits" and "as an end in itself" can be reduced to the three types of hope's objectives mentioned earlier – one's own benefit, another's benefit, and shared life. The reason why this is so is as follows. "Merits" (1) indicate what is instrumental to oneself or others (I desire that particular chronometer on its merits); but if "merit" is not used in this instrumental sense, then *either* (2) oneself or others are possibly instrumental to it (That portrait deserves to survive the war, and I'll do what I can to see that it does), *or* the object is possibly one with which affective union or shared life is desired. "End in itself" usually indicates (2) or (3); so does "for its own sake" and "for itself alone."

Something being desired with willful desire, on the other hand, is desired as a means to rebel and dominate, or yield to and be dominated by, another's will. Can such domination be desired "on its own merits"? Essentially no; at least in adults and in serious matters, e.g., ultimate hopes, domination involves abuse of persons, and is therefore without merit. This point figures in the argument that it is simple absolute desiring that characterizes an ultimate hope that is sound.

a utilizing sort: I desire the object on its merits, but these consist in meeting my need. Yet if the object is incapable of contributing to satisfaction of my needs, I *misuse* it; while my desire *is* measured by the *object*, it is measured badly, and desiring is inappropriate.[12]

If one's ultimate hope is for another's benefit, a similar schematization applies. If I desire to submit to you, then any objective I want is desired as a means for my submission. My desiring is willful. But, if in a different way my ultimate hope is for your benefit, I can want any objective for its excellence as a means for meeting your need. My wanting is simple absolute desiring. Yet if the objective is such as should not be made a means, it would in such a case be abuse, and my desiring would be inappropriate.

Simple absolute desiring, taking its cue from the merits of the objective, is compatible with hopes involving utilizing and being utilized, both the elementary forms and the compound reciprocal-system form; and, in theory at least, it has forms of appropriate use and of misuse and abuse.

When we turn to ultimate hope for shared life, we recognize that it is incompatible with willful desire of both sorts; neither in rebellion nor in submission can I hope for shared life. Nor is the objective of shared life compatible with simple absolute desiring of the utilizing sort, for shared life evaporates when it is used as a means for one's own benefit. The simple absolute desiring appropriate for ultimate hope for shared life is desiring aimed at union or mode of being. Such desiring has an ecstatic character, a readiness for a new form of reality not reducible to anterior intentions of the one who hopes.

The key points in outlining these compatibilities are three. First, simple absolute desiring can be either of a utilizing or unitive sort. But if utilizing, it may be *mis*using. And this leads to our second point: misuse implies relationship of antagonism, of opposition, between used and user; if persons are involved, the relationship is *ab*use. Third: later in this essay it will be argued that for simple absolute desiring, trust is required, and now the simple absolute desiring of such an argument is twofold: unitive desiring, *plus simple absolute desiring that is appropriately utilizing, using well.* To anticipate with examples: trust is required to hope for shared life; trust is also required to hope for needed food.

12. Marcel's portrayal of desire as covetous is psychologically acute and helpful for locating neglected features of significant forms of hoping; but his emphases cut across the lines of the present typology. His notion of desire as covetous or egocentric does seem to apply to desire for what one really needs. The context Marcel intends is that of higher desires, where the objective is not appropriately wanted just for oneself. If Marcel's description is applied to wanting deficiencies remedied, it is inappropriate; if it is applied to ranges of what Maslow calls self-actualization, it is very illuminating.

We will return to ultimate hope's simple absolute desiring when such hope's conditions for soundness are outlined. Presently, it is fundamental hope that requires final elucidation.

Fundamental hope

Lingering on from earlier in this essay is a kind of hope which should now engage our reflection. This hope can be expressed in "I am hopeful" (without delimited objective or focus). It might be labelled *cosmic* hope or umbrella hope – a hope that everything will work out, that things will be all right. Such hope seems to go counter to a principle that all or most hope has an objective. And even in the present context it can seem aimed at an all-encompassing objective, "everything." What is to be said about such a hope, particularly in the context of ultimate hope and fundamental hope?

It is quite possible that such cosmic hope actually does have a focus. The "everything" may turn out to be a genuine objective, perhaps in symbolic form, or it might be a concatenation of unexpressed but quite definite desires. If it is neither of these, if it is truly cosmic or all-encompassing, then a distinction must be made. There is an all-encompassing hope that insofar as it is future-oriented and involves desiring and calculating is undifferentiated. Such a hope is proper to infancy, and is rooted in basic trust. If however such an undifferentiated disposition is carried over into adult life, it becomes a maladaptive optimism.[13] Adult life displays hopes far more sophisticated. Insofar as a cosmic or umbrella hope appears at a truly adult stage, it is better interpreted, not as an all-encompassing ultimate hope, but as a *fundamental* hope. This is especially true when such hope arises in adversity: "Despite the failure of my every project, I still hope things will work out."

Preliminary characterization of fundamental hope presented it as an aspect of possible human existence which could be differentiated from ultimate hope and about which something could be said in its own right. Ultimate hope is always hope with an aim, focus, objective – an event or state both desired and believed possible. There can as well be ultimate fear, where the objective is not desired but dreaded. These constitute two forward-looking dispositions that focus upon some more or less definite outcome. Insofar as any one such disposition is superordinate to another of the same type, it is what this essay terms "ultimate." But the realm of the fundamental – of fundamental hope or its opposite – differs from such dispositions by not having an aim. It is not reducible to yet is concomitant with any ultimate forward-looking disposition. It is the personal or spiritual tone with which I hold my hope or fear (be these

13. "Maladaptive optimism" is Erik Erikson's phrase, and this distinction between cosmic infant hope and mature hope is based upon his epigenetic analysis of human development. *Insight and Responsibility*, p. 118.

ultimate or not). The realm of the fundamental is the *how* of hope or fear. While not identifiable with any definite hope's or fear's reason, cause, or motive, it bears upon what shall count as reason, cause, or motive.

One of the attitudes in the realm of the fundamental is hope. Fundamental hope was presented in preliminary fashion as an openness or readiness of spirit. It faces up to evidence, but also recognizes the limits of evidence. With respect to human desires, it does not deny them, nor does it capitulate to them. It is allied with neither fixation nor fickleness (these latter *directly* pertain to definite hopes). What is intended here is not an argument that fundamental hope is openness, but rather a descriptive pointing-towards a manner or how of hoping or fearing; insofar as one recognizes what is being pointed out, one accepts taking such a disposition as hope insofar as such openness looks to the future.

At this point our exposition of fundamental hope takes another step forward, and does so principally by drawing on the reflective analyses of Gabriel Marcel. His quasi-definitions delineated the pure forms of hope; human hopes meet these definitions in a more-or-less fashion (except for his "absolute hope"). Moreover, some of his definitions point to what this essay recognizes as ultimate hope, others stress fundamental hope, and others treat together the two hopes this essay distinguishes.

For example, hope as essentially a movement by which is challenged the very evidence alleged against it locates this hope as a hope with an aim that is not abandoned in the face of evidence suggesting impossibility. Similarly, taking hope as a thrust of the will that bears upon what does not depend on itself positions it as an aimed hope. So also does taking it as the act by which a clear line of demarcation between what consciousness knows for a fact on the one hand and what it desires on the other is obliterated or denied. These three quasi-definitions all describe hope in terms of desire and calculation of likelihood, and they all express a hope that aims at an objective, and might be an ultimate hope. They give prominent place to how hope relates to judgment of possibility.

Two other quasi-definitions points to this essay's fundamental hope. "Hope is essentially the availability [*disponibilité*] of a soul which has entered intimately enough into the experience of communion to accomplish in the teeth of will and knowledge the transcendent act – the act establishing [better: asserting] the vital regeneration of which this experience affords both the pledge and first fruits."[14] Such a definition takes hope to be essentially an availability, readiness, or openness. It characterizes the person who has entered intimately enough into an experience of communion to be able to look

14. HV 67.

forward to such communion as hope's aim. Hope's essence is such openness; but the soil from which it springs up is the experience of communion.

The quasi-definition Marcel gives which is most important for our present purposes is the one in which hope is identified as the act by which the temptation to despair is overcome. The reason for its present importance is that it captures the heart of what this essay recognizes as fundamental hope, and does so without necessarily setting it within the context of Marcel's larger worldview. Despair in Marcel's understanding and in an understanding now adopted in this essay is the judgment that *all is lost*. (Actually, it is more than this judgment, both in Marcel and for this essay's purposes, as we shall presently see.) Since definition of fundamental hope is now to be approached – negatively – as holding off from making the judgment that all is lost, some care must be taken to see just what this means.

Understandable enough is the judgment that *this* is lost, that *this* case is closed: all the evidence is in, and there is no chance for a favorable outcome. Or, from the side of desiring, *this* is seen to be worthless, and hence it is pointless to want it. For such a specific *this*, hope is given up; it is no longer desired or no longer deemed possible.

The matter is more complex when what is at stake is something hoped for with one's most ardent and basic wish, something which encompasses what one conceives to be the highest and all-inclusive good. If one's ultimate hope has such an all-encompassing character, and *such* hope is dashed, how can one refrain from judging that all is lost? Is not such judgment exactly what the situation calls for? Suppose, for example, that an ultimate hope has this form: I desire to leave this land and go to a new land, where I and my loved ones can begin to enjoy a new, different, and better life. Assume that such is justifiably held to be possible. But then illness, poverty, or political events destroy any such possibility – What then?

In one sense all *is* lost: there is nothing else to be hoped for, that is, no other outcome is possible and worthwhile. Here – and perhaps each of us can formulate his own equivalent case – one must give up not just some specific hope, but one which encompassed, integrated, and gave expression to all one held important. And yet we can, I think, recognize a difference, in the face of such a collapse, between, on the one hand, a response of slowly turning and waiting without knowing what it might be that one is waiting for, and, on the other, a response showing itself through suicide, intoxications of many sorts, or all-pervasive bitterness.

Marcel – to return to his definition – gives greater precision to the notion of despair when he judges it to be not just the judgment that all is lost, but capitulation before a fate we have declared. To "capitulate" is not just to recognize the inevitable as inevitable, to recognize that all is lost, but is further "to go to pieces under this sentence, to disarm," or "to renounce the idea of remaining oneself."[15] Such capitulation shows itself in anticipating or hastening the destructive outcome, and in abdicating one's own person. The opposite of this capitulation is the path of finding some way of retaining one's integrity, some way of interior consolidation, some way of rising above one's fate. The heart of despair, then, consists in not simply judging that all is lost, but in allowing that judgment to destroy or "dismember" one's self.

This approach has some strengths and some difficulties. It does permit taking an ultimate hope seriously, so that for some hopes of an all-encompassing type, disappointment does drive a person to the brink of despair. This approach does not devalue a hope at the prospect of its disappointment. The conceptual framework permits moving from *some* ultimate hope's abandonment to the judgment that, yes, all *is* lost. The difficulties of this approach lie in understanding such notions as abdicating one's person, or retaining one's integrity or interior consolidation. For some, such notions may make immediate sense; for others, they may be quite opaque. These notions do have the value of not leaving despair *outside* the person: they situate it at one's personal core. The "all" of "All is lost" may include one's personal core. Beyond this, such notions require a context of philosophical anthropology to illuminate them.

Another strength, and perhaps the principal one, is that this approach sets up the *reasonableness of despair*. Explaining what this means requires some further comment on the possible sense of "all" in "All is lost." We can conceive of an ultimate hope that is thus all-encompassing – ordering, integrating, expressive – and *justifiably* so, a de jure ultimate hope. Now when this latter hope is rendered null, not only is one appropriately without an ultimate hope; one has no right to shrink from despair. Despair in such a case is the only honest course: all is lost, and *I am lost*.

This essay has been utilizing a key distinction between aimed hope (as in ultimate hope) and the personal tone of openness with which one faces the future (fundamental hope). Now we glimpse the intimate bond between some ultimate hopes and fundamental hope: if there is no possibility of any sound aimed hope, then there is no justification for fundamental hope. And if one hopes fundamentally, that is, holds off from despair, from declaring I am lost while sensing that All is lost, then *implicitly* one believes that there is a way out, a way up, from present entombment.

To conclude remarks on "all": "All is lost" may express the judgment appropriate to disappointment of one's deepest hope. But such disappointment may or may not include one's own personal core (and such inclusion may be a matter of further judgment). Insofar as it does not include my self, the All is lost tempts to but does not require despair; if it does include

15. HV 37.

it, despair is the only course. It is precisely the ambiguity of such inclusion that constitutes the temptation.

It is instructive to compare this essay's conception of fundamental hope, positively understood as openness or *disponibilité*, and negatively as holding off from the judgment that I am lost, with Gabriel Marcel's notion of absolute hope.[16] Obviously the *disponibilité* of fundamental hope is derived from Marcel. But his *absolute* hope focuses on unconditionality: it is an attitude which is not fixated, to the extent that it sets no limits or conditions beyond which one would have no choice but to declare I am lost. As by products of such an attitude, one has absolute confidence, radical security, and is capable of transcending all possible disappointments. Marcel does not claim that everyone is characterized by such hope, or even that some are; it is a theoretical possibility. In our present reflection on his notion of absolute hope, we should distinguish three factors which he, ever hewing to his concrete method, keeps together: the unconditionality of the attitude, the type of aimed hope that goes with this, and the ground that makes such an attitude possible. His notion encompasses the attitude of unconditionality, the aimed hope of communion, and a grounding in relationship to absolute Thou. For this essay's purposes, it seems legitimate to separate the three factors, and recognize in the attribute of unconditionality precisely the pervasive judgment: I am not lost, no matter what aimed hope of mine is voided. Marcel recognizes that *some* aimed hope must be sound if despair is not warranted, but we need not automatically follow him in saying this aimed hope is for the experience of communion. Similarly, absolute hope, if it is not the most radical self-deception, does need grounding, but whether or not to follow Marcel in recognizing this grounding as relationship to absolute Thou is a substantial question of this essay's Part III. Insofar as we distinguish what he sees as one, we can recognize within his notion of absolute hope an attitude quite close to the fullest form of this essay's fundamental hope.

One theme glimpsed in the background of this section must now be brought forward. At some points I spoke of a hope that orders, integrates, and *expresses* all one holds important. Many, if not most, ultimate hopes are capable of *some* expression. The three philosophers considered in this essay give expression to what hope aims at and holds possible. Marcel speaks of the experience of communion; Kant speaks of happiness. And Ernst Bloch marshalls legions of expressions; he takes some to be misleading or partial, and others to be rightly directed; he gives criticism to them all. But even in achievement of what they point to, they are "real symbols": they recognizably begin what finally we have no adequate words for. The point germane here is that language and expression are involved in most ultimate

16. See chapter 12, "Absolute Hope," and "By Way of Definitions."

hopes. Gaps between expressive form and what turns out to be the case permit abandonment of *an* ultimate hope while one perseveres in fundamental hope. But where no gap is perceived, collapse of an ultimate hope seems to require despair. And where the temptation to despair is withstood, one implicitly believes that there is *some* (perhaps unspecified) alternative to one's dashed ultimate hope.

All of this highlights the importance of expression of hopes. Indeed, it raises the question whether in fact one can persevere in fundamental hope, in the face of collapse of all one hoped for, without some image of an aimed hope – to coin a phrase departing from this essay's terminology – even "more ultimate."[17]

This is the ultimate bond that obtains between the realms of fundamental hope and ultimate hope: with the collapse of some ultimate hopes, maintaining oneself in fundamental hope requires at least a "survivor-hope," some sense that there is a way out of present disaster. This may be only by way of an implicit belief that *something* which is worthwhile is still possible.

Sound ultimate hope: its formal characteristics

It would be a gargantuan if not impossible task to evaluate hopes for their soundness. The aim of this section is to set forth some *formal* features of those ultimate hopes which are sound. The approach now being taken rejects evaluating hopes for soundness on grounds of their fulfillment; to do so would be to take a hope as sound if it is sure of its happy outcome, or, after the fact, if it has been fulfilled. This is the approach *not* taken. Aimed ultimate hopes are characterized by desiring and calculation; what is being set forth here is that sound ultimate hopes are those characterized by simple absolute desiring for appropriate utilization or union, and by realistic judgment. Unsound ultimate hopes are characterized by varying degrees and kinds of defection and degradation from sound hope.

Aimed hoping has from the outset been understood as involving desiring and calculation. Ultimate hoping, that is, hoping de facto superordinate to other hopes, can be characterized by desirings and reckonings of all sorts. But sound ultimate hoping is not so indiscriminate. That sound ultimate hopes are those characterized by simple absolute desiring for appropriate utilization or union, and by realistic judgment, is an argument that has its force through explanation of what these characteristics are.

Characteristics of any ultimate hope's desiring were outlined earlier. Any hope's desiring is one of two sorts: either it is simple absolute desiring, aimed at an objective taken on its own merits; or it is willful desiring, with its

17. There is an interesting parallel in Ezra Stotland's notion of higher and lower schemas involved in hoping; cf. *Psychology of Hope*, p. 49.

objective functioning purely as an instrument or token of yielding to or acting against another's will. But if *sound* ultimate hope's desiring *were* to be willful, that is, were for some objective desired in order to yield or dominate, yielding or dominating would have to be desired "on its own merits." In mature persons the desire to dominate or be dominated is not appropriate utilization: it involves abuse of persons, it has no merit. So, as long as abuse of persons is ruled out, desiring domination is ruled out, and thus willful desiring is ruled out; such desiring cannot characterize sound ultimate hope. Since appropriate utilization (or union) characterize sound ultimate hope's objectives, it is simple absolute desiring that must characterize any ultimate hope that is sound.

The companion point concerns sound ultimate hope's calculation: what sort of reckoning is required for ultimate hope's soundness? It should go without saying that hoping that is blind to available evidence is unsound. But within "calculating," a relative contrast should be pointed out. There is on the one hand evidence that is recognizable by anyone, that shows the same face to everyone, that is available to each one without any attitudinal involvement, or with *any* sort of attitudinal involvement, between the one who reckons and the persons, objects, events that go to make up evidence. Whether I fear or desire, hate or love, could not care less or care a great deal, what is given to the reckoning is the same, and what the reckoner contributes is the same. For such evidence, *objective* calculation is required. On the other hand, there are cases where reckoning bears upon not just objectively available facts, but upon matters where the attitudinal disposition of the reckoner makes a difference to what is reckoned and for the reckoning. Marcel gives examples of this, where hoping or withholding hope makes a real difference in the outcome (and therefore should make a difference for the reckoning). In general, whenever the outcome hoped for involves personal relations, achievements, and endurance, the reckoning by the one who hopes must take into account not just factors accessible to the indifferent, but the fact of the desiring itself.[18] We can differentiate between these two types of reckoning, and call the one "objective calculation" and the other "realistic judgment." The latter *includes* objective calculation but recognizes as well

18. Some might want to recognize some hopings as useful fictions. The trouble with "useful fiction" is that a hope can be so labeled only by one who recognizes fiction, that is, lack of basis in fact. In one sense, every hope lacks basis in fact insofar as it bears on the future. But if lack of basis in fact means insufficient warrant for the likelihood of the outcome, then: (A) if the one who hopes recognizes such lack of warrant, he ceases to hope; or if he hopes, he does so willfully; or (B) if an observer judges objective evidence inadequate, *he* may not hope, but the one who hopes may yet have warrant. See Marcel's treatment of this issue in chapter 12, "Reasons and Hoping."

factors that go beyond such calculation. The thrust of this presentation of conditions for sound ultimate hoping then settles on realistic judgment: sound ultimate hoping requires realistic judgment. To include human aspirations when they are immaterial yields wishful thinking; to exclude human aspirations when they are germane is to judge erroneously.[19] "Realistic judgment" is the name for hope's reckoning insofar as it is open to different kinds of evidence and possibility, and, especially in matters where people have a great deal at stake, does not compress evidence into a form that excludes such aspirations.

Though it would seem that in desiderative-calculative hope, soundness is characterized by specificity, and that therefore the *un*specific is unsound, this is not necessarily so. Characteristic of sound hope is hope that knows its limitations. On the side of calculating, I not only reckon accurately what evidence there is, but am ready to recognize the limits of the evidence. Similarly, on the side of desiring, I recognize that while I seem to know what I want, I am ready to have opened up to me possibilities more desirable than what I can presently conceive. In this sense, I both know what I want and yet do not know; what I really want may yet be shown to me. There is therefore a non-fixity to whatever degree of specificity my desiring exhibits. Along this line, sound desiderative-calculative hope can be sound not just in being specific but in being appropriately unspecific. Realistic judgment does not necessarily require restricted hope. Constantly to trim one's hopes to the pedestrian, for example, *might* be precisely to condemn them to being unsound, because they operate from rigidly fixed desire (for example, embittered desire), and from calculation closed without warrant.

Here we glimpse a connection between fundamental hope and desiderative-calculative hope, one that sheds further light on fundamental hope. It would seem that there is a kind of despair permeating rigidly specific aimed hopes – if *this* is not fulfilled, *I* am lost. There can thus be a covert inchoate despair in the marrow of some aimed hopes. Conversely, readiness to have one's desirings amended and one's calculations delimited gives evidence of an openness with respect to the future which is hardly wishy-washy and is at the core of fundamental hope's positive character.

An objection comes immediately to mind: to put it thus is a case of having one's cake and eating it too; we hear condemnation of both doing one's calculating reliably and doing it badly, condemnation of both staying with one's desire and abandoning it. But: the point is not whether desiring should be fixed or labile, nor whether calculation should be carried out well or badly. The point is *appropriate* specificity on both sides.

19. Cf. Bloch on "putschism" and mechanism, p. 76.

And *what is* appropriate specificity? It is that which is well suited to the realities involved. And what are the realities involved? Fuller response to this question is the subject of this essay's Part III, especially its treatment of ontological presuppositions. Suffice it here to say that it makes a major difference whether, to use the language of Martin Buber, reality is exhaustively indicated by the language of I-It, by relationships of use and experiencing, or whether there is not also I-Thou, what Marcel expresses as "the experience of communion."

In such sense of the terms, and for the reasons thus given, an ultimate hope is sound if it has simple absolute desiring for appropriate utilization or union, and realistic judgment, as its formal characteristics. Moving beyond the formal level, and toward perhaps a fuller understanding of sound ultimate hope, I can venture an application of Gabriel Marcel's reflections to the relations between utilization, shared life, and soundness. If my hope is ultimate, and is unconditional in its desiring, it courts despair, for disappointment means the loss of what I desired above all else. If what I desired meant less to me, disappointment would affect me less. I could avoid despair by keeping my hope superficial. On the other hand, what is wrong in hoping deeply and thereby risking disappointment that tempts to despair? Is despair indecent, inhuman? Why not gamble all and risk losing? Such is the risk of an ultimate hope, especially if it is for utilization, for my own benefit.

Gabriel Marcel offers considerations that put the matter in a different light. If my ultimate hope is for shared life, my whole well-being is not put on the line if a specific outcome hoped-for fails to come about. Nor am I avoiding this risk by being vague. Hope for shared life is a hope linked primarily to specific other persons and only secondarily to specific events or states hoped for. Specific disappointments do not preclude shared life. If Marcel's approach is correct, a hope is on the side of being sound if its objective is a complex one with utilization, my own benefit, as *part of* shared life. My interests may not be served, and I am disappointed. But it would require, not just specific disappointment, but refusal or betrayal – or death – to void hope for shared life and bring me to the brink of despair. Hope does not necessarily become more sound by being trimmed; it becomes more sound by being less specifically utilizing and more loving.

Concluding position

Ultimate hope is an aimed hope, which if one has such, is de facto superordinate to other hopes. Its simple objectives are one's own benefit, another's benefit, or shared life; its objective can also be compound in a reciprocally beneficial system. Ultimate hope can be complex, joining different types of objectives as part of one hope.

Concrete analysis of ultimate hope is accurate if it takes hope as challenged by obstacle and characterized by some degree of human inadequacy. Hope-in-face-of-obstacle is the hope portrayed by Marcel (with a sense of *im*possibility); Kant's ultimate hope for the kingdom of God arises in the face of human social propensity to evil, and Bloch's, in the "darkness of the lived moment."

Bloch, Kant, and Marcel converge, and rightly so, in judgment that the agency required for hope's soundness is inadequately found in single individual human beings; the individual is inadequate to ground hope's possibility.

Sound ultimate hope is social. For both Kant and Bloch, sound ultimate hope is for the kingdom of God. And Marcel maintains that the only hope that can surmount disappointments is of the form hope-for-us. But there is a basic ambiguity in the term "social" here. For Kant and Bloch, the highest good or kingdom is characterized by minimized personal abuse and instrumental misuse and consequently by maximized appropriate reciprocal utilization. Needs and wants are met, control is effected, persons treat each other as ends, and suitable instrumentalities serve these ends. The kingdom is a *system*. But for Marcel – though he does not develop a highest good or kingdom as ultimate hope – the sound goal is not system but experience of communion, what this essay calls *shared life*.

This essay does not argue that each of the philosophers cannot but be interpreted in these ways. But there is a difference between the superabundant goal of Kant and Bloch, and that of Marcel, a difference between maximized suitable utilization and shared life. The first is not ignoble, and the two can be incorporated in a complex ultimate hope. But to argue as this essay does that only social ultimate hope is sound is to argue both against individual hope and for a hope that can have two kinds of social objective, system and shared life.

Ultimate hope that is sound is not so by virtue of its fulfillment. Thorough soundness depends on adequate grounds for hope, and discussion of this topic is yet to come. But there are formal characteristics required if any ultimate hope is to be sound, and these are: simple absolute desiring for appropriate utilization or union, together with realistic judgment.[20] Furthermore, a case can be made that an ultimate hope with a complex objective of utilization as

20. Another approach to evaluating hopes is set forth in James Muyskens' *The Sufficiency of Hope: The Conceptual Foundations of Religion* (Philadelphia: Temple University Press, 1979). Muyskens' term of positive evaluation is "justified" (whereas I use "sound"). His criteria apply to what I call aimed hopes, and they are four. A hope is justified if what is desired is *morally* acceptable, if it *pragmatically* fits in with the priorities of other desires, if there are good grounds for affirming the actual *possibility* of what is aimed at, and if the hope's *background beliefs* are justified, that

part of shared life is on the side of sound hoping, inasmuch as specific disappointment does not then require despair. But such a hope does risk being voided by refusal, betrayal, and death.

Ultimate hope that is formally sound and has an objective that is social as system or shared life or both will be the ultimate hope under discussion in the rest of this essay.

Fundamental hope is a holding off from declaring All is lost, I am lost. Absolute (fundamental) hope is doing so no matter what disappointments may overtake a person. But to hold off from despair is to believe that something (perhaps as yet unknown) is worthwhile and possible. Fundamental hope is thus always accompanied by an aimed "survivor-hope." Such a hope would seem to be ultimate, but it cannot be judged ipso facto sound.

With these concluded analyses of ultimate hope, fundamental hope, and absolute hope, this essay now turns to ontological models necessary both for their further interpretation and for drawing implications from such hopes for atheism and theism.

is, if whatever belief a hope presupposes is justified.

Muyskens's four criteria compare with my criteria for sound ultimate hope in the following ways. My selected objectives of appropriate utilization and union pass his moral test. His pragmatic (compatibility/priority) test for justified hope presupposes a notion of preference built into the necessary conditions for *any* hope (*S* hopes that *p* if: "it is not the case that *p* is not preferred by *S* on balance, or that *S* believes that *q*, which he prefers on balance, is incompatible with *p*"); I make preference part of *ultimate* hope and explore compatibility/priority in terms of "parts" of ultimate hope. Muyskens' standard of actual-possibility grounds is compatible with the possibility-side of my realistic judgment. And I have borrowed his phrase "background beliefs" to indicate some of the beliefs implied in ultimate hope, though I do not discuss criteria for such beliefs' justification.

My approach to sound hope adds emphasis on the kind of desiring (simple absolute desiring). Muyskens makes "*S* is disposed to act as if *p*" a necessary condition of any hope; I reserve such dispositions for hope that is *sound*, thereby devaluing velleities while conceding that they do characterize some hopings. I also argue that trust is implied in sound hope. And, in a different vein, I argue that there can be a hoping, possibly sound, that is *not* focused on a target, and this I call fundamental hope.

PART III

ONTOLOGIES, IMPLICATIONS, AND THEISM

CHAPTER 14

ONTOLOGIES

Two models

The explanatory thrust of this essay requires employment of two models. Explanation takes place within a certain interpretive context, and there can be differing interpretive contexts within which hope is situated.

In setting forth two such interpretive contexts, I do not offer a conclusive case for their adequacy or usefulness. But they do seem required for two reasons: to take adequate account of the analysis of hope carried out so far; and to locate in a broader perspective the three philosophers that have figured in a major way in this essay.

The models have a threefold application, ontological, epistemological, and anthropological-societal-ethical: they set forth different understandings of reality; they incorporate different ways of coming to know; and they suggest different patterns of how humankind do and should live together. The principal epistemological thrusts of the two models will be sketched under Implications of Hope. The main themes in present development of the models will be their ontological categories and social implications. The difficulties generally inherent in using models and particularly in using the second model are best addressed after the models have been presented.

Though the models are two, they are constructed from *three* starting points. These can be labelled the way of the object, the way of the subject, and the way of the intersubjective. Something should be said to introduce these emphases before the models are formulated.

The first emphasis is that directed towards objects. What is real is most obviously an object, a thing, an entity or item. Language indicates such with nouns, and with "this" and "that" and "it" and also "he" and "she" and "they." Systematic thinking links objects together according to patterns in space-time and/or according to influences that are causal. To be is, in the first instance, to be an object. Central to understanding the reality of an object is the cluster of characteristics that identify one such reality and differentiate it from another. Such an emphasis lays the foundation for a realm constituted entirely by determinisms.

The second way or emphasis is that of the subject. What is most obviously real is I-myself. There are admittedly *two* emphases here, not just one: there is the self as knower, and the self as agent. Two sets of characterizations are thus possible. The self is taken as (self-) conscious, rational, mind, spirit, thinking; and the self is taken as willing, choosing, deciding, (self-) determining, self-characterizing, originating, responsible. This second array is the dominant one for our subject-emphasis. The emphasis lays the foundation for a realm constituted by self-determination or freedom. For purposes of analysis of hope, the self is taken as one who *wills*, albeit not without some knowing.

The third emphasis is on the interpersonal. What is most obviously real is persons in personal relationship. Employment of language is essentially interpersonal, and the human relationship which shows itself in verbal and body language is the surest reality from which that reflective procedure which ontology is proceeds. This paradigm is inchoate in an infant's relationship to parents, and of full stature in a mature adult's involvement in interpersonal knowing and choosing.

The third emphasis or way is distinguishable from the second only insofar as the second's rational activity can be contrasted with what Martin Buber and others have called I-Thou relationship.[1] Insofar as I-Thou relationship is not reducible to rational activity (understood as the knowing of objects and self determination), this third approach stands on its own.

These emphases have appeared in the history of philosophy. Perhaps the simplest form of object-thinking can be found in the Greek atomists and Epicurus. Subject-thinking is evident from the standpoint of knowing in Descartes and from the standpoint of willing or self-actualizing in Fichte. The interpersonal categories are found perhaps most lucidly expressed in Martin Buber's notion of I-Thou relationship. But every thinker concerned with adequacy must move from the emphasis of the starting point to the difficulties of accounting for the strengths of the other emphases. Descartes must deal with the world, Fichte with non-ego, and Buber with I-It. Many thinkers settle into exploring a bipolar and somewhat paradoxical relationship – subject-object, *pour-soi* and *en-soi*, freedom and nature.

From these three emphases *two models* can be constructed. It is of course possible to sketch a model for ontology using just one emphasis; some of the philosophers just mentioned have done so. But a monopolar model, while facilitating unity of thought, seems less than plausible in view of the analysis developed so far. This essay's two models are labelled *will-nature* and *intersubjective*; some exposition will be devoted to each.

The will-nature model

The will-nature model joins together the object-emphasis and the subject-emphasis, realities given and realities deciding. It could be formulated as the "subject-object" model, but such formulation would tacitly support its being

1. Martin Buber, *I and Thou*, trans. with prologue and notes by Walter Kaufmann (New York: Charles Scribner's Sons, 1970); Gabriel Marcel, "I and Thou," in *The Philosophy of Martin Buber*, ed. Paul A. Schilpp and Maurice Friedman, Library of Living Philosophers, vol. 12 (LaSalle, Ill.: Open Court, and London: Cambridge University Press, 1967), pp. 41-48.

used as essentially a model of *knowing*. Since the subjective side of hoping is primarily characterized by desiring or wanting, it seems better to use "will." And since the objective side of hoping seems better characterized by that which is in relation to human choosing but may have patterns of its own, it seems better to use not "object" but that often ambiguous term "nature." The sense given to these terms will become clear as the model is formulated. There are strong affinities between this model and the approaches of Bloch and Kant.

According to the will-nature model, what is real is twofold: in the sphere of knowing, there are subjects that know and objects that are known. In the sphere of activity, there are agents which are self-determining and entities which are determined by something other than themselves. "Will" points to that sort of reality which is capable of making and using and knowing. Fulfillment lies in mastery, conceptual or operational. "Nature" points to that which is capable of being modified, used, and known. Fulfillment lies in functioning well for others' purposes, in being a perfect instrument (or in organic self-realization). These categories, taken severally or together, more or less exhaust the types of what is real.

These types are not to be taken in a derogatory sense, as if, for example, *using* were a relationship less than appropriate. A metaphysics whose principal categories are will and nature is not a metaphysics of alienation. It may be incomplete or inadequate, but it is not of itself a statement of what is but ought not to be.

This model does however admit of three further alternative determinations. Will-nature may express what is mutually supportive – the environment is basically in harmony with my intentions and is malleable to my activity; the other is ally. Or, the model may express which is mutually at odds – the environment stands counter to my desires and resists my manipulation; the other is obstacle. Or, the model may express a relationship that is neutral – what is situated over against my endeavoring has no bias of its own, either for or against my purposes; I make of it what I will, if I can; the other is instrument.

These same alternatives apply if the will-nature model is construed as involving people. Persons other than myself are objects for me. They may or may not have their own patterns, involuntary or voluntary. And these patterns may or may not, in general or in particular, be in accord with what I want. Persons other than myself may be not only objects but also *wills*; hence I may will in relation to another's will as well as in relation to another's nature – as for example in willful desiring.

The intersubjective model

This second model must be formulated with care. There is the temptation to see it as a complicated form of the will-nature model. At the core of the will-nature model is the relation of using and being used (and – cognitively – grasping and being grasped). The intersubjective model does not consist in multiplying the relation typical of the first model. Nor does the second model consist in reciprocal using or modifying, each willing changes in the other for the sake of oneself. Nor does this second model consist in parallel purposes; it is not a model of alliance of wills, as in Sartre's we-subject.[2] Fulfillment lies in being with, in shared life, in union.

At the heart of the second model is *appreciation*. This means that the other is not merely an instrument for the self, nor merely also an end in itself. More precisely, the relation between self and other is that of a bond surpassing mere utility. What is wanted directly, however, is not the *bond* but rather the flourishing existence of the other. In persons this relation is one of non-covetous love.[3]

Some depth can be given to this model by inquiring into the relationship and asking "*on whose terms*" it is constituted (as if a peace treaty were being negotiated). The will-nature model makes place for interactions on the terms of the self. What is acted upon has its purposes – if it has any – subordinate to those of the self acting. The other is essentially instrument, and can be dealt with without remainder for the self's purposes. Interaction is on the self's own terms. Or, if the other has patterns of its own, interaction may be on the terms of the other as nature or as will; the self can then only either resist or ratify the patterns of the other. Or, interaction may be according to some kind of back-and-forth, reciprocal, or trade-off model.

The intersubjective model begins – but does not end – with stress on the other as an end in itself, as having "its own terms." This model recognizes some accord in Kant's ethical position that persons are not to be treated merely as means but also as ends in themselves. The intersubjective model does not imply that the other must *always* be treated predominantly as an end in itself, but that the other can and sometimes should be.

Yet to stress the other as end in itself, as having its own terms, is only half the account needed for this model. The fuller story is that in the relationship "new terms" may arise. To insist that the only significant terms are those of

2. Cf. Jean-Paul Sartre, *Being and Nothingness*, trans. Hazel E. Barnes (New York: Washington Square Press, Pocket Books, 1966), pt. 3, chap. 3, sec. III, B, "The We-Subject," pp. 547-56.

3. "Non-covetous love" can be understood in two ways: (1) as a synonym for appreciation in contrast to a relationship involving utilization, and (2) as a being-ready-to-serve-as-instrument-for-another (altruism) rather than being-ready-to-treat-the-other-as-instrument (egoism). In the present context instrumentalism is excluded, and the phrase is a synonym for appreciation.

the self makes the other purely instrument; to insist on the other's terms is to make the self an instrument – reversal does not alter the type of relationship. To say that new terms may arise is to say that the relationship is not restricted to the antecedent terms of either party, even if they are parallel. Between the realities in relation the outcomes are not either a yielding or a dominating. The terms of each may be abrogated, or enriched, because of the encounter.

Yet "new terms" does not touch the core of this model, for it can still be construed as reciprocal utility, albeit adaptable. The core of the model is *appreciation*. This means that while the other is indeed an end in itself, the relationship is not primarily characterized by the self's readiness to make itself instrument for the other, or turn third parties to the service of the other – sophistications of a utility-model.

Gabriel Marcel offers a helpful example.[4] I stop a passerby to ask directions. The relation is initially purely functional; a signpost or map would do as well. But in our conversation I discover that we have interests in common, and perhaps friends in common. The conversation may lead to each of us becoming an individual for the other, and perhaps even friends. To utility is added mutual appreciation. Marcel speaks of a threshold between the utilizing and the appreciative (though "appreciative" is not his word), and of gradations in the appreciative. Appreciative relationship is relationship of non-covetous love; towards its zenith such relationship is unitive, is shared life.

The intersubjective model has as paradigm not only appreciative relationship between persons, but appreciation which is mutual. I am not a means to the other's benefit, and the other is not means to mine; I encounter the other with positive regard, and the other does so with respect to me.

The model is taken as personal; it is taken as mutual; but an obvious question arises. Persons can mutually appreciate each other. Does the model apply to what is *non-personal*? Marcel thinks it can. On the descriptive level, he offers an analysis of a "meeting" with a flower.[5] It is not that I use this flower; nor is there the kind of knowledge that asks only "What kind of a flower is this?" His analysis of such encounter seems to accord with this essay's appreciation.[6] And it seems something like such encounter is possible with a work of art.

4. MB 1, 220-21.

5. MB 2, 14-16. Beyond the level of description, he presents reality as intersubjective; see chapter 18, Implication, Ontology, and Indication.

6. Similar appreciative encounter with a flower is explored by D.T. Suzuki in his essay "Existentialism, Pragmatism, and Zen," pp. 270-73; this essay appears in *Zen Buddhism: Selected Writings of D.T. Suzuki*, ed. William Barrett (Garden City, N.Y.: Doubleday, Anchor Books, 1956).

There are admittedly difficulties in recognizing that the intersubjective model is applicable where one term of the relationship is non-personal. Mutual appreciation may obtain where a higher animal is involved, with a pet, for example, but is doubtful where the other is a stone. For a painting there may indeed be appreciation, but it is one-way.

Yet similar difficulty besets utilization and benefit in the will-nature model. My dog may benefit from my instrumental role of feeding him. Does a painting *benefit* from careful treatment? It seems that both models have their difficulties when applied to some relationships where one term is non-personal.

The central motifs of each model seem to be, on the one hand, appreciation for the intersubjective, and on the other, using and being used for the will-nature model. Analogical conceptual extensions of such modelling might range from that which cannot but be used and can never be encountered or appreciated, to that which can only be encountered or appreciated and can never be used. (The case could then be argued whether either conceived extreme finds any instance.)

Appreciation is paradigmatically mutual appreciation. Yet, for purposes of a certain type of logical analysis, mutual appreciation's two-way character will be broken down as if it were two distinct one-way relations that obtained: (1) I appreciate/love you, and (2) you appreciate/love me. This second relation is equivalent to: I am loved by you. In the following logical analysis, which contrasts relationship of utility with that of non-covetous love, just the first of the two one-way relations is subject to analysis.

A logical analysis of the intersubjective model can be made clear through contrast between a relationship of utility and one of love. Compare: I purchase X from Y because of Z (I purchase milk from Fred because his store is open nights) with: I love you. In the first we can distinguish the self (I), the relationship (purchasing milk from), its term (Fred), and the ground of the relationship (because the store is open nights). The term and the ground are separable: should Fred be fired and the store remain, I would still buy there. For Fred anyone else can be substituted; the relationship remains of the same type, but with different terms. (If Fred's departure does mean my ceasing to be a customer, then perhaps an affective bond, or a more complicated utility, is operative.) There is a logical link between the type of relationship and the separability of the relation's term and ground: separability (as substitutability) and utility logically go together. In the case of I love you, things are different. We distinguish the self (I), the relationship (love), its term (you), and ... what ground? The ground may be extrinsic to you (I thought you were someone else) or may only be part of you (you have baby-blue eyes; you saved my life). Such grounds, extrinsic or partial with respect to you, suggest however that the relationship is less than love in its full sense. But insofar as the ground for the relationship approaches identity with the term – moves from "I love you because I need to love somebody" through "I love you because you stood by me" to "I love you because of ... you" – then substitution is not possible. Term and ground are not separable, and there is a *logically necessary link between the type of relationship and the identity of term and ground.* Non-covetous love and identity of term and ground logically go together.[7] The logical core of the intersubjective model is the logically necessary link between the type of relationship (appreciation/love) and the identity of its term and ground.

This intersubjective model and the will-nature model should not be taken as merely subjective frameworks, proposed as tools for imagining what cannot be known. They are indeed frameworks, but they also describe, actually albeit selectively, some features of human living.[8] They express in a simplified way what life presents in ways more complex. They are pure or ideal types, somewhat analogous to the way in which Boyle's Law describes relationships in the ideal gas. At least the will-nature model seems to describe human living, be it the life of *homo faber* or *homo homini lupus*.

There is however a particular set of challenges to the intersubjective model. The first is that the model is only a mirage: human beings do not actually deal with each other in that way. Such dealings can perhaps be conceptually constructed, but actually human beings have personal dealings that are only reciprocal, even dialectical, relationships of utility; it is a misrepresentation to call them any of them anything else. On this reading, even the paradigm case of the intersubjective model would turn out to be not some form of appreciative love, but rather something else – intricate and even exemplary relationships of using and being used. A second challenge adds the objection that even if relationships of appreciative love are not a mirage, they are too rare to be important for ontology or social thought and ethics. These are challenges to the ontological import of the intersubjective model.

There is an additional pair of challenges. A third arises from the "nature" of any model. Theoretically speaking, any model is couched in object-language, and at best selectively describes features "out there" in the world. Any model is object-bound, "third-person." There are objections enough to a model that includes a "first-person" factor, self-determination or will: self as agent seems to be a conceptual 'vanishing point' conceived by negative extrapolation from object-concepts. Add to this that even a realistically

7. "Identity of term and ground" does not mean that my own self and my disposition are not involved as ground in the relationship; the point is that the totality of the other is essential to the relationship's grounding and not just as its term.

8. Helpful on models is the work of Ian Barbour. His definition of "model" is in his *Myths, Models and Paradigms* (New York: Harper & Row, 1974), p. 6.

understood model is selective, partial, or abstractive in content. To think in terms of a model is to think with antecedent conditions, categories, expectations, perceptual sets, hypotheses for confirmation. The fourth challenge is practical: to act in terms of a model is also to have expectations, usually a desire for satisfaction. The intersubjective model is resistant both to theoretical selective attention and to practical limited expectations. What I approach in appreciative love I do not approach merely partially; I am open to whatever fullness the other offers me. And I do not approach with a specific outcome in mind, nor with a design of the dealings in mind. While the nature of the non-partial and non-designed or non-hypothetical character of the intersubjective model is more than I can plumb here, the manner in which Martin Buber explicates I-Thou relation is the way I would proceed in unfolding the non-excluding aspect of the intersubjective model. Some of this non-selective character is pointed to in saying that "new terms" may arise, beyond those antecedent in the self and other.

While the intersubjective model may appear to be a dream of human interactions, its nightmare is the Buber enthusiast, with *I and Thou* in hand, consumed with puzzling out how to "apply it" to her or his spouse! Endemic thus to the intersubjective model is the danger of its deteriorating into one more set of categories, however new or appealing they might be, for use as a technique in dealing with others.[9] Given this theoretical and practical threat, I propose an at least theoretical preventive regimen. The intersubjective model is *a non-model model:* it is an (antecedent) imagined pattern that calls for not being limited to any antecedent pattern.

An inchoate answer to one further question can be sketched here. If the models have some kind of prima facie applicability, in what ways are they related? One is that each offers a perspective logically different from the other. It is fruitful to think of them as complementary, each needing the other if a full picture of human possibilities is to be imagined. In addition, I would propose that one of the ethical implications of considering these two models is that a definition of what is good should not be couched solely in terms of one model. Further anthropological, societal, and ethical implications of these models follow a survey of the ontological and epistemological bearings of the models.

9. In his *Mutuality: The Vision of Martin Buber* (Albany: State University of New York Press, 1985), Donald Berry voices a caution about speaking of models concerning Martin Buber's understanding of relationships between people: "To employ a model is to relate to the other in terms of precedent categories" (p. 58); yet he does admit the term. More importantly, he addresses the possibility of I-Thou relationships both between those who are not peers, in relationships "real but not full," and in the political order.

Ontological bearing of the two models

Conceding descriptive or phenomenological usefulness to these two models, the question still remains: How are these models for *ontology?*[10] Ontology is discourse about what is real qua real. These models could be received as having rough-hewn phenomenological applicability, and yet be rejected as ontological. Persons or flowers or tools or works of art come into existence, perdure, and cease to exist quite apart from whether or not they are used or loved. Hence ontological theory that turns on utilization and appreciation is misconceived as ontology.

Such an objection, however, already has operative within it an ontological model: what is real is what can be located in space-time, that is, as objects. For such, relationships are further determinations, of less ontological significance. If this assumed ontological standpoint is justified, then the objection stands. But if it can be questioned, then some other considerations, perhaps of equal significance, can be brought to bear.

Ontology deals with existents, their interrelations, and their conditions of possibility. We can begin with the position that an ontology points to existents and their *capabilities*, to what is and what can be. We can therefore speak of existents capable of using, capable of being used, and capable of appreciation or love. The question of the intersubjective model's relevance becomes therefore the question whether there are not only existents capable of using and being used but also those capable of loving and being loved.

But there is an ambiguity in "capable" that must be dealt with. The word should not be taken in a merely mechanical sense – someone can be brought to the point of . . . – for this is immediately to restrict the term of one model. "Capable of" should bear the expanded sense "capable-of-and-brought-to-fulfillment-in" and should be contrasted with "capable-of-and-adversely-affected-by." A person, for example, is capable of being a (metaphorical) doormat. There is in this notion of "capable" an inescapable can-and-ought structure, as in Kant's position that persons *can* be treated as means but ought not to be so treated exclusively.

One perspective of any ontology is its categories that answer the question Why. This essay uses the word "ground" aetiologically, to refer to anything that provides such an answer, anything that is a basis for explanation. "Ground" refers to all types of actual influence, to whatever makes a

10. Metaphysics most generally is the study of whatever is real qua real (being), whatever can be real (possible), and whatever cannot be otherwise (necessary). "Ontology" as I use this term refers to such thinking when it is tied to a paradigm, as in the case of this essay's models. The phrase "regional ontologies" has some currency; this essay's models can in a sense constitute such, and their integration would be part of an overall metaphysics.

difference. Ontological consideration of types of grounds follows the lines of paradigmatic types of what is real. Subject-grounding and first-person explanation can be loosely designated as agency, "willpower." The ground of hope's factors is autonomous self-determination. I face the future with openness, I withstand the temptation to despair, because I choose to do so. Explanation ends in the subject as agent, e.g., "*I* called the police."

Of a different type is object-grounding. Actually this is a *set* of types encompassing what might be called impersonal factors. One cluster includes organic factors – genetic, biochemical, biological, and physiological; another encompasses factors which are environmental – social, economic, cultural, political. Hoping has its grounds in heteronomous determinants. Its aspects find explanation in objects, or in the subject understood as object or as a nature. Grounds are *this* or *that*, including *he* and *she* and *they*; such grounds permit third-person explanation, "cause," e.g., "He made me do it."

The third type of grounding is intersubjective. Hope for example would thus arise because I am in positive relationship with you. I face the future with openness, I hold off from despair, because I love you and am loved by you. (A venture in this direction led to the earlier formulation, "Hope. . . is simply the way in which trusting love faces the future.")[11] This type of ground has remained, philosophically, in the background. An early sense of "ground" was the *aitia* of the ancient Greek dramatists: "Who is responsible?" This first-person notion was upstaged by the impersonal in the *aitiai* or causes of Aristotle, and the latter have been operative ever since in thought bearing primarily on the physical.

The types of grounds that follow upon ontological emphases are, at least conceptually, obvious. But an attempt to speak of *adequate* grounds has often gone beyond one single *type* to one of the ontological *models*.

The will-nature model does admit of decision (will) under the influence of the other (causality of nature, including my own nature, or of another's will). This model admits of explanation of hoping as my holding off from despair not simply because I so decide, nor simply because something other than myself makes me, but because I and this other each contribute to the refusal to despair: grounding is bilateral. But on this model grounding *need not be bilateral*; refusal to despair may be entirely willful, or entirely heteronomous, e.g., due to a drug or perhaps hypnosis.

The intersubjective model of explanation, on the other hand, has prime exemplification in effects due to a relationship between persons, effects which are inadequately explained by one party's decision or by impersonal factors, or by juxtaposition of the two. One can deliver a monologue by will power, but not converse. One cannot share by willpower; all one can do is deprive

11. P. 46.

oneself of half or acquire half of something. Sharing, when it is more than partition, seems to depend on mutual appreciation. William Lynch discusses a mutuality which *enables* one to will autonomously, and suggests that a good relationship between psychotherapist and client is of this type.[12] Furthermore, aetiologies of intersubjective relationship are not limited to physical proximity, as couples separated by many miles can testify.

Epistemological bearing of the two models

These two models have application to questions of epistemology: they have relationships to the issues of what we do know, what we can know, and how we know. The primary application of these models to questions of knowing will be restricted to hope, and will be treated under Implications of Hope. Some general and background observations, however, will be made here, though no attempt is made to develop a full epistemology.

A first point to be noted is that both models are interactional and are not therefore primarily models of knowing. Both models reflect the "primacy of the practical"; the knowledge involved is derivative from dynamic interrelationships. What the models do not have in common are the type of knowledge and the basis for knowledge. The will-nature model has knowledge closely linked to observation (objects act on and modify the subject) and experiment (the subject acts on objects to get them to react). Such manners of knowing are for the sake of utilization.

The intersubjective model has knowledge as presence. It reveals the other less as a type and more as unique. Such knowledge obtains within positive affective relationship, and is not fully translatable into objective knowledge.

In both cases distinction should be made between what is known in the relationship – differing according to the different types of relationship – and what is known derivatively, as a consequence of the relationship.

Anthropological-societal-ethical bearings of the two models

The two models have implications not only for the spheres of ontology and epistemology but also for those of philosophical anthropology, social theory, and ethics: they suggest understandings of how people do live in societies, and they offer suggestions on human fulfillment and the good, both individual and social.

The will-nature model fits an understanding of the human person that contrasts freedom in the will and determinisms in other aspects of human existence. Within this perspective the classic problems of free will and determinism are posed. Pressed hard in one direction, this model yields a notion of will that is arbitrary, and a notion of reason that bears on choice

12. *Images*, p. 106.

of suitable means but not on choice of suitable ends. Kant's position, however, does not go so far; will should be rational, yet autonomous; ends accord with this model is the image of person as *homo faber*, man the artisan. It is also the home of willful desiring.

The societal patterns consonant with the will-nature model are those where social relations are primarily instrumental. Where social relations are instrumentally positive, each person is ally or at least instrument for the well-being of the other; where relations are negative, the other is obstacle. In the one case, the person is *civis*, fellow citizen; in the other, *lupus*, predator or competitor.

In the ethical context these emphases yield norms or goods based essentially on interests. The good is one's own individual or group benefit, to be obtained with the instrumentality of the other, reciprocally perhaps in alliance, parallel purposes, and cooperation, and with no loss to the others. Alternately, it is to be obtained in a win-lose situation where one suffers loss in being instrument for another. In both kinds of situation, the optimum is effective utilization of whatever is other.

The intersubjective model is open to an understanding of the human person that makes human existence radically and *positively* "with" other persons. Choosing is recognized as less locked in determinisms or in spontaneity and as more both dependent on others' good will and independent of their determination.

The societal patterns in accord with this model are those closely linked to appreciation and non-covetous love. They mesh with this essay's relational benefit or shared life. As this essay expressed it earlier:

> Shared life, then, can encompass a broad range of positive relationships and bonds – personal intimacy, friendship, familial bonds, and some forms of social, national, and international relations. It obtains wherever using and being used, possession and being possessed, consuming and being consumed, are subordinate to unitive intent.[14]

But as a model applicable to social theory, the intersubjective model falters. Insofar as it is plausible, it seems to be more a statement of an ideal than a pattern of what actually obtains. It has thus a substantial ethical thrust; what it commends are those courses of action which are more open to non-covetous love. Granting its role more as an ideal than as a mirror of the actual, the ideal if presents is quite different from maximized utilization. It presents fulfillment less in terms of possession and consumption and more in terms of

13. On rational beings setting their own ends, see the discussion in chapter 11's note 42.

14. P. 134.

union. One question that the intersubjective model raises is whether it is obligatory (in contrast to supererogatory) not to close oneself off from a possibility the actualization of which does not depend solely on one's own will or one's own nature or on will working on or through nature.

In this essay's Part II, some sample principles of philosophical anthropology and ontology were formulated; there the claim was made that types of actual benefit cannot be described without use of some such principles. The sketches just concluded of our models' bearings on ontology, anthropology, social theory and ethics are elaborations on such principles.[15]

Convergencies and corollaries

What has been said directly about these models, and what has been suggested as avenues for further elaboration, can be gathered together in brief compass. The statements that follow receive little amplification; they are linked principles that seem to "go together." Showing thoroughly how each is linked with its model is beyond the scope of this essay. All the points that follow, however, have a bearing on analysis of hope and each operates as a *presupposition* when the model is employed in hope analysis.

The will-nature model takes the subject as free agent and takes the object as the realm in which agency is carried out. The principal relationship that links the model's two poles is *utilization:* the other serves as instrument for the agent's purposes. This is the model's neutral determination. Conceivable as well is the negative determination when the other is obstacle, and the positive determination when the other is deterministically or freely supportive, is "ally." The type of fulfillment conceivable in this model is mastery – successful possession, consumption, utilization. The model accords place for different types of hope's objectives provided the latter are either the agent's own benefit or the benefit of one other than the agent.

According to the will-nature model, hope is analyzable without remainder into desiring on the one hand and calculation on the other. Calculation is carried out concerning events or states in nature, among objects. Knowledge is by experiment and observation, and has to do primarily with means. A dichotomy obtains between facts and values. The former govern objectivity and are the subject of calculation. Value, however, is valu*ing*; it is arbitrary wanting and has no connection with facts. The will-nature model has will either as arbitrary and imperial or as in accord with, ratifying, nature or another's will.

Two lines of reasoning have their proper site in this model, and each shall be taken up later. The first has to do with how trust is analyzed, and the second has to do with how theism or atheism fits into hope analysis.

15. See p. 137.

The intersubjective model takes realities as related in appreciation, in appreciating and being appreciated, in accepting and being accepted. While the will-nature model's interrelationships admit of further determination as positive, neutral, or negative, the intersubjective model has only positive interrelationship. The type of fulfillment congruent with this model is union rather than successful utilization; the outcome may be beyond the "terms laid down" by the participants. The objective of hope that harmonizes with this model is relational benefit or shared life.

Hope in this model is hope-in as well as hope-that. Knowledge is through appreciative presence, in human persons through personal dialogue. Between fact and value there is no strict dichotomy; knowing and valuing go essentially together, and desiring or wanting is more responsive and less arbitrary. Also in knowing, a gap is experienced between reality and its explanations, a gap which is not just one of lack of details; at issue is not just extent, but depth. Human action is explained not between the dilemma's horns of freedom and determinism, but at another level where choosing and being chosen are not opposed.

And the lines of reasoning that link this model with analysis of trust and with argument bearing on theism and atheism will also be taken up later.

CHAPTER 15

IMPLICATIONS OF HOPE

Both ultimate hopes and fundamental hope have certain implications. The implications of ultimate hope are cognitional, conative, and affective: they include beliefs, kinds of readiness or dispositions, and trust. The implications of fundamental hope also have to do with trust.

The term "implies" means, as far as ultimate hopes and beliefs are concerned, that actual ultimate hoping is such that actual though perhaps unacknowledged believing is a necessary ingredient in it; if a person claims to have such hoping without the related belief, either that person misidentifies his or her disposition as hoping, or fails to acknowledge actual beliefs. Certain kinds of readiness or dispositions are implied when a hope is sound: a person is then prepared to act or interact in ways consistent with and required for the objective's real possibility. If a person is not so disposed, the hope is, in a sense beyond the formal, unsound. Hope's trust also has implications, and this sense of "implication" is made clear when such trust's implications are charted. Both sound ultimate hope and fundamental hope imply trust, and it is through the trust of these two kinds of hope that hope can be not only a climate of the mind, but an organ of apprehension as well.

Implications of formally sound ultimate hope

This essay has developed reflection on hopes that are aimed towards an objective, a future state or event. It has selected those hopes that are ultimate. In abstract analysis, such hopes are aimed at one's own benefit, another's benefit, or shared life. Such objectives may be simple, compound-reciprocal, or complex. Concrete analysis of hope-situations finds hope confronted by obstacles, and characterized by some sense of the hoper's finitude. Arguments showing the implications of ultimate hopes will be limited to those that are, on formal grounds, *sound* ultimate hopes. Such hopes are characterized by simple absolute desiring for appropriate utilization or union, and realistic judgment.

Sound ultimate hope's calculation has the form of what this essay calls realistic judgment. While most of the exposition of such judgment focused on judgment of possibility, it is now time to recall that it is not only beliefs about possibility that characterize hope; in Part I we noted that beliefs about desirability are also involved. Any aimed hope, and a fortiori sound ultimate hope, implies that what is hoped for is believed to be both possible and desirable.

There is an implied *judgment of worth* or desirability in any hoping. Hope implies, therefore, evaluation. But because this essay is now focused on sound ultimate hopes characterized by simple absolute desiring, such evaluation is of an objective assessed according to its own merits (rather than on the grounds involved in desiring that is willful). Earlier we noted that an objective may be desired for its own sake or as a means to something else: "merits" here are thus either instrumental or obtaining in their own right. When it comes to hopes that are ultimate, *parts* of a complex ultimate hope's objective may be instrumental, but the whole is desired for its own sake. Evaluation thus is inevitably evaluation of ends.

But in the matter of hope, ends can be assessed for their desirability in themselves *and* for their possibility: I can calculate worth and likelihood. Evaluation thus exhibits a tension between judging the more worthwhile and the more likely. Judgment could settle on the already present (what is, ought to be), due to its being already at hand. But judgment could also move to the less likely because unfamiliar, to what "eye hath not seen, nor ear heard."

In the concrete, and within the scope of this essay, such evaluation bears upon what is desirable and possible as a social objective. Often utopian visions, compared to the obstacles to their realization, are judged unrealistic; half a loaf is better than none. There may be a *sifting* of social reciprocally-beneficial systems of utility. But if what this essay calls shared life is evaluated, at stake are different kinds of judgments of desirability and possibility.

Judgments of possibility – what a person who hopes believes is possible – obtain on three levels, at least within the framework of this essay. First, there are beliefs about how benefits do come about. It matters in the judging-possible, for example, whether a person believes that he or she can benefit only if someone else suffers. It matters whether benefits are believed to be of a win-lose sort or, on the other hand, can be shared. The second level is close to this: it is the level of one's ontological beliefs. If a person holds, for example, that this essay's intersubjective model finds confirmation in reality, then that person can hope for shared life, believing it possible. But one's range of hope is different if at best only fairminded systems of utility are believed possible.

Presuming the first two levels as hope's "background beliefs,"[1] the third level is that of beliefs concerning the concrete availability of agencies appropriate for bringing about or contributing to the objective. If there are different kinds of objectives, there may be different kinds of agencies required. When silk purses are hoped for, sow ears won't do; for what Marcel describes as an outcome where love and creation are involved, agencies may

1. For this notion of "background beliefs" I am indebted to James Muyskens, *The Sufficiency of Hope*, p. 47.

be different from those required for purely material results.[2]

We can apply these general considerations to the beliefs implied in sound ultimate hopes, especially those social hopes understood as system or as shared life. In doing so, we keep in mind the benefit-theories and ontologies that function as "background beliefs" for such hopes.

Hope for a fairminded system of reciprocal utilization is a compound of hope for one's own benefit and hope for another's benefit. Insofar as this hope is for *another's benefit*, and if this is interpreted according to the will-nature model, then the one who hopes views a specific outcome as a means to another's benefit, is prepared if necessary to be a means to such benefit, and believes that what is required to effect the outcome is available as instrument. Such functioning as an instrument may or may not be at the expense of oneself or of an other serving as instrument. But hope for another's benefit may turn out to be hope for shared life; indeed, earlier discussion pointed to situations where sacrifice required or offered was subsumed under the higher purpose of shared life.[3] If hope for another's benefit can be so subsumed, then the deeper analysis of such hope is that of a complex hope primarily for shared life, with hope for another's benefit as a part. And insofar as hope for a fairminded system of reciprocal utilization includes hope for *one's own benefit*, such hope is more plausibly interpreted according to the will-nature model (though, like hope for another's benefit, it may be able to be interpreted on the intersubjective model *if* one's own benefit is subordinate to shared life). A specific outcome is hoped for as an instrument or means to one's own benefit. If one is not of oneself capable of securing such an outcome, then an other agent is required for it to be possible. Such other is an other agent and in acting functions as an instrument.

Hoping for one's own benefit and another's benefit, in a system of reciprocal utilization, implies believing that instrumentalities needed are available.[4]

If one's ultimate hope is for *shared life* it seems implausible to interpret this on the will-nature model, since on this interpretation each is the instrument of the other. If it is well interpreted according to the intersubjective model, then the outcome is one in which new terms can arise. Shared life requires an other. That other must be well disposed towards me. The other must be capable of entering into relationship in which it is not self-centered, that is, aimed at making of me an instrument. Relationship between the one who hopes and the other is not utilization but union; the other is participant, not instrument.

2. See chapter 12, Hoping's Ontological Import.

3. In chapter 9, Some Complex Forms of Hope's Objectives.

4. Such instrumentalities are believed to be such that they will not make of the hoper an instrument for their own ends, when helping becomes actually using.

Beliefs involved in hope for shared life are not beliefs that instrumentalities are available for me to employ (or which take their course without my involvement). Hoping for shared life implies believing that there is available an other capable of entering into affective union, not as an instrument, and not as ready to make of me an instrument, but as a participant.

But belief concerning instrumentalities available and belief concerning participants available, are two different kinds of belief. Quite apart from whether such beliefs are about another human being, nature, world history, evolution, God, or the cosmos, there is a difference between looking to such "other" as instrument to be counted on, and looking to such "other" as participant appreciated and appreciating. And this leads to consideration of the disposition of the person who hopes, if that person is hoping soundly.

Martin Buber pointed out that a shift from idolatry to faith is not just replacement of the attitude's object, but a change in the attitude itself.[5] Ultimate hopes' different beliefs differ in their requisite dispositions, in the readiness that should characterize the person who hopes and believes, if that hope is not to be unsound. Sound ultimate hope for a fairminded system of reciprocal utilization requires being ready to find in oneself and in public evidence the instrumentalities needed to bring about the objective. Sound ultimate hope for shared life requires one's own readiness to meet the other as participant, and to be participant oneself.

Of course a person can believe that *both* fairminded system and shared life are desirable and jointly possible. Hope for such a complex objective implies both kinds of believing – that instruments are available, and that participants are available – including, in both cases, oneself. It also includes the implicit background belief that utility and communion are not incompatible benefits, and it suggests that a person implicitly believes that both ontological models are appropriate. And soundly to have such a complex ultimate hope for both objectives is to have both kinds of readiness, instrumental and participatory.

Sound ultimate hopes thus have implications of a cognitional sort – concerning desirability and possibility, with their attendant background beliefs – and of a conative sort – dispositions or readinesses, instrumental and participatory. It remains to note the affective implication of sound ultimate hope.

Trust implied by sound ultimate hope's desiring

Sound ultimate hope is characterized by simple absolute desiring for appropriate utilization or union, and by realistic judgment. Sound ultimate hope implies beliefs and readiness; it will now be argued that such hope's simple absolute desiring requires and thus implies trust.

5. *I and Thou*, pp. 153-55.

The notion of trust must be made progressively more precise, not only for the present argument concerning trust implied by hope's simple absolute desiring, but for later argument concerning implications of trust. Set aside from the outset is trust as affectively negative prediction, as in "I trust he'll be as shiftless working for me as he was under my predecessor." Trust of a positive sort has come up in Erik Erikson's notion of Basic Trust, and under the name "mutuality" in William Lynch.[6] Trust's sense in the present argument is not exactly either of these earlier meanings, though it owes much to both.

There is a trust or mutuality at the earliest stage of human existence, between mother and child. Such trust, as it begins, soon sets aside its ties to particular satisfactions – it becomes compatible with particular disappointments, unavoidable pains and separations – but it exhibits ties to particular persons, that is, to parents. It is also, from the beginning, a trust in oneself, in one's capacity to cope with urges. Trust appropriate to infancy develops other forms in the early years of childhood. If relationships necessary to foster such trust are deficient, something like such relationships are needed in later life, in a therapeutic context. (This latter is the primary context of William Lynch.)

Besides childhood or therapeutic trust, there is a trust common enough in adolescents and adults; this is a present affectively positive relationship with individual persons. We could call this face-to-face trust, did it not shade off into relationships joining people separated by great distances. It is characteristically a bond between specific individuals; it can be called intimacy-trust.

The sense of trust central to our present argument, the trust required by simple absolute desiring, is somewhat different from infant and therapeutic trust and from intimacy-trust, although these are involved in its genesis. Its general character is pointed out by Erikson when he maintains that the hope of the infant, signalized by the component of basic trust, is a human ego-strength that is established early, required for later development, and *found throughout all stages of sound human development*. It changes its form, but it does exhibit continuity. It changes, or should change, in sophistication, extent, and depth. The trust is generally social; it is trust in or of significant others, and these others are furthermore located in institutional settings. The relationship with such others is a *positive affective bond*, and "*at-homeness-with*," at every stage. It is not consonant with Erikson's eightfold schema to take these significant others as neutral or hostile – save when the required strength is lacking and the outcome is given basic tone by the schema's litany of negatives: mistrust, shame, guilt, inferiority, confusion, isolation,

6. In chapter 7, pp. 40-42, 44.

stagnation, despair. Insofar as at each stage the relationship with significant others and with oneself is affectively positive, the relationship is what this essay calls trust.

But more must be said about this trust. Some writers speak of a basic trust in one's ultimate context.[7] Such expression usually points up a trust that is in some ways not necessarily linked to specific individuals: it is generic, cosmic, pervasive. Such trust seems at first glance to be trust of everything – or of nothing at all, just a trustfulness. It seems sound to recognize as in *tension* this generic trust and the previously-mentioned trust of significant others. There may well be a twofold development. One side shows sophisticated specificity and depth: I learn whom not to trust, and whom to trust more deeply. The other shows expansion and detachment from specific individuals. The trust of our present context is a trust that *can* be characterized by either or both sides in tension. Such trust may be deep and placed in one person; such trust may be cosmic and perdure without present links to any specific person. There seems a necessary tension and ambiguity to such a trust, drawn to be both concrete and generic; but it is this type of trust, which has forms appropriate to infancy, therapy, and intimacy, that is the trust of present argument.

But can the case be made: when simple absolute desiring obtains, does it require such trust? Such desiring is of two sorts, appropriately utilizing, and unitive. Insofar as such desiring is unitive, for shared life of some sort, it is obvious that whatever is involved in such outcome's possibility is viewed with affectively positive regard. Therefore simple absolute desiring for union or shared life requires trust.

And if desiring is for appropriate utilizing, it is desire that the other be instrument for me, or that I be instrument for the other. If my desire is that the other be instrument for me, for my own benefit, it seems that the relationship, between myself who desires to use and not misuse or abuse, and whatever is viewed as possible instrument, is one not of hostility (engendering my wish to dominate), nor of indifference (if such means both that I care not for any requirements or prerogatives of the other and that I assume the other's absolute malleability to my purposes), but of positive at-homeness with the patterns of the other and myself.[8] And if my desiring is for another's benefit so that I might be instrument, I must have some affectively positive disposition toward something such that I believe my possible utilization will not be a being-abused. Therefore, whether desire for appropriate utilization

7. See, for example, Sam Keen's formulation quoted on p. 187.

8. The differences between indifference and hostility, and between use, misuse, and abuse, are more substantial where persons are involved, and fade towards insignificance where "mere things" exhaust the range of the other to be utilized.

is desire that the other be instrument or that I be instrument, such desiring requires trust.[9]

Trust is thus a necessary feature of simple absolute desiring both for appropriate utilization and for union; it is, therefore, required for sound ultimate hope: trust is implied by sound ultimate hope's desiring.

This essay will argue that fundamental hope also implies trust, and that such trust has implications. What has been said here about sound ultimate hope's trust can be said also of fundamental hope's trust.

Summary

We can sum up our principal points concerning formally sound ultimate hopes and their implications.

Ultimate hopes are of three types. If an ultimate hope is for one's own or another's benefit, then one believes that needed instrumentalities are available. If an ultimate hope is for shared life, one believes that there is the possible presence, not of an instrument, but of a participant.

Believing that there is available an instrument one can count on is different from believing that there is possible presence of a participant. With the former there should be a readiness to find in oneself or in public evidence what is instrumentally required. With the latter there should be a readiness to "meet," that is, to become personally engaged as participant oneself with the participant needed for shared life.

The concrete analysis of this essay focuses on formally sound ultimate hopes in the face of obstacles, hopes for a social objective, that is, a fairminded system of reciprocal utility, or shared life, or both. Hope for a reciprocal system of one's own and another's benefit implies beliefs concerning instrumentalities, and background beliefs concerning how benefits come about and concerning the appropriateness of the will-nature ontological model. As sound, such hope also implies a conative readiness to find and to serve as instrumental agency. Hope for shared life implies beliefs concerning the availability and dispositions of participants, as well as background beliefs concerning shared benefit and the appropriateness of the intersubjective ontological model. As sound, it also implies a conative readiness to be and to meet as participant. A complex sound hope for both social objectives implies both kinds of belief, background beliefs, and readinesses, as well as background beliefs excluding the incompatibility of related types of benefit

9. The third possibility, desire that something or some person other than myself be instrument for you – for example, desire that you be awarded the contract you seek – essentially combines features of the other two: the instrument is presumed – trusted – to be not harmful or the person not inept or malicious, and you are presumed not to be abusive, unreliable.

and of the two ontological models.

In addition, sound ultimate hope implies trust, inasmuch as its desiring is simple absolute desiring and such desiring assumes a developmentally appropriate positive affective disposition toward oneself, instrumentalities of others, and participants.

Such trust figures importantly in the implications of fundamental hope, to which we now turn after recognizing the cognitional, conative, and affective implications of sound social ultimate hope.

Implications of fundamental hope

Fundamental hope is defined positively as openness, readiness, availability with respect to the future. It has an orientation but no focus, no objective – like a window. The focused hopes are those aimed at some objective, some future event or state. Defined negatively, fundamental hope is a holding off from yielding to the temptation to despair.

It seems on balance appropriate to distinguish between fundamental hope and trust.[10] The former is an attitude taken with respect to the future; the latter is a disposition taken with respect to the present. (If trust is rooted in past experience, such experience must carry over into the present.)

Argument that fundamental hope requires trust emerges most easily in connection with such hope's negative definition. Fundamental hope means holding off from declaring I am lost. Holding off from despair would be easy enough in a world without difficulties. Trust would be quite flat in a flat world of facts, and even be perhaps nonexistent. But in a world of difficulties, where hope's context is *ardua*, it seems much more plausible to maintain that holding off from despair requires a positive disposition toward what is in some way present to the one who hopes. In the midst of beleaguerment, some kind of present positive relationship to oneself, to another, to something – trust – is required to warrant holding off from despair. If all relationships are negative and alienated rather than supportive, or, more accurately, if supportive relationships are so only on the surface, then it seems there is no warrant for anything but despair.

Such trust, however, is not to be understood monochromatically. A developmental psychosocial schema such as Erikson's must be kept in mind. Even in the infant, basic trust is not coterminous with the feelings of

10. Whereas I distinguish between fundamental hope and trust, James Muyskens, exploring William James's understanding of religion, finds that James's understanding of trust is close to Muyskens' own understanding of hope (*The Sufficiency of Hope*, p. 102). But this notion of hope is *aimed* hope, not my fundamental hope. There are some similarities between my understandings of trust and Muyskens' analyses of believing-in (*Sufficiency*, p. 42, 122).

particular situations – it is compatible with particular unavoidable pains and separations – though it is tied to particular persons. If, as Erikson insists it should, the characteristic human strength of the infant perdures and supports greater sophistication in later life, it can remain a strength throughout changes in relationships with the particular people that influenced its formation. The trust of fundamental hope should be *trust refined*; if it is not refined, it becomes trust's impostor, eventually unmasked as despair. In a similar way, trust refined is linked to fundamental hope's positive definition as openness, readiness, availability with respect to the future.

There seems sufficient basis for saying that fundamental hope requires and thus implies a developmentally understood trust. Sound ultimate hope also implies trust. The question now upon us is: How should such trust be interpreted or understood? Within what sort of larger philosophical framework can it take a place required for it if from it inferences are going to be drawn concerning hope? Implications of hope are implications of fundamental hope's trust and sound ultimate hope's trust. But explaining such trust first requires situating it in an interpretive context.

Understandings of hope's trust

Two different understandings of trust are possible. at least along the lines developed so far. For brevity's sake, they will be labelled trust as *attitude* and trust as *relationship*. With differences in understanding trust go differences in explaining trust.

To understand trust as an "attitude" is not to suggest it is in no way transitive, that it is other than trust-of or trust-in, that it is in no way a relation. But it is to understand it *primarily* as a disposition characterizing a subject or self. Its analysis falls within the range of this essay's will-nature model. The actuality of trust is due, from the perspective of will, to one's decision to trust; it is an attitude I adopt. There may be motives and reasons, but explanation of trust comes to an end with will: I choose to trust. From the other perspective, that of "nature," trust is a quality of an entity, perhaps an accident of a substance. Actuality of trust is due to third-person factors. The possible range of such factors is not small: I trust because, for examples, I have taken this pill, eaten this food, been shaped by this environment, been influenced by these parents or these friends, by this success; because I "have" this belief; because I have been socialized to trust. Or trust can be due to an interplay of clearly distinct objective and subjective factors, between evidence on the one hand and decision to trust on the other. The first key feature, however, of trust as attitude is separability of trust's term and trust's ground.[11] For example: I trust Fred (term) to do X, because he will lose his

11. See analysis of such separability on pp. 160-61.

job if he does not (ground). My trust of Fred stems from a factor separable from Fred; the ground of my trust is my knowledge of the pressure any employee is under, and if another is substituted for Fred, the new employee is trusted on the same grounds.

If on the other hand trust is understood as relationship, in accord with the intersubjective model, then the formula of such trust is: I trust you because of you. (This trust is closely connected with non-covetous love.) The personal totality of the term is essential to the grounding, must be included in it. Substitution of term is not possible without altering the relationship, that is, without altering the type of relationship. And this brings to light the second key factor in both understandings of trust: there is a link between separability or non-separability of term and ground and the *type* of relation. Consider an apparently relational form of trust that turns out to have its limits: "I trust you only so far." What we have here is closer to sophisticated calculation than to love. It is a counting-on or expecting that is at heart a predicting. It slides toward the impersonal and its term would usually be expressed (to someone else) in the third person: "I trust him only so far." Such trust aspires to have enough accurate calculation to warrant being conclusive and not left open. But when trust is more suitably understood according to the intersubjective model, and approaches its fullest, it exhibits such confidence that when I am disappointed, the lack of favorable outcome is I know not due to the other's ill will; he is still on my side, and it must have been other factors that intervened to prevent his effecting what I wanted. Such trust is betrayed, not disappointed. Trust as attitudinal is disappointed: "Well, he lost his chance; I can't count on him any more."

Understanding trust as attitudinal or as relational is governed by recognizing which of two relationships predominates, that of expecting certain types of behavior, or that of non-covetous love.[12] It should be obvious

12. Coming to know trust in these ways is diverse. The psychological sciences and the sociological can get at trust only insofar as it can be recognized as an attitude, as a characteristic of a subject or group, and they can get at its causes only insofar as these are subject to third-person analysis. Third-person anlysis is truncated, first-person is opaque (the input of freedom), and second-person is elusive, accessible perhaps via Gabriel Marcel's secondary reflection.

Among significant and sophisticated studies of trust are those of psychologist, professor and counselor Carolyn Gratton, *Trusting: Theory and Practice* (New York: Crossroad, 1982) and of philosopher Donald Evans, *Struggle and Fulfillment: The Inner Dynamics of Religion and Morality* (Cleveland and New York: Collins, 1979) and *Faith, Authenticity and Morality* (Toronto: University of Toronto Press, 1980). Also helpful is philosopher and Buber scholar Maurice Friedman, *Touchstones of Reality: Existential Trust and the Community of Peace* (New York: Dutton, 1972) and the works of philosopher and educational theorist Otto Friedrich Bollnow.

that in such matters there can be a scale ranging from purest disinterested reckoning and decision to the utter predominance of intersubjective appreciation. I say "utter predominance" because even in purest love the human process of assessing evidence and being responsible in one's decisions to count on someone goes on, or should go on. The difference between trust as largely counting-on, as attitude, and as largely appreciation or love, as relationship, is an important one. The more the former obtains the will-nature model pertains, the more term and ground are separable and the more the relationship called trust is at heart one of utility. But the more love obtains and the more the intersubjective model pertains, the more closely do term and ground approach identity and the relationship is that of appreciation. These two understandings of hope's trust are a key to grasping further, and most important, implications of hope.

Implications of hope's trust

At the beginning of this essay Thornton Wilder was quoted: "Hope (deep-grounded hope, not those sporadic cries and promptings wrung from us in extremity that more resemble despair) is a climate of the mind and an organ of apprehension." This essay now focuses on the last phrase of Wilder's description. Is hope an organ of apprehension? If so, how does it apprehend? *What* does it apprehend? By pursuing these questions we frame the final question, whether and how philosophical reflection on hope "inclines" toward theism, atheism, or agnosticism.

Among the issues involved here are the kinds of implications that can be recognized in discourse about hope. What does hope logically require? What is meant by "logically" here? And what kinds of hope are we talking about? It can be claimed that some hope implies *belief* in God or in a kind of world history. But to speak of beliefs-implied is to fill out details of the climate of mind; it is not an apprehending of anything.

We can be more precise, and speak of several kinds of connections, only the last of which goes beyond hope's being a climate of the mind and marks out a possible territory for hope as an organ of apprehension. The first kind of connection is that of implication obtaining between statements. "I hope that X comes about" implies "I believe that X is possible" which in turn implies "I believe that whatever is required to effect X is extant." For such implication, however, there functions a major premiss that introduces the second and third types of connection. The premiss is: "If one hopes that X comes about, one believes that X is possible, etc." This premiss has two ways in which it can be true. It can be logically or conceptually true: the notion of hoping contains the notion of believing in such a way that if one claimed to hope but denied having any associated beliefs one would be logically inconsistent. The premiss can also be psychologically true: there is a publicly recognizable pattern according to which one hopes and at the same time has certain beliefs concerning the objective of the hope. Such connection is empirical and psychological; the connection may be frequent or may obtain in every case, universally. It seems to me, however, that the logical truth is derivative from something "stronger" than the psychological truth. It is derivative from something that can be called the factual or existential truth, and can be expressed thus: actual hoping is such that actual believing is a necessary ingredient in it; if one claims to have such hoping without the related belief, either he has misidentified his disposition as hoping – he does not really hope – or he has failed to acknowledge actual beliefs – he may not recognize he has them, or not own up to them for reasons extrinsic to the hoping.[13]

Thus, there is implication that obtains between hope-statements and some belief-statements. And there are connections between hoping and believing – notionally or logically, psychologically, and factually. The last of these, factual connection, links hoping and beliefs in a kind of factual or existential necessity; its beliefs are factually or existentially implied by hoping, and we can label this relationship "implication of *beliefs*." It is one type of implication very central to our continuing analysis. It contrasts with another "implication" also based on a factual or existential connection (and central to our argument), which we can call "implication of *reality*."

This last connection obtains – *if* it obtains – not between hopes and beliefs but between the fact of hope and the actuality of what is related to it. Such hope when actual is an index of the reality of what it is related to as term. It thus has the form: hoping in X implies the reality of X. If a certain kind of hope actually obtains, not only do specific beliefs obtain at least implicitly, but the reality of the term of such hope also obtains. It is not just the case that the one who hopes in such a way cannot avoid thinking of the term as real (when it may not be); the hope here conceived is one the actuality of which is necessarily connected with the reality of the term.[14] To recognize the hope is to know the reality of the term.

But these connections, especially implication of belief and implication of reality, have been clarified here by way of positioning and program. These two kinds of connection will be central to our argument. Hope as a climate of the mind encompasses connections logical and psychological and those factually obtaining between hopes and beliefs (implication of belief); at issue now is whether hope, that is, fundamental hope and sound ultimate hope,

13. Thus I do not admit as existentially possible that a person escape this dilemma by actually hoping without beliefs that, for example, the objective is possible.

14. "Necessarily" here has the sense of what is sometimes termed, in contrast with logical necessity, "physical" or "factual" necessity.

might not also be an organ of apprehension, and its actuality be an indicator of reality.

It is this essay's notion of trust that plays the crucial role here. No strict claim is made in this essay that specific people actually hope in certain ways; but *if* they do, then trust is involved, and if trust is involved, certain of its conditions of possibility actually obtain. The argument moves from assumed hoping to its conditions of possibility.

It is assumed that such hopes' trust is mature and refined, that is, showing developed powers of discrimination between individuals reliable and unreliable, showing depth of appropriate trust of oneself, significant others, and value systems (Erikson's stages V and VI, signalized by fidelity and love), showing readiness to face evidence, readiness to recognize its bearing and limits, and readiness to have beliefs challenged especially by disappointments.[15] Signs of immaturity in trust include maladaptive optimism, pigheadedness or willfullness in the face of challenge, and fickleness. Particular note should be taken of how developing trust moves both *beyond* trust in specific individuals and *more deeply into* trust of specific individuals. In some form, both movements are required for healthy development of trust.

The questions can now be posed: (I) under what conditions is trust correctly understood as an attitude, and its implications as implied *beliefs;* and (II) under what conditions is trust correctly understood as a relationship and its implications as implied *realities*. Spelling out these conditions clarifies how and when fundamental hope or sound ultimate hope is a climate of the mind, and how and when fundamental hope or sound ultimate hope is an organ of apprehension.

The conditions pivotal for answering the questions are whether the trust of such hopes is more accurately understood according to the will-nature model or according to the intersubjective model. Further reflection on these two *models* will be the principal theme of this section. The key issue is whether the connections between trust and its term and ground are contingent or necessary.

Belief-implication is the more accurate understanding of what follows from trust *to the extent that such trust has the form of the will-nature model.* ''I trust X'' implies [16] ''I believe that X is trustworthy'' and ''I believe X is real''

15. It seems clear enough that mature trust is established in respect to challenges. What is not clear is whether mature trust is characterized more by trust unshaken and untroubled by challenges, or by trust undefeated but troubled by challenges.

16. ''Implies'' here signifies what Donald D. Evans identifies as speaker-independent prima facie implication. *The Logic of Self-Involvement: A Philosophical Study of Everyday Language with Special Reference to the Christian use of Language*

because trusting implies believing that what is required to make the trust sound actually obtains. More than belief-that may be *involved* in trust conceptualized via the will-nature model, but no more is strictly *implied*. The reason why no more is implied has to do with the contingency of links between relation, term, and ground in the will-nature model. What this means can be grasped by recurrence to what kinds of explanatory grounds are involved in the will-nature model. Explanatory grounds are of two types, "first-person" and "third-person." In first-person terms, trusting is explained by free decision to trust: I decide to adopt the attitude of trust. Explanation ends in the self's free choice. In third-person terms, however, trusting is due to deterministically understood factors within or around the one who trusts, and this includes reasons and motives; given the actuality of such factors, trusting is automatic. Usual explanations of trusting link free decision and reasons, in a joining of first-person and third-person groundings or aetiology.

This model does not preclude the reality of the term trusted, but it does not require it. The possible unreality of the term is easier to imagine if the trust is somewhat detached from trust of specific individuals, and is also arrested psychologically and exhibits a good deal of willfulness. All trusting involves at least beliefs in the term's trustworthiness and reality. Insofar as the trusting in question fits the will-nature model, such trusting's actuality *may* be due to a combination of first-person and third-person grounds *that are not linked to the term*. I may trust someone actually untrustworthy because of what someone told me. I may even place my trust in what is non-existent. When explanation for trust, and its implied beliefs, come to rest only in free decision and in determinisms within or around the one who trusts, such trust is only psychological; it is only an attitude, a climate of the mind.

The conceptual model of will-nature trust is as follows: the relationship is trust, the term is the one that I trust, the grounds are detachable from the term. The grounds may be attached to the term, but are not necessarily attached. And this is the basis for saying that such trust implies *beliefs* concerning what is required to make it sound, that is, beliefs concerning reality and trustworthiness.

On the other hand, it is *implication of reality* that is more appropriate *to the degree that trust fits the intersubjective model*. Such trust implies, not just beliefs concerning the term, but the *reality of* the term. It would be helpful at this point were we able to produce propositions expressing such implication. But it won't do to offer: "I trust him" implies "He is trustworthy" and "He exists," because such is the language proper to the *will-nature* model and in this latter model it does not follow. Our available

about God as Creator (London: SCM Press, 1963, and New York: Herder and Herder, 1969), pp. 46-50.

language is closely tied to third-person categories, and, to a lesser degree, to those of the first-person. We could play with "I trust him" therefore "He is trusted" and therefore "He exists"; but this sounds like a version of the ontological argument.

The clue to the appropriate pathway is the type of grounding characteristic of the intersubjective model. It can be illustrated least vaguely through relationships between persons. We can admit that someone is trustworthy but that does not automatically mean that *I* actually trust him; I may have no contact with him other than knowing of his trustworthiness. Furthermore, we can recognize how, say, in parent-adolescent relationships, trusting begets trustworthiness: I trust him, and he becomes trustworthy. But here again, the result is not automatic. The crucial factor is the personal affective bond. "I trust *him*" is not the appropriate expression for the intersubjective model; "I trust *you*" is.

There are two key and interwoven factors operative here. The first we notice in human beings as recognition, an intentional turning of one to the other whereby each becomes for the other a *you*. The second factor is the kind of grounding or causation: it is *co*-grounding, mutual grounding; there is "input" from the other, and *without such "input" the relationship cannot be*.

Therefore, if trust fits the intersubjective model, actuality of trust necessarily depends on "input" from the other, and *the fact of such relationship implies the reality of the other*. There is a necessary link between the relationship and the non-separability of its term and explanatory ground. In this model, explanation pointing to factors other than the term is inadequate explanation.

This "input" can range between two extremes. At the one, the "input" is from what the other has at its disposal, that is, separable from itself. The grounds "given" by the other are less than identical with the other, and the good grounds I have for trust are distinguishable from the trust's term. But this to conceive the "input" of the other not consistently with the intersubjective model but along the lines of the will-nature model. There is "input" from the other, but it is separable from the other, not necessarily linked with the other. At the other extreme, the "input" of the other is the other itself. There is the other's self-manifestation or self-disclosure, the other is "in" the "input," and therefore the term is essential, must be included in, the relationship's co-grounding. The other's being "in" the "input" is another way of saying that the totality of the other, and not some contingent and separable feature of the other, is essential to the co-grounding. I trust you, because of you.

Insofar as there is a self-disclosing process going on, there is the possibility of my ideas of the other being corrected. In the will-nature model, there need be no input from the other, and there *can* be input detachable from the other – "putting up a front", "making empty promises"; but if the input is truly from and of the other, and I respond to this, then the intersubjective model becomes the more appropriate.

If the intersubjective model can be appropriate for understanding fundamental hope's trust and/or sound ultimate hope's trust, and if we are seeking to understand whether and how hope is an organ of apprehension, our questions are now three: Is the term of the trust, is what is apprehended, real? Is what is apprehended trustworthy? How is this term apprehended? We therefore address, respectively, the meaning of *is*, the meaning of *trustworthy*, and the meaning of *known*.

Earlier we suggested that to reason from *is-trusted* to *is* sounds like a form of the ontological argument. But between that context and our present one, the proposition has shifted from "*He* is trusted" to "*You* are trusted." The former is appropriate to the will-nature model; the latter approximates the intersubjective model. And in the latter model the proposition is based on a relationship that owes its actuality to "input" from the other as "you." Insofar as the model applies, it cannot be based upon, grounded in, factors which have their reality in the subject alone; and the totality of the term must be included in the ground.

We should distinguish three contexts of *is*. The first appears in implication of beliefs: I trust him, therefore *I believe that he is* trustworthy and a fortiori believe that he exists. This is the *is* of the climate of the mind. It may be only subjective, only psychological. But it may be stronger than naively mental; it may have the force of a postulate in Kant's sense. The second context is that of the *is* of: You are trusted, therefore you are. This is the *is* of presence, of self-disclosure. Only insofar as an other is present to me can I recognize the other as a you well-disposed towards me. The third context is that of the *is* of "He is trusted." To speak of the other as "he" is to cease to be present to the other as a you and to begin to inform a third party about this other. Doing so detaches the term of trust from the actual relationship, and considers the term as an object. "He is trustworthy," "he is" – such locutions direct the addressee's attention to presumably public evidence of his disposition, a disposition which characterizes him whether I trust him or not. The reality of him is the reality of a presumably public fact.

It is important to note that trusting may involve all three. The point being made here is that just two senses of *is* – belief/postulation and public fact – may be inadequate for analysis of trust and its implications, and *are* inadequate to the degree that the intersubjective model applies. This model's sense of "real" or "is" appropriate to the other's self-disclosing "input" is the sense in: "You are trusted," therefore "You are real."

Strictly speaking, the input of the other does not warrant saying "He is trustworthy." "Trustworthy" suggests a reliability which (a) is a disposition, a feature of a subject, like an attribute of an entity, (b) obtains whether or not that person is actually trusted by anyone, and (c) need not be based on relationship to *me*. On the intersubjective model, trust implies not trustworthiness but rather your-being-well-disposed-towards-me. There is relationship to me; there is actual rather than just potential trust; and the you is more than characterized by an attribute: the you is in relation to an I. This understanding therefore permits an implication and warrants an expression of the sort: "You are well-disposed towards me."

When trust is better interpreted according to the will-nature model, trust approaches being a counting-on. Strictly speaking, all it implies is beliefs. But where there is knowledge of facts that warrant the beliefs, such knowledge is of objects as instrumental. If trust's core is counting-on, its knowing is primarily reckoning up or calculating, and such knowing's perfection is closure, cognitional mastery sufficient for prediction. Such knowing is directed to the factual only.

Trust interpreted on the intersubjective model takes trust as primarily appreciation. Its knowing is not confined to the instrumental, but it is knowledge inseparable from appreciation, from presence, from positive affective bond. The reality and benevolence of the term are apprehended in the relationship. The gap between what language can express publicly and the other presented in the relationship leaves an element in mystery, not just extensionally but in depth. Intersubjective knowing attends to self-disclosure of the other. It has an openness which is not the same as allowing for possible error in reckoning. Finally, such knowledge is at once knowledge of fact and value.

From this mutual relationship, conceptual knowledge may emerge as a precipitate: trust of a present other warrants "I trust you," and this latter locution implies "You are real." Of course it also implies beliefs: "I trust you" implies "I believe you can be trusted by me." But beliefs are not all it implies; it also implies the reality and favorable disposition of the other toward me.[17]

Putting this matter of the other's input and trust's implications into the framework of the contrast between the order of reality and the order of coming to know (*ordo essendi* and *ordo cognoscendi*), we can say: my being appreciated makes intersubjectively-understood trust possible – an aetiological connection; my intersubjectively-understood trusting makes my

17. These points about intersubjective trust and what it implies are similar to the relationships between hoping and its precipitated or derivative assertions as these are found in Marcel's definitions of hope, chapter 12, pp. 125-27.

being appreciated known – a cognitive connection. In this way, fundamental hope can be an organ of apprehension.

And so can sound ultimate hope. This is not to claim that a formally sound aimed ultimate hope brings about, "creates," its objective. For the objective desired, *any* hoping's wish is at most father to the thought (belief). But *sound* ultimate hope requires trust. If this trust fits and thus requires interpretation on the intersubjective model, it is logical to conclude, as in the case of fundamental hope's trust, to the reality of thou or you, because this type of trust requires co-grounding. This does not guarantee such hope's success; it does make it subject to betrayal and death rather than to specific disappointment.

Absolute trust

Gabriel Marcel speaks of absolute hope, "the inner disposition of one who, setting no condition or limit and *abandoning himself in absolute confidence*, would thus transcend all possible disappointment and would experience a security of his being, or in his being, which is contrary to the radical insecurity of Having."[18] Without at the moment attending to the framework within which Marcel's absolute hope is situated, we can recognize in his "absolute confidence" a disposition we can term *absolute* trust. Absolute hope is for Marcel a theoretical possibility; for us absolute trust is theoretically possible. We can now inquire into its import and conditions of possibility.

Absolute trust is trust unshakable; as the core of fundamental hope, it would characterize a person who holds off from despair no matter what disappointments are visited on him. The basic statement of fundamental hope is that no disappointment necessitates despair. *No* disappointment? There is a paradoxical character to fundamental hope, such that while no frustration of a hoped-for outcome necessitates despair, there is yet some sort of an at least implicit aimed hope that survives disappointment: beyond all conceived limits there is still some favorable forward path which is not impossible. Should such survivor-hope be adequately conceptualized and be then proved impossible, despair is the only course.

Trust has a term, and care should be taken in elucidating what might be the term of absolute trust. However trust be interpreted, according to the will-nature model or the intersubjective model, trust has at least an implicit intentional term. But absolute trust is not trust of everything. At least it is not trust of everything if it follows the patterns outlined in developmental psychology, according to which maturing means learning what *not* to trust. But neither is it *necessarily* a vague, cosmic, or all-encompassing trust that

18. HV 46, emphasis added.

precludes specifying a term. Unshakable confidence theoretically might be attached to a quite individual person.

Once such theoretically possible trust is interpreted according to the two models of this essay, differences emerge. According to the will-nature model, trust is counting-on, and what is counted-on may be so on grounds not necessarily identical with the term. Thus, because of an idea, or because of one's willfullness, one might absolutely trust someone or something. There are explanatory grounds for such trust, but these are not necessarily sufficient to justify the trust, to establish its soundness. According to the intersubjective model, on the other hand, trust is an appreciative affective bond, and its term is inseparable from its grounding, since this model entails "input" from the term for the relationship to be actual. Thus absolute trust of this type implies the reality of and the favorable disposition of the term. But knowledge of such obtains only in the relationship; the sticking point is in figuring out whether one's trust is of this type. Yet even if it is, such knowledge does not yield "It is certain that . . . ," for such discourse is proper to the object-side of the will-nature model. Insofar as such trust depends on the input of the other, it is subject to betrayal. Betrayal is the appropriate term, for insofar as this model applies, the relationship includes some type of mutual recognition of each other as a *you*.

Discussion very hopeful for focusing reflection on absolute trust, its term, and its interpretation can be found in some writings of Sam Keen. One text, admittedly considered in isolation, raises the issues clearly (Keen is speaking directly, not of experience of absolute trust, but of religious discourse):

> It is not difficult to see the continuity between basic trust and the central affirmation that constitutes the religious consciousness. It is the function of religion to nourish and restore the sense of basic trust by affirming in symbolic language that *the ultimate context of life is succoring and trustworthy*.[19]

This text elicits three attention-focusing remarks. (1) Religion has a language that *affirms* trustworthiness. The thrust here is not on experience of trustworthiness but on affirmation or message. The role of this language is to "nourish and restore the sense of basic trust." (2) Keen's description of the term of such trust is "the ultimate context of life." It seems quite differentiated from any specific entity. (3) Keen's language at least suggests he is thinking in, or is entrapped by though not intending to think in, the will-nature model. Religion affirms that the ultimate context is succoring and trustworthy. This is third-person language about the ultimate context. It has its meaning apart from anyone's personal engagement with "the ultimate

19. Sam Keen, *Apology for Wonder* (New York: Harper & Row, 1969), p. 204.

context.'' Furthermore, religion has its function, ''to nourish and restore the sense of basic trust'': such language suggests that religion is an instrument, and an instrument for effecting a subject's sense of something – basic trust – rather than effecting the trust itself. Perhaps too much weight is placed on just one text of Keen; perhaps other ways of speaking are equally problematic; but his language does serve as illuminating contrast with, for example, some formula like this:

> Religion, as a form of life, nourishes and restores basic trust by being a situation of meeting with the ultimate context. *In such meeting one knows that this context succors and is well-disposed towards me.*

Keen speaks of ''the continuity between basic trust and the central affirmation that constitutes the religious consciousness.'' Continuity there certainly is between trust and *affirmation*; but even closer is the connection between basic trust and the central religious *relationship*.

The models of this essay, however, offer *two* relationships, utilization and appreciation. Care must be taken to note whether religious (or non-religious) affirmations present or promote the other as instrument (or myself as instrument), or speak of the other as involved in appreciating and being appreciated. In our present context, sound absolute trust is not just a matter of getting the correct other in focus, but of getting the trust correct: Does sound absolute trust have the form of counting on, of appreciating, or of a combination of the two?

To summarize our analysis of absolute trust as the core of fundamental hope: (1) absolute trust is a theoretical possibility; (2) what is required to ground it and serve as basis for explaining its actuality varies according to the type of trust and the type of model used in seeking explanation. Absolute trust on the will-nature interpretation is a counting-on, for which adequate grounds need not be due to the term itself. It can be only psychological. Absolute trust on the intersubjective model is a mutual appreciation, and its grounding necessarily includes ''input'' from the term. Such absolute trust is inseparable from the presence of its term, and from such term's favorable disposition sufficient to ground it. Finding the appropriate description or name for the actual term necessarily implied when such trust obtains is quite another matter, and no easy one. But any description or name should be compatible with the type of relationship that the trust is recognized to be.

Integration and soundness

It is a major question whether the two ontological models sketched in this essay can be formulated in one unified theoretical metaphysical system.

It is a different question whether the two kinds of trust sketched according to the models can be integrated *in human living*. It seems to me that they can. How such integration might obtain takes two forms. The first is not problematic and occurs when trust is *only* of the counting-on sort. The intersubjective model remains only a theory; all trust is a utilizing relationship.

The second form is when trust admits to intepretation according to the intersubjective model. But it seems that such trust is always *shadowed* by will-nature trust. Trust as intersubjective (in which knowledge of the term's reality and disposition are given in the relationship) is usually accompanied by trust of a will-nature sort (in which the relation can be adequately grounded by factors separable from the term). The former is not subject to doubt in the relationship but cannot muster adequate public evidence; the latter is subject to doubt, but public evidence which does bear on this doubt cannot, since we are dealing with the core of a disposition oriented to the future, yield objective certainty. Or perhaps it can – depending on one's understanding of how past and present are related to the future.

So far we have spoken of these two types of trust and their variously conceived grounds, and of how identifying the latter yields explanation. But though we have mentioned disappointment and betrayal, we have not dealt directly with trust that is *sound*.

Intersubjective trust can only be judged sound by its parties in relation; will-nature trust can be judged according to public evidence. Justification for one type of trust may be insufficient for justification of the other. She may be trustworthy but I am not in relation with her : or I trust her (as you) but I cannot prove she is trustworthy.

What if the two are in conflict? What if what I know publicly goes against the implications of my appreciating relationship? An approach to this question can be developed from Gabriel Marcel's reflections on the question whether I can hope when reasons are against it.[20] We can ask whether I can trust (intersubjectively) when reasons, that is, reckonings, are against it. We can recall the case where trusting begets trustworthiness, but not automatically. And, along Marcellian lines, we can say: (1) if I recognize that I do not have adequate basis for trust, then I am not really trusting. (2) There can be two levels of trusting. One is I trust (intersubjectively); the other is: I calculate trustworthiness. Were there only the latter, trusting would be automatic: she is trustworthy, therefore I trust her. In many cases only the one level does operate and the trust *is* automatic. (3) After Marcel, we can inspect a third question: *May* I trust when reasons are not sufficient? If only one level is involved, No, I may not trust; it would be unsound. But if two levels are involved, then when reckoning falls short of supporting intersubjective trust,

20. See chapter 12, Reasons and Hoping.

I *may* trust. Such trust is unsound insofar as it is connected with results that reckoning will not admit as likely; such trust is sound insofar as it is ordered essentially to the mutual appreciation or love of the parties that trust each other.

Applied to hoping, these reflections on integration of two types of trust suggest as a concrete possibility a case in which a person's aimed hope's trust is of a calculative sort, assessing reliability and thus predictability, and perhaps doing this erroneously; yet this person does not cling to the definite outcome hoped for or give it a deadline. Such flexibility or patience is rooted in fundamental hope, and the latter may contain a relationship of trust that is correctly interpreted on the intersubjective model. In such a case, *two* kinds of trust obtain within, respectively, this person's two kinds of hope.

And if two kinds of trust can obtain in a lived situation of hope, perhaps on the theoretical level the two ontological models can be at least dialectically integrated. It would be unfortunate to have something which worked in practice but not in theory.

Summary

The implications of hope are implications of both formally sound ultimate hope and fundamental hope. Sound ultimate hope implies belief-that adequate agency is available: if the objective is a system of utility, appropriate instrumentalities are believed available; if the objective is shared life, participants are believed available. Sound ultimate hope also implies kinds of disposition or readiness, and its desiring implies trust. Fundamental hope also implies trust.

Hope's trust interpreted on the will-nature model implies belief – that what is needed is available as instrument; interpreted on the intersubjective model, it implies reality-of a thou, since such trust requires co-grounding. Thus, insofar as the will-nature model applies, deep-grounded hope is a climate of the mind; insofar as the intersubjective model applies, it is an organ of apprehension, in touch with the reality of a thou.

It remains to be seen how this analysis can be applied to atheism and theism, in dialogue with the atheism of Ernst Bloch and the theisms of Immanuel Kant and Gabriel Marcel, and in the concluding position of this essay.

CHAPTER 16

BLOCH'S ATHEISM AND ONTOLOGY: A SKETCH

The aim of this chapter is to bring to light the kind of atheism in Bloch's thought, the reasons he has for this atheism, and the ontological model that underlies what serves as a reason – at least insofar as such ontological presuppositions mesh with one of the ontological models presented in the preceding section, namely, the subject-object or will-nature model. This purpose serves this essay's larger intent, to see how hope-analysis and analysis of grounds for hope incline towards theism or atheism, particularly as mediated by certain ontological presuppositions. For this larger purpose, then, Bloch's thought serves as a paradigm of one kind of atheism and one type of ontology.

Much of Bloch's evaluation of religion has been dealt with earlier. Religion is not simply the opium of the people; it is also their outcry, their protest against oppression. But it must be correctly interpreted, it must be "inherited," and Marxism provides the general canons for correct interpretation. The basic message of religion correctly interpreted is messianism. Bloch maintains that the history of religions establishes this. From Cadmus to Moses and Jesus, religion has been characterized, in an ever stronger and clearer way, by three features: the proclamation of deliverance and the promise of the kingdom of God (messianism); increasing identification of the message and the messenger insofar as deliverance is proclaimed by one who is himself the deliverer; and increasing clarity that the deity referred to is not a Lord above, but is rather an open future ahead – the corollary of this last feature is atheism.[1] In Moses Bloch finds a shift from the Sinai Lord of heaven above to the Exodus-God. Moses himself is one who not only announces liberation but also leads his people out of Egypt.[2] Bloch typically understands Jesus through interpretations of the Anselmian phrase *Cur Deus homo* and the passage from the Gospel According to John "I and the Father are one."[3] Bloch takes traditional *homoousios* doctrine in a radical anthropological sense: corrected, message and messenger declare *homo*

1. This is the gist of the argument of PH's chap. 53, translated in MO as "Man's Increasing Entry into Religious Mystery." The argument is carried out concerning Christianity in *Atheism in Christianity*.

2. PH 1402, 1450ff., 1456f., MO (MIE) 150-51, 165ff., 171f.

3. The Anselmian phrase is employed to the indicated effect in PH 1417, 1515, MO (MIE) 165, 209, and in AC 218/170. The Johannine text is cited in AC 214/167.

homini Deus – whatever is humankind's God is really humankind itself.[4] What is really proclaimed and declared possible is the kingdom of God – without God.

Bloch's principal argument for atheism is thus one from the history of religions: correct interpretation of religion's message and of religious founders brings to light an atheism for the sake of the kingdom. The style of such interpretation is derived from Feuerbach. There is, hoewever, an implicit secondary argument in favor of atheism, one that proceeds from the very kind of deities found through history of religion. God shows up in the manner of a Lord and Pharaoh; beneath such deity humanity is in thrall. But religions' message is that the kingdom *is* possible, and this kingdom is not possible with a "throning" deity.[5] Therefore no such Lord-above is consistent with the core of religions' message.

Yet while Bloch follows Feuerbach, he also has a quarrel with him. Feuerbach's God was bourgeois, and consequently so was his Man. But, correctly interpreted, the future which religion proclaims, and the hope it urges, is "explosive, total, and incognito." "Totally Other" still applies – to humanity. *Deus absconditus* is actually *homo*, but no less *absconditus*; it is still hidden what man can become.

It is beyond the paradigm-character of this sketch of Bloch's atheism to review his long analysis of the history of religions and give detailed evaluation of his approach. His atheism involves an unmasking of a God lording it over man; he does this for the sake of declaring for *human* possibilities.[6]

4. PH 1521, MO (MIE) 213; PH 1493, MO (MIE) 190-91; AC 215-17/168-69. See also Bloch's use of the phrase *Eritis sicut Deus* in PH 1504, MO (MIE) 202; TEP 183, MO (RT) 114; PH 1556.

5. "Where there is a great master of the world there is no room for freedom, not even for the freedom of God's children. Nor is there any room for the figure of the kingdom, for the mystical democracy of chiliastic hope. The utopia of the kingdom wipes out the fiction of a divine creator and the hypostasis of a God in heaven, but precisely does not wipe out the final space in which *ens perfectissimum* has the abyss of its yet unthwarted latency. The existence of God – indeed God as such, as a distinct being – is superstition; faith is solely the belief in a messianic kingdom of God, without God. Therefore, far from being an enemy of religious utopianism, atheism is its premiss: *without atheism there is no room for messianism*." PH 1413, MO (MIE) 161-62. God is "überflüssig." PH 272.

6. On Bloch's atheism, see Ronald M. Green, "Ernst Bloch's Revision of Atheism," *Journal of Religion* 49 (1969): 128-35; Theodor Heim, "Blochs Atheismus," in *Ernst Bloch zu ehren: Beiträge zu seinem Werk*, ed. Siegfried Unseld (Frankfurt a. M.: Suhrkamp, 1965), pp. 157-80; Jürgen Moltmann, "Hope without Faith: An Eschatological Humanism without God," in *Is God Dead?*, ed. Johannes Metz, Concilium: Theology in the Age of Renewal, vol. 16 (New York: Paulist Press, 1966), pp. 25-40.

But Bloch retains an important place for divine predicates and for a kind of ontological import they have. Elimination of a Lord-above leaves behind a vacuum. The grade of being denoted by *ens perfectissimum* does not cease to have reference once the hypostasized God-on-high is recognized as a projection. *Ens perfectissimum* refers to a "space" or "topos" which is not above but rather *ahead*. The future is neither closed nor confined merely to the pedestrian. Religious language speaks of a future that is beyond the presently conceivable; *ens perfectissimum* refers in a veiled manner to what humanity can become. This phrase and others indicate transcendence-ahead – or, as Bloch put it, "transcendence without heavenly transcendence."[7] The "space" from which the certainty of being has been cleared out is admittedly open to two interpretations; the first is emptiness, pure void, nothingness, and the second is as an open sphere for the human subject and nature, is as a "front."[8] This second is the interpretation Bloch gives to the remainder of deity-language, applying it to the possibilities of human future.

But this future is not already decided, is not determinate. Bloch is at great pains to elaborate various senses of possibility, and his category of the really-possible – the unfinished character that can receive determination in the interplay between definite forces of nature and history and the imagination and action of human agency – is the ontological category that locates the type of determinateness characteristic of the genuine future. The future is "partially conditioned." Bloch's original ontological category, the Not-yet, is not the Will-be. It is not yet decided whether resolution of indeterminacy will yield nothingness or All, destruction or fulfillment as the *regnum humanum*, the kingdom of God without God.[9]

Bloch's thought reveals a tension between taking history as undecided, and taking it in a sense freighted with optimism. The former position is supposed whenever Bloch would stimulate and warn against complacency. But at times he also seems to hold that all human beings have to do to effect change is to become aware of what is in the process from the outset. Consciousness of need for change coincides with the emergence of the conditions which make such change concretely possible.[10]

In recognizing Bloch's continued use of *ens perfectissimum*, in noting the vacuum or empty-space-ahead for human progress, in adverting to his

7. PH 1515-34, MO (MIE) 209-26; PH 1522, MO (MIE) 213; PH 1625, OKM (KMH) 41.

8. PH 1530-32, MO (MIE) 222-24. The chain of being is really an incomplete chain of becoming.

9. PH 1531-33, MO (MIE) 223-25.

10. Bloch quotes Marx to this effect, PH 1613, OKM (KMH) 27-28. See also PH 1608, OKM (KMH) 23, where Marxism's future is spoken of as inevitable.

category of really-possible, we have begun to close in on his basic ontological categories.[11] Bloch's basic ontology is Marxian. Reality admits categorization as subject and object, and this categorization has similarities with the will-nature model of this essay. Subject and object are dialectically opposed on a functional level. But functional opposition is not ultimate in its source, because both the subjective and objective pole stem from the same single principle, matter or being.[12] Matter is an active principle; it has what Bloch calls *Tendenz*, active potentiality.[13] When, like an opposable thumb, matter shows up not only as objective processes in nature and history, but also in human subjects, its active potentialities are "*identisch*," that is, not at odds, but mutually supportive.[14]

Bloch's basic ontological stance is therefore that subject and object are mutually supportive. Yet alienation often obtains in the present; this suggests that subject-factors and object-factors are related in a manner mutually destructive; enslaving relationships, alienated labor, and so forth, characterize human existence; the humanization of nature and the naturalization of humanity are not yet accomplished. But because the underlying ontological structure is one of support, because nature is a world of "allied potentials in value-material," the alienation is not necessarily final. Indeed, it is the role of religion to proclaim an alliance, not simply between humanity and nature, but between humanity and history.[15] Subject and object, one in their ultimate source, are one as well in their ultimate though veiled goal.

There remains a problem of conceiving the favorable outcome. The kingdom of God is ushered in through the twin activities of revolution and mysticism.[16] Alienation is overcome, subject and object become one (or are grasped as one). Yet it seems that the reconciliation of human beings with each other and with nature, or, more ontologically expressed, of subject with object, is in relationships of *control* and of *labor*.

> Naturalization of man – that would mean his incorporation into the

11. On Bloch's ontology, see *The Encyclopedia of Philosophy* (1967), s.v. "Bloch, Ernst," by Franco Lombardi; Egenolf Roeder von Diersburg, *Zur Ontologie und Logik offener Systeme: Ernst Bloch vor dem Gesetz der Tradition* (Hamburg: Meiner, 1967).

12. That matter is the basic principle is Marxism's usual understanding. Bloch also speaks of this principle as *being*. PH 299f., 303, OKM 69, 73.

13. On matter's *Tendenz*, see PH 2, 4, 8, 273, 277; PH 331, OKM, 103.

14. PH 1570.

15. PH 152lf., MO (MIE) 213-14.

16. PH 1534-40, MO (MIE) 226-32.

> community, his final this-worldly awakening, so that, free from all alienation, we could really control our *hic et nunc*.[17]

Labor is no longer alienated; destructive social institutions are turned to humanity's true service; yet the mode of relation is control. Reciprocal misuse becomes, it seems, reciprocal utility. The kingdom is not characterized, it seems, by what this essay calls appreciation. Subject and object are reconciled, but as agent and instrument.[18]

The point of this brief sketch is not to present thoroughly, nor is it to evaluate, Bloch's arguments for atheism. Nor is it immediately aimed toward evaluation of Bloch's ontology. My intent is to point out general features of his approach, and make clear his options, his presuppositions, and the corollaries of his position.

He derives his atheism from Feuerbach and Marx, but with some differences. Religion has value as expression of commitment to ultimate human possibilities, to the humanization of nature and the naturalization of humanity. The religious notion "kingdom of God" points to this; but, since "God" means "throning-Lord-above," such a deity is incompatible with achieving human possibilities. Therefore the non-existence of God is a logically necessary condition for the possibility of human fulfillment.

Bloch's ontological presuppositions fit, in part, this essay's will-nature model of ontology. Bloch maintains that beneath current historical destructive oppositions between these two poles, there is underlying mutual support, at least in principle. Religion reminds us in a veiled way that this alliance can be realized in a final overcoming of alienations.

But glimpsed behind the veil is a structure of such overcoming, a structure of control, a structure where subject and object are reconciled as agent and instrument. ("Mysticism," however, may augur another, non-controlling, mode of subject-object unification.)

To heed the message of religion inherited is to have a "faith [which] is solely the belief in a messianic kingdom of God, without God."[19] Such faith counts on the process without having objective, that is, detached, certainty concerning the outcome. The form of hope this yields is a *dialectical* meshing

17. AC 352/271.

18. Bloch cautions against such reconciliations being taken as bourgeois. It is, on the contrary, explosive. *Seligkeit* is *hereinbrechende*, bliss breaks in. It is tempting to suggest that this incursion comes from outside the process. But Bloch's explosive character of the Novum is better understood psychologically: the ordinariness of present expectations will be surprised by the positive future that can come.

19. PH 1413, MO (MIE) 162.

of accurate reckoning and ardent desiring, an adapting balance between what Bloch calls the cold-stream and the warm-stream in Marxist thought.[20]

20. PH 1620-21, OKM (KMH) 35; AC 349-50/268-69.

CHAPTER 17

KANT AND BELIEF IN GOD

The purpose of this chapter is to survey the principal Kantian themes and arguments that relate hope and theism. More precisely – since earlier treatment of Kant developed his understandings of hope – the present section attends to his position and arguments bearing on what hope's intelligibility requires in the matter of God. This chapter initiates a dialogue between Kant's approach and that of this essay concerning hope's implications for theism.

The threshold to Kant's approach to theism is postulation of reason. Postulation of the existence of God, however, is in two stages: the first is postulation concerning causality adequate for the highest good, and the second is the specification of such causality as God rather than nature.

Postulation of adequate causality

The first stage is situated against the background of the limits of theoretical reason. The existence of God cannot be known as spatio-temporal sensuous objects are known. Proof of the existence of God is impossible. But something more can be said from the standpoint of reason's practical employment. Practical reason supplies determinations to the executive will; theoretical reason thinks through the structure and conditions of possibility for such determination as *obligatory*, that is, it thinks through the conditions of possibility for moral obligation being what it is.

Moral obligation includes obligation to promote happiness as it requires promotion of the highest good. But while virtue does lie within the power of rational beings to effect, happiness does not; needs are not met, wishes are not fulfilled, at least not with the consistency and fairness that deserved happiness requires. Hence, if I am obliged by the moral law, either the moral law is, with respect to happiness, practically self-contradictory, or inadequacy of finite rational causality is not where theoretical reason must come to a halt in thinking through the highest good's possibility. If the demands of the moral law are *not unreasonable*, there must exist, ultimately, causality which is *adequate* for assuring to the virtuous the happiness deserved; and if the moral law is *to be obeyed*, whatever is necessary for its obligatory character must be assumed. Such assumption, on the part of theoretical reason, is called "postulation."

Illusion is the stumbling block to postulation of causality adequate to ensure the highest good's possibility. One recognizes obligation to promote the highest good, therefore one must believe the highest good possible; virtue is possible but happiness as satisfaction of needs and wishes is a problem. Is it not illegitimate to argue from the reality of a need or wish to the availability of what is needed or wished? And is not this just what postulation is about?

Kant saw this objection in the argument of Thomas Wizenmann: the latter argued that one cannot "argue from a need to the objective reality of the object of the need."[1] In response, Kant distinguishes between a need based on inclination and a need of reason, and concedes that Wizenmann is correct when it comes to a need based on inclination, but not when a need of reason is concerned. Concerning "a need of reason arising from an objective determining ground of the will, i.e., the moral law," Kant maintains there is a priori justification for "the presupposition of suitable conditions in nature."

> It is a duty to realize the highest good as far as it lies within our power to do so; therefore it must be possible to do so. Consequently, it is unavoidable for every rational being in the world to assume whatever is necessary to its objective possibility. The assumption is as necessary as the moral law, in relation to which alone it is valid.[2]

In dealing with Kant's response to Wizenmann's objection, three levels must be distinguished. The first is Kant's concession to the objection: when it is a matter of needs based on inclination, indeed one cannot argue from the need to the reality of the object of that need. The second is Kant's own point: when it is a matter of a need of reason arising from the moral law, one does have warrant for arguing from such need to the *assumption* or *belief* that what the moral law requires in theory be available. The third would be a formulation that strictly parallels Wizenmann's point: in a matter of a need of reason arising from the moral law, one can argue from the need to the *reality* of the object of that need. The question whether Kant argues in this third manner is postponed until the differences between the first and second are clarified.

Differences between what can be argued from inclination-needs and what can be argued from a need of reason arising out of the moral law can be elucidated as follows. Needs of reason arising out of moral law require certain beliefs, and these latter are allegedly *justified* because they are connected with the moral law; but there is a difference between a belief justified because its content actually obtains (belief-that-X-exists is justified because X exists) and a belief justified because it is related to reason and moral law. This latter is a curious kind of justification, and suggests that other beliefs might not be justified because they are not related to reason but to *inclination*. The key to the difference seems to be this: I can *recognize* an inclination without being

1. As summarized by Kant in KpV 143, note, CPrR 149, note 6.
2. KpV 144, note, CPrR 149, note 6.

required to believe that there is available what will satisfy that inclination. But I cannot *pursue* satisfaction of a need based on inclination unless I believe such satisfaction is available. But with reason and moral law, matters are different. *Recognizing* the moral law *as obliging me*, and committing myself to what its form implies, i.e., *pursuing* its object because I am obliged to do so, are inseparable – or so Kant seems to suppose; any distinction between recognition and pursuit collapses. Hence, while a faith-of-inclination is required for pursuit-concerning but not for recogniton-of an inclination, a faith of practical reason *is* required for recognition-of moral law as obligatory, because no one can be obliged to pursue what is believed to be impossible. Hence, for theoretical reason to see its way clear for obligation, it has to assume what is necessary for the moral law. Belief related to moral law has warrant in the consistency of theoretical reason. But any further warrant beyond such consistency is veiled. Theoretical reason cannot *know* a moral world order, nor how it is effected; theoretical reason cannot assure itself of the existence of adequate causality. But belief in adequate causality is required by theoretical reflection on the moral law and its object, the highest good. Whatever is required for the latter's possibility *must* be assumed; "the assumption is as necessary as the moral law." (*How* it is to be specified is not thus necessary; it involves choice, as we shall see.)

Belief in adequate causality

We now return to the third level of response to the Wizenmann objection; could one argue that in the case of a need of reason arising from the moral law, one can – one has sufficient warrant to – argue from the need to the reality of the object of that need?

It should be made clear that the object of the need of reason is the possibility of the highest good, and therefore the reality in question is, in the argument, derivative: it is the reality of that which makes the highest good possible.

Kant is clearly saying that full respect for the moral law (in its form as including the highest good as object) requires belief-in the reality of causality adequate to effecting the highest good. Allen Wood, however, judges that Kant's argument excludes *denial* of the existence of (in our current terminology) adequate causality, but "this is not the same thing at all as requiring or even justifying a positive *belief* in" adequate causality.[3]

Kant seems to have thought his arguments entailed more than morally justified belief-in. He says the practical use of reason does yield cognitions, and cognitions of existence, though nothing more can be said of such

3. Wood, *Kant's Moral Religion*, p. 30; he speaks here of God and immortality rather than of adequate causality.

existents.[4] But strictly speaking, the argument supports only a necessary *belief* that adequate causality is available without giving enough justification of such belief to warrant a reality-claim. Thus, Kant does not really argue a case clearly counter to Wizenmann's objection.[5]

Thorough grounding of such a belief, that is, *theoretically* sufficient warrant for the faith of pure practical reason, lies behind the veil that conceals from positive human recognition a reasonableness for finite rational existence as commanded by the moral law.

But perhaps the issue can be pursued a little further. Belief in the availability of causality adequate to effect the highest good is as necessary as the moral law. Is "belief" here to be taken as "unfounded conviction"? (It is obviously not probability-judgment.) It is as founded as the moral law is founded. Kant's position is clear: were the highest good not possible, "then the moral law which commands that it be furthered must be fantastic, directed to empty imaginary ends, and consequently inherently false."[6] But the moral law is not false; "duty is based upon an apodictic law, the moral law, which is independent of... and needs no support from theoretical opinions... in order to bind us completely to actions unconditionally conformable to the law."[7]

Thus, belief that adequate causality is available is such that with its (unprovable) truth there stands or falls the moral law's truth, and the reliability of reason, as well. (Supposed in all of this is that the experience of human causal *in*adequacy in securing proportionate happiness is not deceptive.) Moral law, reason, and adequate causality: if the first two are not illusory, the third is real.

But the moral law and reason are not separate: the moral law is reason in its practical exercise. In its practical use reason can go beyond the limitations of its theoretical use, and, of the two uses, the practical is primary.[8] "Every interest is ultimately practical, even that of speculative reason being only conditional and reaching perfection only in practical use."[9] And for what speculative or theoretical reason presented as ideas of Reason, practical reason supplies reality: "Here we have to do not with theoretical knowledge

4. "Thus it can be seen why in the entire faculty of reason only the practical can lift us above the world of sense and furnish cognitions [Erkenntnisse] of a supersensuous order and connection, though these cognitions can be extended only as far as is needed for pure practical purposes." KpV 106, CPrR 110.

5. Cf. Beck, *Commentary*, pp. 253, 260-64.

6. KpV 114, CPrR 118.

7. KpV 142f., CPrR 148.

8. KpV 119ff., CPrR 124ff.

9. KpV 121, CPrR 126.

of objects of these ideas but only whether they do have objects or not. This reality is supplied by pure practical reason."[10]

Not only is practical reason at issue here, but practical reason as a *ratio cognoscendi* (manner of coming to know). The moral law reveals the reality of freedom,[11] and thus gives cognitive access to the realm of the noumenal. In postulation of adequate causality, we seem to have similar inferential cognitive access to adequate causality as noumenal; but such is not known as objects are known.

Specification of the postulate as God

The second and for this essay's purposes crucial stage is now upon us, namely, the specification of what is postulated – causality adequate for proportionate happiness – as God rather than nature.

Such specification proceeds through several stages. To begin with, a need of theoretical reason requires all morally engaged finite rational beings to assume whatever is necessary for the possibility of the highest good. This possibility is "objectively grounded (in theoretical reason, which has nothing to say against it)."[12] Assuming what is thus necessary is postulation.

The next stage brings to light a difficulty. There is a problem in the thinking-through of the conditions required for this possibility: "as to the manner in which this possibility is to be thought, *reason cannot objectively decide* whether it is by universal laws of *nature* without a wise Author presiding over nature or whether only on the assumption of such an *Author*."[13] There are no objectively sufficient reasons for one assumption (concerning the basis for the highest good's possibility) rather than the other; therefore "the manner in which we are to think of it as possible is subject to our own choice."[14]

Such choice, however, is not arbitrary; it is not without reasons, though these are not compelling. There is a negative reason, a *subjective* impossibility of conceiving the highest good's possibility in terms of nature.

> Our reason finds it impossible to conceive, in the mere course of nature, a connection so exactly proportioned and so thoroughly adapted to an end between natural events which occur according to laws so heterogeneous. But, as with every other purposive thing in nature, it still cannot prove that it is

10. KpV 136, CPrR 141.
11. KpV 4, CPrR 3.
12. KpV 145, CPrR 151.
13. KpV 145, CPrR 151, with emphasis added.
14. Ibid.

> impossible according to universal laws of nature [only], i.e., show this by objectively sufficient reasons.[15]

And there is a positive reason: there is "a free interest of pure practical reason [which] is decisive for the assumption of a wise Author of the world."[16] This "interest of pure practical reason" seems to be what Kant refers to when in the same passage he says, "Now a subjective condition of reason enters." Some explanation should be given both to the negative reason, the subjective impossibility relating to nature, and to the positive reason, the interest of pure practical reason.

An interpretation of the subjective impossibility of conceiving nature as a causality adequate to ensuring deserved happiness can run as follows. Universal laws of nature, as laws and universal, are not in the world, but in theoretical reason; they express the ordering of phenomena. Happiness has to be worked out in the world, and its vicissitudes stem both from lack of knowledge and from lack of reliable effectiveness of the finite moral agent's noumenal causality. Hence theoretical reason cannot but recognize a gap between, on the one hand, phenomenal universal laws of nature and, on the other, that realm of nature where happiness is worked out through noumenal moral agency. This is the *conceptual* problem in harmonizing the two realms: such conceptual harmony is impossible in terms of one realm alone.

Such a difficulty in conceptualizing does not, however, burden finite reason if adequate causality is taken as God, and this leads into elaboration of the positive reason, the interest of reason which is decisive, the subjective condition which enters in. This subjective condition is a realization that specifying adequate causality as God is the only way two conditions can obtain: "it is the only way in which it is theoretically possible for it [theoretical reason] to conceive of the exact harmony of the realm of nature with the realm of morals as the condition of possibility of the highest good," and "it is the only way conducive to morality."[17] Adequate causality is subjectively inconceivable solely in terms of laws of nature. What is required and sufficient is well formulated by Allen Wood: "the practical possibility of a systematic causal connection between worthiness and happiness where this connection itself is regarded as an object of purposive volition and action."[18] Human volition is finite and cannot reliably shape nature to its intentions. Agency for such connection is for us conceivable, as Kant puts it, "only on the supposition of a supreme cause of nature which has a causality

15. KpV 145, CPrR 150.
16. KpV 145-46, CPrR 151.
17. KpV 145, CPrR 151.
18. Wood, *Kant's Moral Religion*, p. 132.

corresponding to the moral intention," and postulation requires specification of that "which is capable of actions by the idea of laws," that is, a will.[19] Finite reason cannot see how nature meets this requirement, and cannot see how this requirement could be otherwise. The concept of an Author of both nature and the moral law is the only theoretically satisfactory concept harmonizing virtue and proportionate happiness.

The other part of the subjective condition is a realization that conceiving adequate causality as Author of both realms is "the only way conducive to morality." Morality can benefit from whatever theoretical conceptions support its precise character as morality, that is, decisions in accord with and out of respect for the moral law. Theoretical conceiving of adequate causality is a free decision; as a decision conducive to morality it should accord with obedience to and respect for the moral law. There are perhaps two reasons why free specification in terms of Author of both realms is more conducive to moral decisions than specification of required causality as nature. "Nature alone" is a principle that renders impossible what reason needs to conceive moral obligation, that is, freedom. And furthermore, "Author of nature and the moral law" permits finite reason's viewing the moral law as divine commands; such as Kant's first definition of religion.[20] Pure practical reason has a stake – "a moral interest turns the scale"[21] – in not having inadequate or treacherous conceptual backing for the moral law.[22] Hence, since theoretical reason has no objectively compelling reasons against it, it can defer to the interest of practical reason in deciding how to specify the causality required if the moral law is not to be recognized as practically self-contradictory.

The decision is on subjective grounds; something must now be said about "subjective."[23] In the *Critique of Pure Reason*, Kant distinguishes between knowledge, belief, and opinion. Knowledge is that which is sufficiently grounded both objectively and subjectively, opinion has sufficient ground neither objectively nor subjectively, and belief has objectively insufficient but subjectively sufficient grounds. Speaking of practical contexts, Kant writes:

> Once an end is accepted, the conditions of its attainment are hypothetically necessary. This necessity is subjectively, but still only comparatively, sufficient, if I know of no other conditions under which the end can be attained.[24]

19. KpV 125, CPrR 130.
20. KpV 129, CPrR 134.
21. KpV 145, CPrR 150.
22. On "interest" in Kant and the *Critique of Practical Reason*, see Beck, *Commentary*, pp. 249-50; cf. KpV 119-20, CPrR 124.
23. See Beck, *Commentary*, pp. 217, 255-56.
24. A 823-24/B 851-52.

The term "subjective," both when applied to the impossibility of conceiving nature alone as adequate, and when applied to the subjective condition decisive for Author of the two realms, seems plausibly interpreted in the following way: if I decide to obey the moral law, I accept an end it contains, and once I accept such an end, I am necessitated to the conceptual conditions its attainment requires. Of such conditions I can conceive of only two ("I know of no other conditions"); one is ruled out on grounds not objectively compelling but for which I have no alternative – nature – and the other is decided-for because I have to have *some* theoretical clearance for my moral commitment to be reasonable.

The decision on how to conceive adequate causality is not based on a subjective condition in the sense that it is arbitrary or without foundation; it is not opinion. Once the limits of theoretical knowledge have been determined, there is a practical legitimacy available for convictions that go beyond such limits, a legitimacy that is based on the needs of the subject especially as these are consequent upon adoption of a viewpoint that is moral. Kant judges that theoretical needs of morally committed subjects can be met in only a limited number of ways, and that, given the limits of conceiving, one way has better grounding than another. It is thus that the theoretically better grounded decision, the faith of pure practical reason, is in the Author of both the realm of nature and the moral law.

Faith as trust

Postulation yields belief-in adequate causality (specified as Author of both nature and the moral law); because of the connection this belief has with reason and the moral law, it may be a kind of inferential cognitive access to the noumenal. However this latter issue be resolved, it seems that such belief can be interpreted as trust, and this interpretation constitutes a bridge between Kant and this essay's exploration of trust in part III, chapter 15.[25] That Kant's faith of pure practical reason is a trust in God is an argument of Allen Wood, and he cites many Kantian texts to support this, such as, for example: "Faith, then, denotes trust in God that he will supply our deficiency in things beyond our power, provided we have done all within our power."[26] Insofar as this interpretation is warranted, it means that God-as-believed-in is God-as-counted-on to effect something beyond human powers. The notion of trust developed in this essay that is closest to that of Kant's faith is that of trust as a counting-on-to-do. Belief in God is belief in an Instrument, albeit One that is intelligent and free. What is believed-in is a God of the gap, so well-

25. Pp. 179-86, 190.

26. Wood, *Kant's Moral Religion*, p. 162, quoting from Kant's *Lectures on Ethics*, trans. Louis Infield (New York: Harper & Row, 1963), p. 95.

disposed towards human beings as to be reliable in fairly apportioning happiness.[27]

A further observation, on hope and trust, and asseverations concerning trust: in Kant, hope for the highest good/kingdom of God requires belief in God, and this belief in God is belief that God will do what human beings cannot do, effect the highest good/kingdom of God.[28] If I respect the moral law, theoretical reason has subjectively sufficient grounds for my saying "I trust God." There is no objective claim here, as in "God is trustworthy," or "God exists." The asseverations subjectively warranted are "I believe in God" and "I trust God." Such a pattern of thought and implication falls within this essay's subject-object model of hope and trust; Kant's thought is essentially of this type.

Nature and history

In *Perpetual Peace*, nature alone guarantees perpetual peace. Why could not nature alone guarantee the highest good/kingdom of God? The principal answer to such a question is indicated above; that argument we can cap with the observation: if nature is all, there can be no virtue, since there is no freedom. The highest good as a concept collapses.

But the question of nature returns as the question of *history*. The "nature" of *Perpetual Peace* is human nature active through history. The question is clearly put by Lucien Goldmann, discussing Kant:

> Why must we believe not in a *human, historical*, and *immanent* realization in the *future*, but in a *superhuman* and *supernatural* realization in *eternity*? Why must practical interest lead reason *not to a philosophy of history but to a transcendent religion*?[29]

Goldmann does acknowledge a difficulty in principle which Kant would have with some notion of "natural progress": it would evacuate morality either through heteronomy or through being a doctrine of necessity without human freedom and hence without virtue. But Goldmann presses a judgment on Kant: it was the concrete social situation of Germany and especially of Prussia that made any hope in a *historical* future appear to Kant as utopian.[30]

27. Wood argues (pp. 166-67) against taking faith as a means in Kant's thought; but it does seem that Kant has *God* as a means.

28. The dual phrase "highest good/kingdom of God" here functions under the supposition that the latter notion, especially as developed in RLR, requires no major change in this section's analysis or argument.

29. Lucien Goldmann, *Immanuel Kant*, trans. Robert Black (London: NLB, 1971), p. 198.

30. Ibid., p. 199.

But a difficulty based on historical improbability is a difficulty of *varying* weight in times of varying subjective judgments: another age might judge it likely that history will see not only perpetual peace realized, but the kingdom of God as well. The choice seems between history and God, or between history without God and God without history.[31] The point here is not to enter into Kant's philosophy of history, though this, for the present question, is important.[32] But Goldmann's question of Kant is prototype of every question of aimed hope: is aimed hope sound only on the supposition that God, or historical mankind, or both, is adequate to ensure a hope's possibility?

It is clear enough that Kant's hope is grounded in God, and Ernst Bloch's, in history. In the thought of each, grounded hope implies *belief-in*, and this becomes *trust that* a specified agency will effect what is required for aimed hope's reasonableness. Both Kant and Bloch, concerned with the gap between human intent and felicitous world outcomes, do their thinking in the subject-object mode. Another mode appears in the thought of Gabriel Marcel.

31. Cf. pp. 47-49 on "Hope, Society, and History."

32. See, for example, Emil L. Fackenheim, "Kant's Concept of History," *Kant-Studien* 48 (1956-57): 381-98.

CHAPTER 18

MARCEL AND ABSOLUTE THOU

Full hope, implication, and thou

This chapter returns to the thought of Gabriel Marcel on hope and explores relationships that obtain between hope, theism, ontology, and especially inquires whether his thought confirms and furthers the interpretations of hope developed in the early chapters of Part III. Earlier treatment of Marcel ended with his notion of absolute hope, and such hope is the prime focus of this chapter. But since absolute hope is an unconditional form of what this essay terms "full" hope, and since relations between absolute hope and theism are similar in type to relations between full hope and what it implies, it is with re-examination of several features of full hope that we begin.

Full hope, approximately expressed in the locution "I hope in thee for us," is first of all an attitude; *disponibilité*, openness-availability, is at the heart of this hope. Secondly, it is also an act, and is precisely a *transcending* act: it is an act in which are overcome challenges to its right to hold off from declaring All is lost, I am lost; it is an act that declares "the case is not closed." Such transcending is not total; it simply means that one has surmounted obstacles of some type or other. In full hope there is at least *some* transcending. Thirdly and importantly for our purposes, hope is an act *implying an affirmation* of a certain sort. This feature of hope links it to the treatment of hoping's trust and its implications earlier in Part III. Marcel's formulations support this interpretation: hope involves "the transcendent act *par lequel elle affirme...*"; "it affirms as if it saw"; "hope consists in asserting that..."[1] These converging formulae seem to mesh with the theme of this essay that at least certain types of hope imply beliefs of some sort.

Beliefs of what sort? The first and generic belief is the conviction All is not lost, I am not lost. Furthermore, full hope's primary form is expressed as "I hope in thee for us," and this formulation permits beliefs to be specified as possibilities of the "us." The "us" is pluriform, and the possibilities are not strictly predicted. There is however an orientation toward *la perennité vivante* of the communion that grounds the hope – what this essay calls "shared life." And such hoping "for us" does imply beliefs that whatever is required to effect the outcome glimpsed but not grasped is available. Insofar as that which is required for some outcome to be possible is not specifiable precisely to the "thee" of "I hope in thee for us," then what Marcel said more

1. See chapter 12, By Way of Definitions; texts are from, respectively, HV 67, HV 53, and PE 28.

generally obtains in its generality: "Hope consists in asserting that there is at the heart of being, beyond all inventories and calculations, a mysterious principle which is in connivance with me..."[2]

But here, still in the arena of full but not necessarily absolute hope, *there arises an ambiguity concerning the "thee" of "I hope in thee."* On the one hand, the thee seems suitably interpreted as what Marcel will speak of as an "empirical thou." On the other hand, the phrase "a mysterious principle in connivance with me" admits interpretation as something more than a specific individual "empirical thou." Insofar as this tension shows up when texts are juxtaposed that refer to full but not necessarily absolute hope, this tension seems to characterize at least some full hopes. It seems that analysis of full hope generally admits of not only empirical thous but also supra-empirical – "mysterious" – factors. Hope as attitude therefore involves beliefs or assertions concerning possibilities linked to empirical and perhaps supra-empirical factors. The tension between these two lines of categorization becomes acute when we turn to hope that is absolute.

But before doing so, another remark should be made concerning full hope's implications. So far, the model of analysis has been that of hope implying beliefs-concerning. But it is obvious that the second line of this essay's hope-trust implication, in which hoping's trust implies the *reality of* the term, is also germane. Such implication holds only when the intersubjective model is appropriate. If it is appropriate anywhere, it certainly is for Gabriel Marcel's thought, and therefore one implication of hope of the form "I hope in thee for us" is *the reality of the term* of such hope's trust, "thee." But ambiguities in describing such a thee further – empirical? mysterious principle? – are now emerging. And this ambiguity remains when absolute hope's implications are under scrutiny.

Absolute hope

As we turn to absolute hope, and its putative relationship to an absolute Thou, it is important to attend to Marcel's manner of contrasting an empirical thou with an absolute Thou; he sketches it thus. Someone I meet almost as an object – I ask directions of him – can, when common interests and experience are recognized, become a thou for me. A felt unity arises. But he can "always relapse into the neutral region of objectivity"; he can become a bore; I can upon leaving him wonder what he does; I can doubt or distrust him.

> But if I follow this line of thought to the end, I arrive at the idea of a being in whom my faith and trust is so absolute that I shall never fall back into that

2. PE 28.

> state of doubt or distrust; or at least if I do, it will mean that I deny him utterly. This is the Absolute Thou. It is obvious that I cannot assert Him without an act of faith . . .[3]

It is at least theoretically possible that a person hope in a full and *absolute way*, that is, set no conditions or limits, abandon himself or herself in absolute confidence, and thus transcend all possible disappointment and experience radical security in his or her being; this is absolute hope. Central for the relation between absolute hope and theism in Marcel is relationship between absolute hope and absolute Thou. What is such relationship?

It is clear that absolute hope "appears as a response of the creature to the infinite Being to whom it is conscious of owing everything . . ."; the absolute Thou is its "only possible source."[4] This manner of absolute Thou's being such a source requires further examination; the type of relation between absolute hope and absolute Thou should be made as clear as possible. Clarity is very necessary because the status of the empirical thou in this matter is obscure; in the best available phrasing "I hope in thee for us," is the "thee" an empirical thou or an absolute Thou? Admittedly the "us" can be pluriform; but what more precisely can be said of the "thee"? A text of Marcel treating any full hope merits careful scrutiny.

> "In thee – for us": between this "thou" and this "us" which only the most persistent reflection can finally discover in the act of hope, what is the vital link? Must we not reply that "Thou" is in some way the guarantee of the union that holds us together, myself to myself, or the one to the other, or these beings to those other beings? More than a guarantee which secures or confirms from outside a union which already exists, it is the very cement which binds the whole into one.[5]

Here we have hope in the lower-case thou, as in myself, in one other, in others; such are empirical thous, and such an empirical thou is the thee in which I hope. But the link between that thou and the I who hope (for us) is upper-case Thou, and this latter's "role" is variously conceived, as guarantee, and also and preferably as "cement" since in speaking of absolute Thou "outside" and "inside" are not appropriate terms.[6]

Any full hope, Marcel thus maintains, involves not only an empirical thou (although the thou and the us in each case appear only to the "most persistent reflection") but also absolute Thou. In this manner Marcel addresses the

3. "Theism and Personal Relationships," (TPR), p. 37.
4. HV 47.
5. HV 60-61.
6. TPR 38.

ambiguity noted above concerning the thee of "I hope in thee." In any full hope, and a fortiori in absolute hope, there is involvement of *both* an empirical thou *and* absolute Thou.

If this serves to place in Marcel's context the empirical thou and the absolute Thou, attention to other texts can place in similar context hope related to "a mysterious principle . . . in connivance with me." This phrase does suggest a cosmic or pervasive hope, a hope without specific referent or term. There would appear to be no thou – at least no empirical thou – in which I hope. (In other cases there might appear to be an empirical thou, a specific term, but no absolute Thou.) In putatively cosmic hope there would appear to be a hope with no degree of specificity to the thou, and, while there might be an absolute Thou, the formula "I hope in thee for us" would capture no finite thou as the term of the relationship. But Marcel offers a comment that calls into question any interpretation of absolute hope so cosmic as to be term-less. He writes of "fundamental existential assurance," and says it consists in "the affirmation of an original link, one could even say an umbilical link, which unites the human being, not to the world in general, which would mean nothing, but to a certain determinate ambiance which is as concrete as a cocoon or a nest."[7] In this text Marcel declines to speak of a link to the world-in-general; linkage is determinate, concrete to the point of being nest-like, conferring a sense of at-home and nurturing. Here Marcel's thought supports interpreting a cosmic hope as not without a thou, a term with some degree of determinacy. It seems plausible to conclude that Marcel resists taking absolute hope, or any full hope, as being utterly without relationship to a determinate thou, to a determinate term.

Implication, ontology, and indication

Such is a sketch of relationships between absolute hope (and any full hope) and both empirical thous and absolute Thou. In any full hope absolute Thou is involved, though grasping how is almost impossible. And even when hope seems term-less, there is a welcoming and fostering determinateness that precludes total vagueness in the term-ground.

The question joining Marcel's thought and this essay's question is now upon us: Is Marcel's absolute hope an "organ of apprehension"? Does its reality imply the reality of its term, and not just imply belief concerning the reality of its term? On an intersubjective model for ontology, hoping's trust

7. I use this more detailed translation provided by Joan Nowotny ("Gabriel Marcel's Philosophy of Hope," Ph.D. dissertation, University of Toronto, 1974, p. 285) from *Pour une sagesse tragique et son au-delà* (Paris: Plon, 1968), p. 67, rather than that in *Tragic Wisdom and Beyond* (Evanston: Northwestern University Press, 1973), p. 38.

implies the reality of the "you" that is trusted. The other as "you" is in the input. It *would* seem that all that this essay now needs is a survey of how Marcel's thought meshes with this essay's intersubjective model, and how absolute hope would be an organ of apprehension of absolute Thou.

It is quite appropriate to characterize Marcel's philosophy as an intersubjective philosophy. He identifies it as such.[8] His approach to an ontology starts from intersubjectivity and presses the question "Can we say that being *is* intersubjectivity?"[9] He is cautious in the extreme in his answer, saying it is impossible to agree to this proposition if it is taken literally, and stressing that the matter, being more subtle, requires strict and more intricate expression: the ego cannot be the sole starting and reference point; yet one should not speak of the ego as part of a numerical totality inclusive of other egos; he does finally find an acceptable formula:

> I concern myself with being only in so far as I have more or less distinct consciousness of the underlying unity which ties me to other beings of whose reality I already have a preliminary notion.[10]

This formula embodies a cautious yet resolute approach to being as intersubjective, and thus aligns him with an intersubjective model of ontology. And the "other beings of whose reality I already have a preliminary notion" would lead, in the case of hope's trust, to a consonance with this essay's doctrine of implication of the term's reality – *were it not for* the ambiguity in the *thou*.

The ambiguity of the *thou* in the phrase "I hope in thee for us" has already been noted. Marcel contrasts an empirical thou and absolute Thou, and these contrasting notions, applied to analysis of absolute hope, give rise to a dilemma: on the intersubjective model a relationship of trust implies the reality of the term; the thou that is the term can be either empirical or absolute; if it is empirical and presumably finite, this term-ground is inadequate to ground absolute hope; if it is absolute and presumably without empirical character, then its reality cannot be distinguished from non-reality. Absolute transcendence of the thou-term is indistinguishable from no term at all; thorough immanence of the term is inadequate for grounding unconditional confidence.

But Marcel overcomes the dilemma insofar as in full hope and a fortiori in absolute hope *both* an empirical thou *and* absolute Thou are involved. But for this same reason, any strict implication (on the intersubjective model) of the

8. MB 1, 223.
9. MB 2, chap. I. Citation is from p. 18.
10. MB 2, 19, with emphasis omitted.

reality of absolute Thou is impossible. Intersubjective strict implication of this essay's intersubjective model seems to get purchase only on a term as empirical thou.

A form of hope may be full, may be absolute, may fit this essay's intersubjective model. The relationships involved *may be* grounded in God and thus admit a theistic interpretation.[11] Whether this latter grounding is so is not lightly to be presumed. God is not "cause" of any such relationship. Marcel maintains that testing is necessary and not quickly carried out, yet it does not in any case yield an "object of knowledge."[12] Such knowledge and "cause" too – indeed all description and categorization – have their range in the will-nature or subject-object model. What may obtain here is not knowledge, but presence.[13] Marcel maintains that absolute hope is inseparable from an equally absolute act of faith.[14]

Yet insofar as third-person conceptualization of a second-person empirical thou as term-ground reveals on will-nature grounds a causality that is *inadequate for a relationship stronger than the relata*, the "cement" metaphor seems appropriate, and this may *indicate* what might be called absolute Thou.[15] Of such "cement" Marcel is chary of descriptions, and we should be as cautious as he is when he speaks of the "powers" it is philosophy's delicate task to bring to light:

> What are these powers? It is very hard to name them, first of all because words are most often too withered, too lifeless for the task. But speaking very generally I would say that these powers are radiations of being.[16]

This radiation-image is helpful, and parallel to one applied to many human relationships:

> I should say without hesitation that a living personal relationship becomes itself a source of heat and light, even for those who are not directly involved therein; it is moreover in this way that a relationship proves itself to be rooted in God, whatever opinion of God's nature these friends or lovers may entertain.[17]

11. See Marcel's TPR, esp. p. 41.
12. TPR 38.
13. BH 81.
14. HV 46.
15. "Indicate" [*indique*] is adapted from Charles Widmer, *Gabriel Marcel et le théisme existentiel*, Cogitatio fidei, no. 5 (Paris: Cerf, 1971), p. 181.
16. *Tragic Wisdom*, p. 14. The original reads "comme des irradiations de l'être." *Pour une sagesse tragique*, p. 32.
17. TPR 40.

Every attribute of God is a *Grenzbegriff*,[18] and ''absolute Thou'' is no exception. But whatever certain human relationships, full and absolute hope among them, may *indicate*, the final ground of such relationship is better conceived as Thou rather than as It. But such does not show up as an item to one who surveys; it is perhaps met as a Presence.

18. BH 169.

CHAPTER 19

CONCLUSION

The thrust of this essay's conclusion is toward hope's bearing on theism. Analysis of deep hope yielded a distinction between ultimate hope and fundamental hope, and yielded arguments concerning what contributes to soundness in ultimate hopes. What is said of ultimate hope, fundamental hope, and absolute hope at the end of Part II is presumed here. This essay then set forth, with the aid of two models for ontologies, two different kinds of implication involved in hope's trust. This was followed by presentation of how each of this essay's philosophers linked hope and theism or atheism, with each's own ontological framework as background.

Now we turn to implications of such hope-analysis for theism. Such implications range over hope as climate of the mind, and yield beliefs about the future and about what would make such future possible – sketches of what is to be looked for, the finding of which would establish an ultimate hope as *thoroughly* sound because adequate causality is available. Here we have indications of kinds of theism. Implications of hope-analysis also pertain to hope as an organ of apprehension. Here we have inclinations concerning the plausibility of theism. Conclusions ventured are as much charters for further exploration as they are reports of findings.

Is the future open?

The person who hopes *believes* that the future is open, that is, believes that something personally worthwhile is possible. But there are different breadths to the future's "aperture," and a survey of these is a survey of hope's being a climate of the mind.

Minimally, there is "survivor hope." This is the aimed hope entailed by fundamental hope: if I do not declare All is lost, I am lost, I implicitly believe there is some way out, up, or forward beyond present straitened circumstances. The objective may be vague; yet something is believed still worthwhile and possible. This hope is presumably an ultimate hope, but not necessarily sound.

Is the future open for me?

Here we locate the problem of history and sacrifice. It besets especially any system of thought that envisions my hoping for a future in which I will not share, a future effected perhaps at my expense. Here I hope for other's benefit, perhaps at a loss of my own. This problem seems unavoidable for any ultimate hope that is both social and historical, such as that total hope presented by Ernst Bloch.

We can assume this hope is ultimate, and is sound in its formal characteristics. But if such hope's fulfillment requires my exclusion or suffering, is it *sound* to hope thus for an objective that is not worthwhile and possible for the one who hopes? In this formulation – as an ''altruistic'' hope – it remains a question.

But the problem can be reformulated. Recall Marcel's example of the patriot who hoped for his country's liberation, knowing his dying would precede that day. With such an outcome, and those who would see it, this patriot is linked. In the terms of this essay, the objective is a form of shared life rather than others' benefit at the patriot's expense. There is a love of what the patriot would create, a bond between him and those who will see liberation; indeed, his hope is vital to the outcome's possibility. If such ''altruistic'' hope, such as that of Marcel's patriot and Bloch's Red hero, can be legitimately viewed in the light of experience of communion instead of simply as someone's being used for others' gain, then there may be far less objection to its soundness. This essay's formula of complex ultimate hopes permits benefit-loss hope to be subsumed under hope for shared life.

What sort of a future is believed open?

Here we return to the ultimate hope presented as sound by Bloch and Kant. Theirs is a total ultimate hope, a hope for the highest good, the kingdom of God. We took note earlier of the ambiguity in the kingdom's character as social. It seems a fair interpretation of these philosophers' views to take the kingdom as minimized abuse and misuse, and maximal appropriate reciprocal utilization. Persons are treated as ends, nature and other persons are instruments in suitable fashion, persons are reconciled with persons and nature in alliance and control. This is the kingdom as system; it is no ignoble goal.

Marcel does not speak much of total hope; he does see superabundance as part of sound hope's objective, and a foretaste of this is experience of communion or shared life. If total hope be hope for shared life, then it is not (merely) appropriate utilization that is hoped for, but affective union.

The point of rehearsing senses of total hope's objective as system and as communion is to indicate the difference it makes in the beliefs such hope implies. If I hope for system, I believe that needed instrumentalities are available and that I can serve appropriately as instrument. If I hope for communion, I believe that participants are available and that I am ready to respond appreciatively to others.

Differing total hopes thus require differing beliefs. They also require different attitudes: personal readiness to serve and be served is distinguishable from personal readiness for affective response. Kant, for example, views the moral law as rationally requiring promoting the highest good as system; the appropriate and obligatory attitude, then, is one of readiness to treat persons including oneself as ends in themselves. Yet the two attitudes, readiness to serve and be served and readiness for affective response, are not incompatible insofar as their respective objectives are not.

The kingdom of God – without God?

We now confront what is believed adequate in the matter of causality or grounding for the highest good as kingdom. It is safe to say that any individual human being is, as individual, inadequate.

Reflecting first on kingdom as system, we recall that Bloch presented historical humanity as adequate to make possible the kingdom. Historical humanity, i.e., human nature, might in Kant's view at most effect civil peace. But effecting a moral world order is another matter. Kant judged that reason could not see how Nature could ensure systematic deserved happiness, and it is hard to gainsay his judgment short of fusing the two as *Deus sive Natura*. Adequate causality has to be specified as Author of both the moral law and nature, that is, as God.

The question of causality believed available and adequate is the question, not exactly of the Almighty, but of the Sufficiently-mighty. Sufficiency requires at least humankind for both Bloch and Kant (though not historical humanity for Kant), but not God for Bloch.

It seems that between Bloch and Kant we find a simple disjunction: belief that adequate ground is available is belief in humanity or God, Prometheus or Zeus. One who hopes for the kingdom counts on historical humanity without God or God without historical humanity. Or, one who unconditionally refuses to despair is believed grounded in humanity or God.

Perhaps Marcel offers a third approach. If hope for the kingdom (as communion, of course) can be construed along the lines of Marcel's analysis of "I hope in thee for us," then the following is germane. The thee (individual or group) in whom I or we hope is linked with those who hope by a Thou as "cement." Hope is always in a term that is an empirical thou, yet this bond is established, as "guarantee" from outside or "cement" within, by a Thou that is absolute. What this schematization suggests is hope in Prometheus *and* Zeus, thou and Thou; full hope, at least if it is absolute, cannot be absolute without Thou but cannot exist without thou. However this thou and this Thou are named, both are involved, and each is involved not merely as instrument but as participant.

What to look for, and how: images of God

If hope implies belief that causality adequate to effect its objective is available, then the content of that belief specifies what counts as confirmation that the hope is thoroughly sound because the hoped-for is possible, that is, is not just believed possible. Such content of belief is therefore a sketch of *what to look for* in order to know whether the hope is thoroughly sound. This content is like the sketch an artist composes from instructions of a film's casting director: Look for someone who looks like this. The sketch conforms to reality if there is someone who looks like that, but it is derived from the imagination of the casting director. The latter imagines what is needed for a certain role. There may or may not be such a character; even if there is, he or she may not be found.

If I hope for benefit, I believe that an instrument is available; I look for an instrument. In ontological terms, I believe that first-person or third-person aetiologies are available, and look for these. If I hope for shared life, I believe that second-person efficacy can be "met"; I look for a participant.

If my hope is ultimate and total, and if it has the form of kingdom as system, then I look for adequate first- or third-person causalities as instruments for effecting such system. If it has the form of communion, I look for adequate second-person efficacy, a thou. If the total hope is both for appropriate utilization and union, then adequate grounding must include both that which can be characterized as instrument and as thou. If the grounding is absolute, then it is both Almighty and Thou.[1] An Almighty seems to be what Bloch denies and Kant affirms. Marcel's Thou must not be taken as (third- or first-person?) cause, he says. But such causality must be sought if system is involved in the kingdom. It seems an Almighty must be sought "outside" both mankind and nature, at least in a Kantian context; Bloch would prefer "inside" – and "ahead." But Marcel's Thou can be met "between," in meeting with empirical thou, be this latter a label for aspects of oneself, for another person, or for one's natural or social milieu.

Hope's implied beliefs present not only what to look for, but *how to look*. To have hope for one's own benefit is to believe in the availability of an instrument; to hope for shared life is to believe in the availability of a participant. To look for the latter is not just to conduct an inventory of instruments; it is to be ready to meet a thou on terms other than one's own. One can therefore do one's looking in differing ways – as a spectator-utilizer, or as one ready as a person to meet, or as a combination of the two.

Hope: organ of apprehension?

Hope has implications for theism not only in the area of implied beliefs and images of God, but also in the area of reality-claims. The former is hope's climate of the mind, the latter, hope as organ of apprehension.

To investigate whether and how hope is an organ of apprehension is to

1. "Almighty" here connotes power and *benevolence*. Bloch's portrait of the Pharaoh-God is one of power and *abuse*.

evaluate it as possibly cognitive, as a *ratio cognoscendi* or manner of coming to know. That which may be so apprehended is real. In the matter of hope and God, at issue is whether any form of hope indicates that God is real. But, insofar as different models of ontology apply, "real" has different senses – as object, as subject, as thou.

Whether anything concerning the reality of God is implied by hope, divides, as a question, into implications of ultimate hope and implications of fundamental hope.

When ultimate hope is a total hope, when it has the form of hope for the kingdom as system, as it probably does in Bloch and Kant, then a person who so hopes at least implicitly believes that causality adequate to effect this system is available. This is an implied belief-that, and as such is part of hope's climate of the mind.

Fundamental hope requires trust (so does sound ultimate hope's desiring). This trust can be differently understood. When it is appropriately construed according to the will-nature model, as it seems to be in Kant and Bloch, such trust may likewise imply no more than belief-that the term of the trust is reliable. But when such trust is appropriately understood according to the intersubjective model, then the actuality of such trust implies the reality of its term. In this case, hope is an organ of apprehension; it is in touch with its term's reality.

Kant's approach may not fit smoothly into these two classifications. There may be more to hope-implication than belief-that, warranted, as he put it, subjectively but not objectively. It seems that postulation of adequate causality is a counting-on the Author of both the moral law and nature such that in my finite rational existence I cannot rationally refrain from such counting-on without denying the reality of the moral law. If this is so, then experience of the moral law gives, in the matter of adequate aetiology, *inferential cognitive access to the noumenal*. Freedom as noumenal is known through moral experience. Similarly but inferentially, adequate aetiology as noumenal (i.e., real) is known.

If this interpretation of Kant holds up, hope for the kingdom is an organ of apprehension. But it is so under the following conditions and with the following consequences. First, reason functions (and can only function) within the will-nature model. What is postulated is a will that can universally bring about effects in nature. Second, granted that this causality is specified as Author and recognized as God, this God is Instrument only; there is no encounter, no appreciation, no shared life; God assures deserved benefits in circumstances where humankind cannot guarantee them. In this frame, prayer or union with God is inconceivable. Third, this Author is clearly extrinsic to both the realm of finite rational beings and the realm of nature; in relation to these two noumenal realms, divine transcendence is extrinsic.

If this interpretation is valid, there *is* a reality-claim, but the reality is interpreted in terms of will and nature; God is the fairminded Almighty.

In contrast with this inferential cognitive access to the real understood in will-nature terms stands the intersubjective approach. Borrowing on its key cognitional term "presence," it can be called *presential cognitive access to the real as thou*. Such is the implication of reality stemming from interpreting hope's trust on the intersubjective model. Its form of trust indicates the reality of the thou in whom I trust, that such is real and well-disposed towards me.

When would knowing the reality of such a thou also involve knowing absolute Thou? Supposing intersubjective knowledge of thou as real, one would then have to say in addition that Marcel's analysis is plausible when he says that in any full hope what is involved is both empirical thou and absolute Thou. Some support for Marcel's analysis arises insofar as the trust in question is a relation stronger than the relata. This adds to the question of grounding the notion of comparative degrees of adequate input. Of course both an empirical thou and an empirical I can have degrees of input that enable the one who hopes to withstand proportionate degrees of trial. (There is, of course, the question of how one knows the strength or other characteristics of one's hope.) But if both I and thou are inadequate to explain the strength of hope's trust, then there is a "mysterious principle" involved as "cement" or "guarantee." And finally, if the hope is unconditional, then there is plausibility in taking the ground as including, not just thou, but thou which is absolute, that is, strong enough to enable me to withstand any disappointment.

This approach, too, requires comment on its conditions and consequences. First, transcendence here has the form of a bond stronger than its terms. Second, the ground of this bond's strength functions both from within ("cement") and from without ("guarantee"). Third, there is here an instrumental role: the Thou serves to confirm a bond. Fourth – however – it seems that such Thou can also be encountered, in presence. Yet, fifth, encounter with absolute Thou seems (always?) to be mediated by empirical thou. Such encounter seems likely to be characterized developmentally by both a deepening and an expanding, both with respect to an empirical thou and with respect to Marcel's "mysterious principle."

Does this essay attempt a proof of God's existence? Is it claiming that if anyone anywhere had absolute hope, such would prove the existence of God? The question as formulated brings out the ambiguities of the term "proof." A proof is presumably a procedure available to anyone, regardless of his or her personal attitude. Proof, and evidence bearing on proof, pertain to the object-side of the will-nature model. It is third-person categories that are the tools of philosophical proof. Kant seems to assume this when, contrasting knowledge and belief, he explains the latter as subjectively but not objectively warranted. So absolute hope is not basis for a proof. But, if the intersubjective model makes sense, absolute hope is an *indication* of the reality of absolute Thou – either this, or such hope is the greatest delusion.

The reality of absolute *Thou* is not *implied* by hope's trust understood on the intersubjective model; the reality of *thou* is implied. The reality of absolute Thou is *indicated*, i.e., possibly involved and therefore knowable, insofar as both the intersubjective model applies and the relation is stronger than the I and empirical thou. Should hope be recognized as absolute, however, it is difficult to see how its adequate grounding could be other than absolute Thou.

This essay wondered at the outset whether hope analysis *inclines* towards theism or atheism. There is no question of proof. But a theistic inclination seems to obtain insofar as the following claims are true: (1) the moral law, in Kant's sense, is not false; (2) sound ultimate hope is characterized by simple absolute desiring for appropriate utilization (thus meshing with Kant) or union, and such desiring requires trust; (3) fundamental hope requires trust; (4) such trust admits to analysis on the intersubjective model; (5) there are, actually, some hopes; (6) these hopes exhibit totality or unconditionality.

To hope is to risk. At risk is not just disappointment, but betrayal and self-betrayal. The greater risk is in declining to hope at all, if declining to do so is to depart from human duty, or reason, or developmental possibility. Philosophical analysis of hope does not reveal readily-comprehensible warrant. And lived hope is burdened by death and tragedy weighing against it – essential issues this essay lacked scope to deal with.

This essay began with the tale of Prometheus, Epimetheus, and Pandora. Prometheus' story reflects the antagonism between Zeus Almighty and humanity's hero. But perhaps hope's theism or atheism need not turn on a choice between God and historical humanity. And when Epimetheus risks espousing Pandora, he has no assurance that her dowry of hope is not a curse. Prometheus counseled against the marriage. Maybe Prometheus was right. But I doubt it.

CHAPTER 20

EPILOGUE ON SOME RELIGIOUS AND THEOLOGICAL THOUGHT

Few these days are concerned about Pandora, Prometheus, and Epimetheus; more are concerned with recent theological and religious thought. The issues are perennial, the historical forms these issues take vary, and as the year 2000 approaches, concern in some quarters will increase.

This epilogue sketches some bridges between this essay's themes and some features of religious and theological thought, especially some features of more recent thought. It is not a concluding unphilosophical postscript; my method is that advocated by Paul Ricoeur: the philosopher deals with theological discourse by "approximation," by coming up close to theological discourse to listen, to use reason in its fullness, neither subordinating philosophy to theology nor prescinding from anything the philosopher believes essential, even religiously essential. Reason need not be a priori committed either to religion or to scepticism or to solely autonomous usage; reasonable listening can be exercised in a community of dialogue among people of reason and commitment. Nor does reason require distinguishing a priori between natural and sacred theology; employing this distinction is a theological, not a philosophical, position. Yet I do not merely listen; I also speak, suggesting some implications of my argument for religious and theological thought.

It is a common Christian teaching that hope is a virtue. Faith, hope, and charity are theological or theologal virtues, human excellences in human relationships between a person and God. Long ago Josef Pieper proposed the centrality of hope, and more recently Karl Rahner, Gustavo Gutiérrez, and Jürgen Moltmann have argued for the primacy of hope among these three virtues.

But another major stream of religious thought challenges hope's reputation as a virtue, essentially by naming desire a vice.[1] In Buddhism and in Advaita Vedanta Hinduism, for example, there are doctrines that desiring is to be overcome, even annihilated.[2] The Advaita Vedanta school teaches that I

1. Perhaps hope is a virtue for some cultures but not for others. There are cultures where people simply do not plan for the future, and in that sense they could be said not to hope. Or perhaps hope is a virtue only for children, the weak, or the old. Alastair MacIntyre and Michael Slote, among others, have stressed that the virtues of one culture and age are not necessarily the virtues of another.

2. On desire in Vedanta and Buddhist thought, see, for example, Ernest Wood, *Vedanta Dictionary* (New York: Philosophical Library, 1964), p. 58; S. G. F. Brandon, *A Dictionary of Comparative Religion* (New York: Charles Scribner's Sons, 1970), pp. 214-215; Nyanatiloka, *Buddhist Dictionary: Manual of Buddhist Terms and*

should be free from both every desire-for and desire-against (fear). The Buddha taught that desire in the sense of craving is the root of all suffering; I should be free of desire for rebirth and free of desire for no further rebirth, free even of desire for desirelessness. It is fairly clear that "desire" – "craving" – here means at least selfish desire. But would not even minimally ruling out selfish desire thereby rule out desire for fulfillment of what I really need? Hope for satisfaction of my real needs does seem to be part of an acceptable or honorable hope-for-me. Maybe also ruled out would be the desire to serve well and to be well served. Hoping is thus charged with being inescapably infected with desire, and true liberation requires leaving all desire behind.

This is not just a matter of hoping for the right thing. Clearly hope with its sights set on the illusory, on *maya*, on the worthless or the impossible would be anathema not only to Buddhists and Advaitins but to Marxists and Christians as well. It is a matter of the kind of hoping, whatever be the object hoped for – the kind of desiring, whatever be the object of desire. Is there so deep a division between West and East on this matter of desire, and therefore on the worth of any kind of hope?

My response to this objection that hope is infected with illusion and desire begins with my proposal for sound aimed hope. An ultimate aimed hope is sound insofar as it is characterized by simple absolute desiring, not willful desiring. In willful desiring, someone else's will is the pivotal factor: does she want me to want this, or want me not to want it? I choose my course in reference to another's will, not according to the merits of what is before me. "Willful" wanting is a matter of yielding to or dominating another's will. Hope to dominate, at least in a person's ultimate hope, is a vice; equally a vice is a hope to be dominated by another's will. Simple absolute desiring, freed from a contest of wills, is a necessary condition for any sound ultimate hope. Whether this simple absolute desiring seeks union, shared life, appreciative presence, or whether such desiring seeks fair relations of serving and being served, such desiring is on the side of the human. This simple absolute desiring seems less open to the critique of Buddhism and Vedanta than desiring colored by antagonism, consumerism, and greed. This point is not only a non-Western one: Dag Hammarskjöld points out somewhere that we do not pray simply by pointing out to God our cravings and asking God to attend to them. Furthermore, simple absolute desiring can experience an "education." I can begin in fear and craving and grow toward openness. The education of desiring is a matter in which religious traditions

Doctrines, third rev. and enlarged edition, ed. Nyanaponika (Colombo, Ceylon [Sri Lanka]: Frewin and Co., 1972), p. 198, s.v. "Vipassana"; Christmas Humphreys, *A Popular Dictionary of Buddhism* (London: Curzon Press, 1984) p. 64, s.v. "Desire."

have much to suggest to an understanding of hope. For example, while Wayne Davis wisely distinguishes between appetitive desire (what I'll call "given" desire) and volitive desire (what I'll call "chosen" desire), he maintains that appetitive desire affects volitive desire but volitive desire does not influence appetitive desire.[3] I would go further: it is not inconceivable that a person can desire that some desires be effective, even dominating other desires: a person can want to have a certain kind of will, and this kind of "second-order desire" is indeed morally meritorious, as Harry Frankfurt has pointed out.[4] The kind of desires a person wants is also highlighted in the *Spiritual Exercises* of Ignatius of Loyola: key is not only the question "What do you really desire?" but also *imagining* having different desires.[5] Compatible both with conceptions of desiring and with actual desiring is the view that some movements arise from within and without that move towards satisfactions, and a person can choose which ones to ally himself or herself with. With desires, it would be a matter of choosing to ally oneself with different given movements of desiring, and in hopes, of choosing to ally oneself with different occurring movements of hoping.

I'd add three further comments. First, choosing-to-ally-oneself can be due to what is not just I-myself. To use the Buberian phrases, hope's desiring can be not just a matter of will but also of grace; indeed, such desiring comes "not by seeking." This leads to my second comment: at some point paradox seems a necessary way of speaking of such matters. "Desiring comes not by seeking." "Desire to have the desire to have no desires, and then give up that desire." "The desire to serve well can only lead to serving badly." Applied to hopings, these two comments suggest that I may be able to "have" simple absolute desiring for some worthwhile possibility only if another communicates to me that this is not a matter of winning or losing, but of being

3. Wayne A. Davis, "The Two Senses of Desire," *Philosophical Studies* 45 (March 1984): 181-96.

4. Harry G. Frankfurt, "Freedom of the Will and the Concept of a Person", *Journal of Philosophy* 68 (1971): 5-20.

5. Ignatius also proposes that each particular individual not antecedently fix his or her desires on what is admittedly a good but perhaps erroneously assumed to be an embodying part of the ultimate good appropriately hoped for by that individual. As long as we are not bound by some obligation and have a choice, "we should not fix our desires on health or sickness, wealth or poverty, success or failure, a long life or a short one. For everything has the potential of calling forth in us a deeper response to our life in God" (number 23, Fleming translation-paraphrase). Such fixation seems a way of understanding the "craving" denounced in Buddhism and Hinduism. See also E. Edward Kinerk, S.J., *Eliciting Great Desires: Their Place in the Spirituality of the Society of Jesus,* Studies in the Spirituality of Jesuits 16, No. 4 (St. Louis, Mo.: American Assistancy Seminar, 1984).

present to the merits of what I am now enabled to imagine. Third and finally, what I now imagine is not simply a matter of the future. William Lynch has criticized Jürgen Moltmann for so stressing the future as determinant of present choices that it becomes impossible to imagine really facing the present, living in the present. It is the present experience that Lynch will take seriously: the captive who hopes for future freedom must nonetheless wash and shave in the present.[6] It is easy to formulate dichotomous questions about living in the present versus living for the future; it seems however to me that paradox may be a portal for walking through such a divide: a willful-less Zen of the present may balance Moltmann's stress on the future.

If there is one feature common to all religions, it may be the message that there is a way out, a way up, from the slough of despond or the cave of presumption. We shall be healed, free at last, lifted up, reconciled: such is religion's prognosis. There is also diagnosis of the ills and illusions, and prescription of the cure.

My essay calls for realistic judgment about both the possibility of and the desirability of what is hoped for. Thomas Aquinas, for example, is cautious about misplaced reliance: unwarranted dependence on God is worse than presumptuous reliance on one's own resources.[7] And the commandment against idolatry bears also upon images of hope's desires. Especially in religious hopes where what is desired is different from what has been, we need to be ready to smile but not lose heart as we realize that what lies ahead of us is to some degree our own image, reflected enlarged and distorted, fun-house mirror style. Hopes, even as Ernst Bloch surveyed them so comprehensively, should become educated, *docta*. The more misleading images of what might be hoped for should yield to the less misleading. Such a changing of one's course seems possible, however, only once a person is underway, as in sailing. Giving up on one image of hope does not mean that a person has lost hope. Whether salvation is seen as seraglio or alone with the Alone, we need to be critical as well as reverent when dealing with weak human imaginings: to have fundamental hope means holding off from presumption as well as from despair. Thus this analysis of desiring (and later of what is desired) must be balanced by my stress on fundamental hope, the disposition that endures when desiring has been abandoned: fundamental hope has a lot in common with desirelessness. And the interplay between aimed ultimate hope and fundamental hope provides theoretical place for the abandoning of some image of what is hoped for.

6. William F. Lynch, S.J., *Images of Faith: An Exploration of the Ironic Imagination* (Notre Dame, Ind.: University of Notre Dame Press, 1973), pp. 136-40.

7. Thomas Aquinas. "Hope," *Summa Theologiae* II-II, 17-22 (Blackfriars, with New York:McGraw-Hill, and London: Eyre & Spottiswoode, 1966), s.v. Presumption, Q. 21, a. 1, ad primum.

Imagining and conceiving what is hoped for: eschatology

Some have proposed that there is one thing all people do hope for, happiness, salvation, eternity, the kingdom. This much does seem sure: the images are different for what people hope for. Even granting the differences between the desires that stir as "given" like appetites, and the desires that a person has chosen to be his or her own, it is not obvious that on the deep level of inbuilt desires all people are the same. And certainly how they specify what they want diverges, even granting the symbolic or token role their hopes may reveal. Anthropologies, empirical, psychological, philosophical, theological, need to be thoroughly worked out to say whether all people at some level hope for the same thing.

Pursuing answers to such questions is helped by seeing some of hope's objectives as contributing to other objectives. There may be a "big" hope which little hopes are part of. Here is where religions' eschatological hopes come into view: what finally is there to hope for? Is there a definitive future, "after" which, if there is history, it is of quite a different sort? Is what I am doing now, is what we have done, merely to be left behind, or does it contribute to something that lasts? Are what we hope for merely steppingstones, or are they foretastes of what will mean fulfillment in the end?

John Macquarrie offers a matrix useful for locating the themes of Christian (and by extension other) discourse about the future.[8] The categories are in pairs: individual, social-cosmic; this-worldly, otherworldly; evolutionary, revolutionary; realized, future (or, between these, inaugurated). I would add an additional group concerning what brings matters to pass, fulfillment's aetiology: human effort, nature, God.

Questions about the future are sometimes social-cosmic and sometimes individual in the way they are posed. Collectively asked, the questions are: What will become of the world, finally? Will it end? Answers speak of the kingdom of God, the Second Coming of Christ. Sometimes the questions are asked in so individualistic a way that doctrines imitating the collective "end" have been developed for each person: What will become of me, finally? Answers speak of immortality of the soul, of resurrection, of seeing God or being damned in final individual judgment prior to final collective judgment.[9]

How "final" is the eschatological condition hoped for? There are difficulties imagining any such condition, difficulties conceiving of time, duration. Bluntly put, almost as threatening as eternal punishment would be

8. John Macquarrie, *Christian Hope* (New York: Seabury Press, 1978), p. 87.

9. Collective and individual eschatology are respectively surveyed and summarized in Zachary Hayes, O.F.M., *What Are They Saying About the End of the World?* (New York: Paulist, 1983) and Monika K. Hellwig, *What are They Saying About Death and Christian Hope?* (New York: Paulist, 1978).

heavenly boredom. A line from Jürgen Moltmann captures the problem: "If at the end of everything there had to be a goal that could be reached, it would probably be better if this goal were never reached, for once this goal were reached, life would have no goal."[10] Addressing a traditional understanding that at the end faith yields to vision, love endures, but hope comes to an end, Karl Rahner argues that hope endures. Hope is not just the virtue for the *viator*. This is because hope is the origin and center which binds together the other two theological virtues, faith and love. It is highly questionable to understand the final blessed condition of human beings according to the model of "possession". According to Rahner, this "possession" really is

> the radical transcending and abandoning of ourselves into the truth of this unfathomable mystery, and the radical self-alienation and self-transcendence of love. This love cannot attract the love of the beloved by any self-giving. Rather, this love draws its own life totally from the beloved's – which is grounded only in itself. "Possession" is pure reception, and so brings the intercourse of mutual love, but is not itself produced by this intercourse.... The word "hope" expresses this one, unifying self-abandonment into the mystery of God, and thus hope is this unifying center between faith-vision and imperfect-perfect love. In the final analysis, therefore, hope is not a provisional modality of faith and love. It is the permanent clearing away of what is provisional and the making room for the radical, bare unfathomableness of God. Hope is the constant destruction of the illusion that the real, absolute truth is what we comprehend, and that love is what is produced by our love.... Hope, therefore, is basically not the modality of all that is historical as it moves through time to its final state. It is rather the basic modality of our relationship to what is final, and hence it "sets in movement" the true movement. In the light of this, presumption *and* despair are basically and in the same way the refusal of the subject to let himself be grasped by what is unfathomable, and thus torn from himself.[11]

Moltmann's objection is apparently met by Rahner's doctrine, that if saved I be not less alive. Yet it would seem also to be important that any hope that would continue, as Rahner suggests hope will continue, be hope without anxiety, and in that sense I could also hope to have no craving/fearful hope. Indeed, Rahner says it is abandonment trust.

How then to imagine what is hoped for? John Hick, discussing

10. As quoted by Henri Desroche in his *The Sociology of Hope,* transl. Carol Martin-Sperry (London, Boston, and Henley: Routledge & Kegan Paul, 1979), p. 38.

11. Karl Rahner, S.J., "The Theology of Hope," *Theology Digest* Sesquicentennial [of St. Louis University] Issue (February 1968): 81-82. This essay is also "Zur Theologie der Hoffnung," in his *Zur Theologie der Zukunft* (München: Deutscher Taschenbuch Verlag, 1971).

eschatological verification, proposed that a child could know what it means to be an adult, with verification of any statements about adult life still in the future. The child would not fully know, but statements about adult life would not be meaningless.[12] Analogously, a person can hope to be an adult without really knowing what being an adult is – yet know when that has come to pass. Some hopes promise surprises, more than we have dreamed of: What eye has not seen, nor ear heard, nor the mind of man conceived – this God has prepared for those who love him. It seems that only pedestrian hopes are accompanied by a clear sense of what exactly would count as their satisfaction. A total hope need not have an objective that is clear and distinct. A total hope may be comprehensive but not comprehend*ed*. Marcel and Rahner, and Ricoeur, stress the inability to comprehend a total hope, and the inadvisability of presuming to do so.

Ricoeur is a convert to Moltmann concerning the centrality of hope, rather than faith, for theology.[13] His is a philosophy of limits that nonetheless recognizes the theoretical and practical impulse towards completeness. He acknowledges, with Kant, that reason looks for totalization: practicality, for example, demands the completion of virtue with happiness. But this is a preliminary and abstract totalization. In the concrete, as Hegel noted, will does not universalize; in the concrete will struggles with other wills concerning what can be possessed. In the concrete, therefore, hope's willing must deal with community and possessions. Also with Kant Ricoeur recognizes that will works in the face of temptation to evil. Therefore, a concrete philosophy of hope must deal not just with what is desirable and possible, but with what is possible for a community threatened by evil and what is desirable in relation to the desires of others. Ricoeur is akin to the liberation theologians in taking human community, not the willing of the individual, as the actual locus of thinking about hope, and in taking evil, especially evil in social, political and church structures, as the place where concrete thinking about hope must take place. Ricoeur is right: a full philosophy of hope must listen to theology of liberation, lest its use of reason be less than full. But it cannot expect to achieve complete "understanding." Ricoeur finds an excess of meaning in hope: hope asks for more than can be understood. Can reason understand the kind of society hoped for? This essay identifies two sound ultimate hopes: for fairminded system and for intersubjective communion. These need not be alternatives; communion is the ideal, the leaven, and the challenge to

12. John Hick, *Philosophy of Religion,* third edition (Englewood Cliffs, N.J.: Prentice-Hall, 1983): 103-105.

13. Paul Ricoeur, "Freedom in the Light of Hope," in his *The Conflict of Interpretations: Essays in Hermeneutics,* ed. Don Ihde (Evanston: Northwestern University Press, 1974): 404.

fairminded system. But these two outcomes imply with Ricoeur that willfulness should not be imagined as the final hoped-for outcome. Covetous adversarial possession is not what reason need stop at in imagining what can eschatologically be hoped for. And yet possessing in a social context is a concrete setting for hoping and despair, as theology of hope and liberation theology have taken note of.

Theology of hope and liberation theology

In the 1960s a number of theologians first in Germany and then elsewhere began to give hope and history high prominence in their writings. Among them were Jürgen Moltmann, Johannes Metz, Wolfhart Pannenberg, and as often as not they were writing in response to the work of Ernst Bloch.[14] Concern with hope became "theology of hope." Focusing then and since on the individual were writers such as Ladislaus Boros and Joseph Owens; but most focused on humanity considered socially.[15] From one point of view, such theologians promoted a primacy of eschatology; after the "anthropological turn," primacy belongs to hope. The philosophical and theological backgrounds of theologians in the hope movement include process thought, existential Thomism, Marxism, continental evangelical thought. The applications of their thought include social theory and ethics.[16] Many of these theologians came to take eschatology and hope as "normative," that is, as the perspective from which other sectors of theology and theological

14. Substantial bibliographic and analytical surveys can be found in and through William P. Frost, "A Decade of Hope Theology in North America," *Theological Studies* 39, No. 1 (March 1978): 139-153. Writings of Ladislaus Boros, more personal in tone, and those of Pierre Teilhard de Chardin, more cosmic and scientific, can complement Frost's bibliographical surveys.

15. Individual hope is addressed by: Ladislaus Boros, *We Are Future* (New York: Herder and Herder, 1970; New York: Doubleday, 1973; orig. *Wir Sind Zukunft,* Mainz: Matthias-Grünewald-Verlag, 1969), and *Living in Hope: Future Perspectives in Christian Thought* (Garden City, N.Y.: Doubleday, 1973, orig. *Aus der Hoffnung leben,* Olten and Freiburg im Breisgau: Walter-Verlag, 1968); Joseph Owens, C.Ss.R., *Human Destiny: Some Problems for Catholic Philosophy* (Washington: Catholic University of America Press, 1985); and Monika K. Hellwig, *What are They Saying About Death and Christian Hope?* In addition to those listed in Frost, the more social view is addressed by Zachary Hayes. See note 9 above.

16. Among these are, besides authors mentioned earlier, Vincent J. Genovesi, S.J., *Expectant Creativity: The Action of Hope in Christian Ethics* (Washington, DC: University Press of America, 1982); Langdon Gilkey, *Reaping the Whirlwind: A Christian Interpretation of History* (New York: Seabury Press, A Crossroad Book, 1976); and Philip J. Rossi, S.J., *Together Toward Hope: A Journey to Moral Theology* (Notre Dame and London: University of Notre Dame Press, 1983).

anthropology would henceforth be thought out.

Recent theology of liberation is from one point of view an extension of theology of hope: considered from the top down, i.e., dogmatically, the theology of liberation builds on the work of hope theologians especially in concern for history and social structures. In its primary intention, however, liberation theology proceeds from the bottom up, from local experience of poverty and oppression, read against the Gospel. Roger Haight offers a clear overview in "Suppositions of Liberation Theology": the fundamental underlying experience is the experience of poverty; human awareness is awareness of temporality, of the fact that the present is a product of the past and of the fact that human beings are responsible for human history; *this* world is important; particular contexts, histories, and humanity's essentially *social* existential situations are what are to be brought to the Gospel in a method of reciprocal correlation; the challenge of Marxism has to be recognized, and the methods of social analysis and the social sciences have an important role in theology; human solidarity is an ideal; God wishes all to be saved, and there is a close connection between salvation and liberation; the essence of Christianity is love, but love must be linked with the demands of justice.[17]

Characteristic of both hope theologians and liberation theologians are the centrality of hope in understanding human existence, the weight that images, discourse, expectations, and promises about the future, especially the "final" future (the eschata, the kingdom) should have in religious and even political discourse. The religious and especially the Christian hope, they propose, is properly understood as primarily social and even cosmic, and as not otherworldly. They divide over whether the kingdom of God is more continuous with or more discontinuous with human history. Pierre Teilhard de Chardin, for example, is most associated with an evolutionary view and a sense that the kingdom has been begun, whereas the liberation theologians stress the distinctly un-Godly present realities, and recognize the need for radical change for the kingdom to be realized.

What does theology of hope and theology of liberation have to say to the argument of this essay? And what does the argument of this essay have to say to these theologies?

These theologies support the contention of this essay that hope is *a* if not

17. Haight, Roger, S.J. "The Suppositions of Liberation Theology," *Thought,* Vol. 58, No. 229 (June 1983): 158-169; this essay is also the first chapter in his *An Alternative Vision: An Interpretation of Liberation Theology* (New York, and Mahwah, N.J.: Paulist, 1985), in which he takes the themes of liberation theology especially as found in Latin America and forms them into a general approach to theology that is transcultural, indeed, universal.

the central human experience. Especially the liberation theologians point out a structure of captivity and release: it is poverty in all forms but especially economic poverty that signalizes the captive state of humankind, and the inchoate and definitive overcoming of such captivity is the good news of the Christian gospel: the kingdom of God is not far; it is near. The call is for human solidarity, and for a love that does justice; these are promised as really possible.

To such theologies this essay can say that genuine hope should eschew the optimism that Marcel dissects, the secret knowledge that claims to know how matters will turn out. The justice of concern to liberation theologians can be understood in terms of this essay's appropriate relationships of serving and being served – serving without servility and being served without dominating. One target of sound ultimate hope is a system of fairminded instrumentality, and this meshes well with justice as a goal in liberation theology.

But love is in liberation theology, and love adds more. This essay's "communion," a sharing of life beyond reciprocal utility, can serve as an outline of what liberation theology's doctrine of Christian love has in mind.

But what is the relation between the two, system and communion, justice and love? Sound ultimate hopes are characterized, I maintain, by realistic judgment and simple absolute desiring for appropriate utilization *or* union, for fairminded system or communion. The one target *or* the other suffices for the target of sound ultimate hope. But liberation theology – and other theologies and indeed the spiritual and moral teaching of many religions – proposes love *and* justice. To this extent, then, they propose an ideal and not just what will suffice; they propose more than a hoping that avoids forms filled with illusion or craving.

Borrowing an insight from Immanuel Kant, I propose that to hope for less than the ideal is to set in motion a shift away from sound hoping. To hope for no more than a fairminded system, to accept as unrealistic any hope for shared life or communion, is to jeopardize even the soundness of hope for a just system. Why so? I suspect that the argument, if it can be made on grounds other than religious grounds, is nonetheless most readily found in religious sectors. Martin Buber makes the argument best: there are two ways, not just one, of relating to the world. There is the I-It way, of using and experiencing what is other than myself according to partialities of self and other. And there is another way of relating, which sometimes arises but cannot be caused or planned or even "desired": the way of I-Thou. It is in I-Thou relationship that fullness of human existence is to be found. And while I-It is not evil, it is evil to so set out as to seal off any possibility of I-Thou arising.

The difference between I-It or serving-and-being-served love and I-Thou or appreciative love is like the distinction theologian Frederick Crowe has pointed out in Thomas Aquinas and proposed himself between "concern" and "complacency."[18] "Concern" is the love that moves, desires, goes toward its object; "complacency" rests, is receptive. Concern-love seems significantly similar to I-It or will-nature love; the latter seeks to be served or to serve; it is need-love and gift-love. (This essay's simple absolute desiring is part of concern-love.) Complacency-love (Aquinas's *complacentia*) is akin to my own "appreciation," an attentive presence of one's whole person to what is present.

It is a message of many religions that I-Thou relationship or appreciative love is possible and supremely worthwhile. And therefore my essay's doctrine of *sound* ultimate hope is complemented by a doctrine of *ideal* hope: ideal hope is characterized by realistic judgment and simple absolute desiring for appropriate utilization *and* union. How these two *logically* could both be possible has been sketched in chapter 13. But it is part of religious proclamation to say that they are together *factually* possible and that some of the necessary conditions for their compossibility are fulfilled.

There is an objection to this compossibility. While appreciative love or I-Thou relationship can mesh with reciprocal utility in intimate dealings between individuals, there is no place for such relationship in the social and political sphere. Reinhold Niebuhr's *Moral Man and Immoral Society* is often cited as a source for such a theological and political doctrine. It is dangerous romanticism to hope that I-Thou relationship – which the intersubjective model outlines – come to pass in civil society. Justice, not love, is the practical ideal in the *polis*. This view does not claim that the intersubjective model cannot ever be embodied in practice. The claim is that the realm of politics, more broadly the realm of institutions, cannot be a place where communion could ever obtain.

The response to this objection is twofold. First, Gabriel Marcel's understanding of the "us" for whom a person hopes included the bond between a person and his country. Marcel did not conceive communion to be envisioned only for pairs of individuals. While Marcel may have been mistaken in this, the plausibility of his being in error is reduced to the degree that a point Martin Buber made applies. Buber proposed that there can be 'real but not full' I-Thou relationships. These obtained between those not ontological peers: between a person and nature, between teacher and student, between therapist and client, pastor and penitent. Donald Berry argues that

18. Frederick Crowe, S.J., "Complacency and Concern in the Thought of St. Thomas," *Theological Studies* 20 (1959): 1-39, 198-230, 343-395. Crowe's magisterial study includes comparisons with eros and agape in Nygren, as well as with the thought of existentialists. He also discusses whether Aquinas conceptually integrated these two kinds of love.

relationships 'real but not full' can obtain between *groups* when they move towards each other.[19] Healing a breach between two families would be an example of this. Admittedly, Martin Buber judged that relations with "institutions" were of the I-It sort. Yet his category of "spiritual beings" could be the category for that with which Marcel's captive patriot kept faith: my country. As Berry observes, it is not just that a particular theology of original sin or a particular history of distrust and friction should be acknowledged; such a theology and political history actually affect the possibility of what can arise between groups. I would add a further point: hope for nothing more than a just social system is vulnerable to a temptation to hope for domination, in the sense of hoping that *they* will be instruments for *us* even without their so choosing. Hope for liberation can be tempted to no more than the reversal of master-slave relations. Hope for communion can weigh against such an inclination.

Sometimes hope for liberation is disappointed or endlessly postponed, and the temptation to despair, or to violence, springs up. And sometimes the image of what is hoped for becomes tarnished, and people feel they have to cling desperately nonetheless to that image lest they fall into despair. Here is where fundamental hope needs to be recognized: the holding off from despair in the face of temptation to say "All is lost." It is important to be able to name a hoping in those who have no vividly imagined future: they just

19. Berry puts it well: "The contention is that the way of mutuality is inapplicable to social and political structures since only one person can speak "Thou" to one other person. This objection, however, as natural as it may appear, rests upon a fundamental error. It confuses principle with procedures, confuses the idea of applying the concept of mutuality to the larger social situations with the manner or mode(s) of such an application. Reinhold Niebuhr's influential view about the relation of religious understanding to social ethics was noted for its realistic analysis of the possibilities of human community in the light of a particular view of human nature that recognized continuing human sinfulness, especially in societies. For Niebuhr, when the philosophy of dialogue is extended to organized groups or nations, it becomes utopian romanticism.... Now there is no question that it is much easier to see the relevance of the way of mutuality to the sphere of the interhuman when only two individuals are involved, than to any other sphere. But there is no necessary contradiction in making such a move. Just as there are 'degrees' of mutuality, real if not full, that are possible in the sphere of nature, so there are 'degrees' of mutuality, real if not full, that are possible when groups of human beings move toward each other. These possibilities are diminished when that encounter is prefaced or its future prejudged by a theology of original sin (Niebuhr) or by bondage to a prior history of distrust, suspicion, and animosity.

"The communal realm, the realm of the *polis,* the coming-to-be-of community, is precisely the realm in which the renewal of human life is to occur for Buber." Berry, 92-93.

survive, hang on. (Yet the dialectic returns: no one can hang on without some sense that captivity is not final.)

A final point about a theology of hope and theology of liberation, the issue of agency: are we to hope and *work*? Are we to hope and *wait*? Who will do what we hope will be done? For those who wait, bliss or salvation breaks in, deliverance punctures our sealed present. The attitude implicitly called for here is receptive: we do not close our hands to what is given. Moltmann seems to be a theologian associated with God's deliverance breaking into our captivity. Others seem close to *providentia est nos ipsi:* we provide for ourselves.

An aetiological observation is appropriate here: discussion of agency and instrumentality is couched in language of the will-nature model. This is appropriate, of course, for results where outcomes are recognizable events. But where outcomes are relationships between subjects, the intersubjective model suggests that the "agency" is not will-nature but of a different sort, where responsibility is not alternately or reciprocally attributed, but shared.

Healing, body, and time: John Macquarrie

Some of the issues raised by theologies of hope and liberation theologies find clear expression in John Macquarrie's *Christian Hope*. Macquarrie outlines not only the larger or social eschatological hope, but also the eschatological hope for the individual. He proposes a manner of reconciling corporate and individual eschatology in a "total hope." He understands Christianity to offer such a total hope, and his aim is to show that the fulfillment of such a hope is possible, in the sense that it is conceivable: coherent and consistent both with what Christian theologians have said and with the fruits of contemporary philosophy and science. His total hope encompasses both universal renewal for corporate humanity and fulfillment for each individual.

His proposal for the larger hope for corporate humanity is in line with eschatological thought that draws on evolution, including evolution occurring with sudden jumps. The passages from life to consciousness and from the animal to the human are arguably such emergences. Another such emergence is pointed to by phrases of Christian theology, the "resurrection of the dead," "the kingdom of heaven," "the final coming of Christ." The later emergences are different from the earlier ones: what was, ages ago, nature taking its course is now dependent on human choices. What Christians imagine as the kingdom of God is not inevitable, but will to some degree depend on human choices and actions. Pierre Teilhard de Chardin has offered an understanding of such an evolution, but Macquarrie faults his thought for neglecting choices and evils; there is not enough emphasis on the contingency of the outcome hoped for. The Anglican theologian Lionel Thornton, many decades ago, drew on process philosophers Samuel Alexander and Alfred North Whitehead to draw a portrait of successive stages of evolution where each recapitulates what went before. The Incarnation rules out sharp discontinuities between earthly realities and what is promised for the future. Thornton finds the image of the "body of Christ" suggestive for the gathering up of creation and human history in a new social reality, in forms of community we cannot now imagine. Macquarrie's own position incorporates aspects of the thought of both Teilhard de Chardin and Thornton:

> The end to which we look forward in our historical epoch is a new social unity, though its nature cannot be grasped by us short of its fulfilment . . . We can say further that even if the nature of this end is in large measure veiled from us, we have an anticipation of it in Christ and in his body, which is the Christian community; and that when this end is realized, new vistas will open up beyond it. Such a cosmic vision is surely a great encouragement and source of hope to the human race as it struggles to build up peace, justice and authentic community in the world.[20]

It is when Macquarrie turns to the destiny of the individual that he proposes a view different from those conventionally outlined by Christian theologians. The issue is: what shall become of the individual? Is the death of a person who dies before the final establishment of the kingdom a mere steppingstone to the hoped-for future? Macquarrie judges "there would be no true gathering up or summing up of all things in Christ if so much had to be discarded and if the goal demanded that people be used as means and not treated as ends."[21] Though he acknowledges the recent efforts to make bodily resurrection and immortality of the soul intelligible conceptions, Macquarrie proposes what he considers a third possibility, akin to but different from a doctrine of resurrection. It is based on the temporal conception of selfhood.

The self or soul is seen as effecting a pattern in time. While "the soul is inseparable from the body (and so the view I am expounding is closer to the resurrection than the immortality hypothesis), soul and body are distinct in the sense that the soul is to be understood in terms of time, body in terms of space."[22] What is characteristic of human selves is the way they gather up moments of the past with a present and a future to form a "span of time"; for example, given what happened yesterday, I can now expect some difficulties to crop up tomorrow. It is not just that we remember; rather, what we have in memory enters into our conceptions of future and present.

Macquarrie applies this analogy to the experience of God. "May we

20. Macquarrie, *Christian Hope,* 111.
21. Macquarrie, 112.
22. Macquarrie, 117.

suppose that God gathers up all time, so that past and future are both present in their fullness to him?''[23] Recalling the Christian eschatological statement that all things are gathered up in Christ, and that persons become members of Christ's body, Macquarrie asks ''Could we suppose then that our destiny as individuals is not to live on as immortal souls or to be provided with new bodies, but to be summed up or gathered up in the experience of God as the people we are or have been in our several segments of time and in our bodies?''[24]

Macquarrie acknowledges the obvious challenge to this approach, that this is equivalent to saying little more than that God will remember us. Macquarrie intends to say more than this: persons would have new experiences, ''including a deeper awareness of and communion with God.'' The central image Macquarrie uses is that of healing: God is *healing the past*.

> God is not changing the past by changing the facts that have happened (this is not possible even for him) but by bringing it into what I have called 'an ever wider reconciling context.' The supreme example of this is the cross of Christ which is turned from evil to good and finds its completion in the resurrection – and we remind ourselves that Easter is not a reversal of Good Friday but its conversion. This is God's reconciling work, and its reaches into all time, including the past which is still present to God. It is the costly atoning work of God, by which he draws out and absorbs and overcomes the poisons of history.[25]

It is indeed helpful to imagine the final condition of humankind as a healing of the past. Commendable as well is the priority Macquarrie gives to the larger hope for renewal and elevation of humanity, a hope imaginable in spite of threats to peace, life resources, and human community. The body of Christ is a helpful image for this, as is the related theme of recapitulation of all things in Christ.

But there are matters which, in light of the argument of this essay, can be clarified, expanded, and perhaps even improved upon. Such are points about what is healed and how, about the self, and about the agency or agencies involved in the healing.

The analogy of God healing the past should be complemented by God healing *us*. Our past facts are indeed irreversible, and what has happened is no longer subject to alteration either by our deciding, by natural causes, or by God. I agree with Macquarrie and Aquinas that God cannot change the

23. Macquarrie, 118.
24. Macquarrie, 118.
25. Macquarrie, 120-121.

past. Macquarrie's point is that something *about* us, about our past facts, is made different, made new.

> The value of these facts can be changed and often is changed. It is in this sense that one can quite properly say that the past can be healed and transformed. The hardship that someone suffered at a certain period of her life seemed like a bitter evil, but it has turned out to be the adversity coefficient that has made that person a woman of character.... What I experienced as a bitter disappointment, I now recognize to have been very much for my good.[26]

This seems to mean, first, that I come to view, interpret, "recognize" the unchanged past differently. Overlapping with "recognizing" is a second way of dealing with the past: I have a different *attitude towards*, a different valuing of, my unchanged past. I see my being fired, for example, as lucky, though I did not think it so at the time. A third reading of "healing" between my past and me is that I *use* it differently: the recovering alcoholic has sensibilities that make him of greater help to other alcoholics. And a fourth reading focuses on *integration*: my past joys and sorrows are no longer disconnected, nor is my seeing them as connected merely an interpretation that leaves me presently unaffected. I see, value, and grasp my life as a whole, rather like the final stage of psychosocial development Erik Erikson termed "wisdom." It is this latter linking-up of unchanged events into a new pattern of meaning and value that I think best captures what Macquarrie has in mind.

There is also a question of agency, of who does the grasping of a life as a whole. Who links up unchanged events into a new pattern of meaning and value? Macquarrie's analogy begins in the first person: "The person whom I used to despise I now see in quite a different light and desire a new relation with him."[27] This and his examples suggest that the person who had the experiences deals with them in a new way. But when the analogy is applied to the eschatological context under discussion, it is *God* who heals the past. Is it therefore *God* who views my life in a new way? If that is all, does that not leave me *un*healed in some important way? Would not a total hope be fuller if *I myself* saw things as all working unto good? What Macquarrie seems to be employing is an Augustinian theodicy as a model: God sees light and shadow; God makes something fine out of human joys and sorrows. But it would be better if what God makes out of our lives were in some way to be appreciated by us, in a kind of active receptivity. We at least should be able to say "Amen." That God alone see things in a new light seems not enough.

26. Macquarrie, 120.
27. Macquarrie, 120.

The question of who heals can be in part answered through some attention to the ordinary process of human healing. For a damaged tree, the caring person arranges matters so that if possible the tree can heal itself. In a sense, physicians do heal their human patients, but being healed is not just passive. Medicine does not proceed as auto collision work, nor even as an artist making something splendid out of flawed materials. Surgery is unlike carpentry or sewing: the surgeon operates when the patient is strong enough to recuperate. A good physician knows, acts, and assists the body's healing of itself. One limitation of healing as an analogy obtains when healing is understood to be only passive. Of course the physician does work on the patient, but the patient also does her or his own healing, with the physician instrumental to the process.

But there is something else. In some kinds of therapy, if not in all kinds of human therapy, the therapist is not purely instrumental. Such a not-purely-instrumental role can be clarified by reference to Martin Buber's work and the argument of this essay. Instrumentality is a characteristic of what Buber termed I-It relations. Yet the therapeutic relationship, as he saw it, need hardly be I-It without remainder. Granted, it is not a symmetric relation between peers, and it is not a full I-Thou relationship. As Donald Berry has traced these, the therapeutic relationship, like the master-disciple relationship in teaching and the religiously ministerial forgiving relationship, is one where some "degree" of I-Thou relationship can arise.[28] These are relationships "real but not full." This essay's intersubjective model, furthermore, includes the stipulation that the other is not capable of being substituted for without changing the relation; substitutability is a feature of purely instrumental relations. Thus the analogy of healing is stronger insofar as it includes both the possibility of fuller dealings, and insofar as it resists being understood as implying mere instrumentality. God should not be understood purely as instrumental Healer (despite the weight, and simple appeal, of a Kantian understanding of God as Provider of happiness to the virtuous).

I also propose that the aetiology – agency or causation – involved in fully human healing is not exclusively divine. There is also agency and responsibility on the part of the one being healed. Indeed, viewing the relation through Buberian concepts and those of the intersubjective model will lead to questioning the distinction between agency and passivity, and thus calling into question the thought-model employed in seeking to apportion and attribute correctly the agency involved in eschatological healing.

Gabriel Marcel's thought has offered a further perspective on *us* and on healing. According to Marcel, full or genuine hope is aimed at *us*. While the

28. Berry, "The Helper," Chapter 2 of *Mutuality: The Vision of Martin Buber,* 39-68.

obvious paradigm for "us" is a pair of individual human beings, Marcel's examples and text indicate that the *us* can be pluriform: a relation between several sides of myself (as in terminal illness), between myself and another person (in promises made and kept), and between a person and his country (with the captive patriot and his occupied nation). The healing need not be imagined exclusively between individual persons. And if the range of the us extends along lines of Buber's I-Thou relationship with a being of nature and of *The Letter to the Romans* Chapter Eight, healing can also obtain between humanity and nature.

Marcel also offers insights concerning aetiology. We recall his claim that it is inaccurate to say that it lies in my own individual power to fulfill my hope for us; it depends also on capacities in the other, and indeed in capacities, for unconditional hope, in a Thou which is not empirical. Marcel's contrast between an empirical thou and an absolute Thou permits imagining divine healing as operating with empirical agencies, yet not in purely instrumental ways. Healing can be an I-Thou process, albeit between those not peers. Yet a "full" healing, like a "full" hope (beyond the capabilities of the empirical I and the empirical thous involved) is mysteriously effected by absolute Thou, active "from within" or "from without," these internal and external spatial analogies pointing up both the intimacy and the transcendence of the agency. The Physician assists and enlists powers in the ill that lie beyond what they were capable of. God heals by mysteriously enabling the initiatives of Is and thous to be the vehicles for overcoming wounds and estrangements. When a relation is "stronger" than the strengths of myself and any empirical thou – a side of myself, another person, a community – its strength is due to the active but non-empirical presence of an absolute Thou. Crudely imagined, this is God as glue, joining the broken parts together. Using a traditional term in a Marcellian way, this is God as mediator, bringing together, reconciling, what has been estranged.

The healing is not just physical and not just personal. Its range encompasses the social as well as the intimate. To return to Macquarrie's phrase, there is "an ever wider reconciling context." The full range is not just recovery of health, or wholeness, on the individual scale; it is the movement towards wholeness of all humanity in the body of Christ that is hoped for. Full healing is both of body and body politic, of both individual and community, granting that personal (and community) survival is a necessary condition for intersubjective healing. The overarching category is Marcel's *us:* individual, interpersonal, social, and sometimes institutional.

Macquarrie uses contemporary physics, and specifically the time-relativity of simultaneity and succession to suggest how what is past for us can be present to God. Macquarrie seems correct in using the understanding of time proper to relativity theory to indicate how even for human beings the past can be present. He applies this to God, and plausibly so.

Concerning human persons, Macquarrie distinguishes between time and space: self or soul is understood in terms of time, and body is understood in terms of space. But applying this distinction to healing the past requires keeping united what has been distinguished: in the contemporary understanding, time and space are distinguishable but inseparable concepts: there is no "past" without spatial distance, and no "elsewhere" without an "elsewhen." Therefore healing of our past requires, in some sense, healing of our spatial bodily existence.

Human conceptions of time can indeed be used to speak of God's timelessness, and to speak as Macquarrie does of God as present to the past. But then God, present to the past at least the way human beings are present to the past, is also present to the distant, at least the way human beings are present to the distant. Granted there is no past to God, and no elsewhere as well, but if there is to be a past to persons, there seems also to have to be a distance to persons, and therefore a spatiality to persons. Healing of persons, then seems to require in some sense *body*. Macquarrie does see his third way as closer to a traditional doctrine of the resurrection than to a doctrine of immortality of the soul. The requirement of spatiality for any temporality supports some sense of body for any sense of self, and thus confirms Macquarrie's reading of his doctrine as not too far from a doctrine of bodily resurrection.

A final comment on a model influential in Macquarrie's thought: process thought often takes the category of the organic as a model for thinking about relationships between past and present, or between individuals and societies. It seems to me that a process model that relies on organism as a metaphor, even when "organism" is social, is probably close to employing as its depth-model what this essay calls the will-nature model. One reality acts on another; even when the actions are reciprocal, the relations are instrumental. Thus, in an eschatological healing, God heals us. Or gathers us. Or raises us up.

But what if the *intersubjective* model is used to explore "the larger hope" and "the destiny of the individual"? First of all, this model engages the *us* of Marcel and the complexity of answering the question "Did I do this myself, or did someone else do this?" Marcel judges that neither autonomy nor heteronomy characterize the fullest human life. A different conception of God and the individual human's destiny might arise from applying Buber's concept of time (and space) in I-Thou relationships (together with the intersubjective model generally) to the problems of universal and individual eschatology. Some kind of "active receptivity" would have to obtain, and thus some kind of continuance and agency after death. But one thing seems clear: a doctrine of life after death in which the individual is diminished seems at odds both with Macquarrie's intent and with any doctrine of Christian hope.

Perhaps the problem of integrating corporate eschatology with individual eschatology is a problem of the standpoint of the observer-questioner. What is over and done with about us from the standpoint of one observer is not necessarily over and done with in relation someone else. What we have done (to our point of view) is not necessarily finished to God. There might be yet an altered and enhanced relationship to the cosmos and its Sustainer. Whatever is being healed is present to God; nothing can be healed – no aspects of ourselves integrated, no divisions overcome – without being present to God. This renders problematic the terming of anything as "past." Perhaps the standpoint from which something could be called past in the end-time would be only that of someone not present to God. Being "at some remove" from any activity of God would have to be "spatial" as well as "temporal." If *we* are present to God, then calling our deeds (granted they are "done" and no longer in one sense subject to our determining) "past" and therefore possibly "lost" is possible only for one not present to God; *ex hypothesi* one in the presence of God could not raise the question. Only we *in statu viatoris* can ask; those *in patria* cannot. It seems necessary therefore to employ the term "past" in two senses: the "completed" character of what has been subject to our own agency or nature's causation; and the characteristic of being beyond the range of God's efficacy, understood as intersubjectively engaged with our own agency. The former sense expresses the past as we experience it; the latter may perhaps express a past of which, in the end, there will be no experience for those in the presence of God.

I have scope here only to point out another avenue that might be fruitful. There is in Buber's thought, especially in his understanding of God as eternal Thou, a possible understanding of time and inclusivity that would enrich any attempt to integrate individual and corporate eschatology in a way that overcomes dilemmas about activity and passivity, present and past. Even of "ordinary" I-Thou relationships, Martin Buber said:

> When I confront a human being as my You and speak the basic word I-You to him, then he is no thing among things nor does he consist of things. He is no longer He or She, limited by other Hes and Shes, a dot in the world grid of space and time.... And even as prayer is not in time but time in prayer, the sacrifice not in space but space in the sacrifice,... I do not find the human being to whom I say You in any Sometime and Somewhere.[29]

Such a text calls into question some phenomenologies of time, and, given Buber's preference for speaking of "depth description" rather than of "ontology," some ontologies of time as well.

29. *I and Thou,* Kaufmann translation (New York: Charles Scribner's Sons, 1970), 59.

Hope's trust as cognitive: Küng, Evans, Buber

One part of my overall argument is that hope can sometimes be not only a climate of the mind, but also an organ of apprehension. It is not just that the person who hopes also believes, explicitly or implicitly, certain things about the desirability and possibility of hope's objective. In addition, sometimes the person who hopes has, as a concomitant feature of that kind of hoping, a heightened ability to be in touch with reality. Some kinds of hope have a "sense of touch." The person who hopes has powers that a person who does not hope lacks.

Hope's manner of knowing is not a kind of foreseeing. Aristotle ranged hope with memory and sensation as cognitive faculties dealing respectively with the future, the past, and the present. Such a view takes hope as the having of an opinion about what will happen.[30] My argument is not that hope grasps the future, however modest that grasp might be. And my proposal is not just that evaluation of hope should include assessment of desiring as well as of conditions of possibility and therefore of predictable agency. Hope as an organ of apprehension is not forward "looking" ultimate hope, but rather fundamental hope.

An image for this is the acute ear, alert hand, and careful step of a blind person. Such a person may be satisfied with not feeling any object: the way is clear, there is no obstacle on the path. The one who hopes "with open outstretched hand" is alert to more than her or his own sensations. Hope reaches into the dark, prepared to meet what is there. Granted, sound ultimate hope's desiring implies trust, and trust is the pivot of hope's apprehending. My central proposal is that fundamental hope includes trust, and this trust can be of two sorts, either directed by one's own will towards the nature of or the will of another, or oriented towards an other in an intersubjective way. The kind of trust that involves will and nature can at most admit trust (and its hope) as a climate of the mind: the one who trusts believes. But the kind of trust that admits analysis on the intersubjective model is in touch with what is the term of that trust. The person who trusts in this way is present to what is real, and is not just believing certain things to be so.

Among religious thinkers three stand out as addressing this sort of approach and these differences. Hans Küng's *Does God Exist?* takes trust (his term is "fundamental trust") as central, but his analysis of fundamental trust seems to go no farther than that of a climate of the mind. Donald Evans in

30. Divination is *episteme elpistike* in Aristotle's *De Memoria*. Memory, sensation, and hope are reviewed in Gauthier, René Antoine, O.P., and Jolif, Jean Yves, O.P. *L'Éthique à Nicomaque: introduction, traduction, et commentaire,* 2ème edition, (Louvain: Publications Universitaires de Louvain, and Paris: Éditions Béatrice-Nauwelaerts: 1959; 2ème edition 1970), p. 233.

Struggle and Fulfillment and in *Faith, Authenticity, and Morality* proposes that trust can be a way of discerning what is ultimately real. Trust does more than just imply some beliefs. And in the thought of Martin Buber already referred to there is a teaching on access to the ultimately real that is quite similar to my own argument.

In *Does God Exist?*, Hans Küng proposes that whether or not a person has what he terms fundamental trust is the most basic issue, not only in matters of religion, but also in science and ethics.[31] Trust is a pre-condition for all kinds of knowledge and every moral reflection and decision. Fundamental trust is not to be equated with faith in God. But there are important connections between the two. The movement of *Does God Exist?* is a spiral descent through modern philosophy, science, psychology, and social analysis: the paths lead through Hegel, Feuerbach, Marx, Freud and converge in Nietzsche: do all paths lead to nihilism? Küng proposes a trusting Yes to reality as the alternative to nihilism. Paths to a Yes to God as alternative to atheism, and to a Yes to the Christian God, constitute the second half of the book. The crossroads, however, is at the point of trust.

Küng defines fundamental trust as affirmation and attitude.

> Fundamental trust means that a person, in principle, says *Yes to the uncertain reality* of himself and the world, making himself open to reality and able to maintain this attitude consistently in practice. This positive fundamental attitude implies an antinihilistic fundamental certainty in regard to all human experience and behavior, despite persistent, menacing uncertainty.[32]

''Reality becomes apparent to me,'' Küng writes, ''in this fundamental trust'': as one despite all disunion, as true despite all meaninglessness, as good despite all worthlessness, both concerning my own existence and concerning uncertain reality beyond myself.[33] Justification of this trust comes within the trusting, neither antecedently nor as a consequence of this trust nor by external rationality. Fundamental trust, however, is not just effected by an act of the will. ''Reality itself must make my trust possible despite all uncertainty.... Fundamental trust is a gift.''[34]

Because fundamental trust in reality is not to be equated with belief in God, a person who has fundamental trust is not (yet) someone who believes in God, i.e., believes that God exists and relies on God. This distinction between fundamental trust and theistic belief is the point where J.L. Mackie offers his criticism of Küng. In *The Miracle of Theism,* Mackie argues that Küng's

31. Hans Küng, *Does God Exist? An Answer for Today* (Garden City, N.Y.: Doubleday & Company, 1980; orig. *Existiert Gott?,* München: R. Piper & Co. Verlag, 1978).

32. Küng, 445.

33. Küng, 445-6.

34. Küng, 451.

postulation of a god is neither needed nor comprehensible, given Küng's distinction between fundamental trust, which is self-justifying and sufficient to ground a positive response to nihilism, and belief in God which is a further determination.[35] The gap Küng identifies between fundamental trust and belief in God is a key divide that any argument linking trust and God will have to cross.

There is a further charge against Küng's argument. Fundamental trust is merely a climate of the mind, is in no way an organ of apprehension: fundamental trust does not lead to reality becoming apparent to me. Assessing this charge thoroughly is more than this essay's scope permits, but the key question is whether fundamental trust as Küng understands it can be analysed according to the will-nature model or according to the intersubjective model. An intersubjective model of trust admits justification emerging within the trust itself; otherwise, trust may be chosen or caused, but not necessarily with justification. And the way in which fundamental trust is a gift is also more comprehensible within the intersubjective model. Insofar as the will-nature model captures fundamental trust, such trust is not necessarily even in touch with reality, let alone in touch with God.

For Donald Evans, on the other hand, there is little difference between basic or fundamental trust and belief in God, and therefore a gap between trust and religious belief does not obtain. Furthermore, Evans proposes that basic trust is cognitive. While part of the argument of *Struggle and Fulfillment* is a not uncommon argument that trust as an attitude implies specific beliefs, the innovative argument is that trust enables a person to discern what is ultimately real. The argument is more intricate than present limits allow, but its general lines can be sketched. In its generic form, the argument has a metaphysical contention, a reflective contention, and a conclusion. The metaphysical contention is: "What we discern as ultimate from attitude *x* really *is* and really is *ultimate*." The reflective contention is: "What we discern as ultimate from attitude *x* is best articulated as *d* (a description)." Conclusion: "*d* is and *d* is ultimate."[36]

Made specific for what Evans calls basic trust, the argument would read as follows: what we discern as ultimate from basic trust really is and really is ultimate. What we discern as ultimate from basic trust is best articulated as (fill in this description). Therefore there really exists as ultimate what the

35. J. L. Mackie, *The Miracle of Theism: Arguments For and Against the Existence of God* (Oxford: Clarendon, 1982), 250-51.

36. Donald Evans, *Struggle and Fulfillment: The Inner Dynamics of Religion and Morality* (Cleveland: Collins, 1979; Philadelphia: Fortress, 1981), 180. His *Faith, Authenticity, and Morality* (Toronto: University of Toronto Press, 1980) has other major treatments of both attitudes implying beliefs and attitudes enabling discernment; see pp. 67-72, 238-40, and 253-263.

description portrays. Whether this description should employ traditional predicates of God, especially "one," "personal," "good," is linked to just what perceptions of reality arise for a person of basic trust; much of *Struggle and Fulfillment* is devoted to exploring the features of basic trust (and to the proposal that basic trust is preferable to its rival basic mistrust or suspicion). That exploration suggests the appropriateness of a number of traditional predicates for God. With the ultimate understood in this way, there is little difference between basic trust as Evans understands it and religious belief in God.

Whether trust is cognitive in Küng and Evans, or is only a climate of the mind, turns on whether trust is analysable in terms of the will-nature model or the intersubjective model. There are texts of each that support each interpretation. I am inclined to take Küng's thought as closer to the will-nature model, and Evans's as closer to the intersubjective.

In the thought of Küng and Evans there are then differences concerning the term of trust, and perhaps differences in whether and how trust is cognitive. They seem to be similar, however, in proposing for the most part a trust the term of which – reality or God – is relatively unmediated. And in this they differ from the argument of this essay. I propose a difference between empirical thou and absolute Thou. Gabriel Marcel employed the distinction, and I think it is an important one. Martin Buber also indicates the difference between the (empirical) thou of I-Thou relationship and the "eternal Thou" glimpsed or "mediated" through the relationship. My own view is closer to that of Buber and Marcel than perhaps to Evans and Küng, at least on a first reading of these two. My conclusion employed a kind of mediation, distinguishing between empirical thou and absolute Thou: insofar as hope's trust is correctly understood according to the intersubjective model, such trust apprehends the other – the empirical other. But insofar as the relation of trust is stronger than the parties of the relationship, insofar as the appreciative love is more than I and the empirical other can explain, there is "indicated" the efficacy of that which is the absolute Thou Marcel speaks of and the eternal Thou Buber identifies. As I put it: "A theistic inclination seems to obtain insofar as . . . fundamental trust admits to analysis on the intersubjective model . . . [and] hopes exhibit totality or unconditionality." Warrant for following such "inclination" may not be available with conceptual clarity – which clarity, of course, would be pursued within the will-nature model.

I think trust is a necessary condition for discerning what is ultimate. I do not think it is sufficient for distinguishing appropriately between what is "empirical" and what is more than "empirical" in the relationship. This may seem a modest conclusion to a long argument, especially when compared with the work of Küng and Evans. But it seems quite important to be cautious in taking *the other* of some kinds of relationship as the *Absolute simpliciter*. It seems more in accord with human experience to see any such grasp as mediated, "partial," "indirect," even if apparently unmediated. As Hegel reminds us, the Absolute is not delivered up snared on the end of a stick. It seems better to be open to the possibility that what believers would call Thou is active in mysterious ways in the best forms of human relationships with others and themselves.

The term "mediation" needs a look. Mediation is not instantiation. The term can be taken in a means-end context, according to which that which mediates is that through which something or someone else is dealt with. Such a medium is quite "self-effacing." This understanding of mediation takes the medium or mediator as purely a means. But sometimes the medium or mediator is not just a means, but rather a participant in or inchoate form of the reality of that which is "mediated." "Embodiment" could serve as a term for this relationship, and the Buberian and Marcellian distinction-and-relation between empirical thou and absolute Thou offers some framework for conceiving such an embodying form of mediation. Ernst Bloch's *real-symbol* can be understood in a similar way. The embodying form of mediation seems preferable both to a relatively unmediated relationship (between one who trusts and the term of that trust, cosmos or God) and to a means-end mediation, say, with God as the ground, support, and goal for (non-divine) reality. *Does God Exist?* takes this latter approach.

Embodying mediation seems more at home in the intersubjective model of trust. The "thou" character of the term of trust suggests finitude, and a Marcellian text suggested that "nest" rather than "universe" is a better label for the "thee" in whom I hope. On this kind of reading, it seems that the term of trust must in some sense be finite, be not without definition.

A finite thou as the term of trust (supposing that the relation gives access to absolute Thou) opens up discourse to the role of finite persons and institutions: can religiously significant trust be in a finite person or institution?

Avoiding idolatry seems to require saying "Of course not." While there is truth in this, we should also recall that in Judaism and Christianity there is the select community, corporeal election, the body of Christ, the ecclesia. Martin Buber essentially locates institutions as It-realities. To deal with structure or institution is to deal with It. Donald Berry felicitously paraphrases Buber: "Without structure man cannot live. But he who lives with structure alone is not a man."[37] And yet, as we have seen Berry point out in our discussion of liberation theology, Martin Buber does have some opening to institution as thou, in relationships "real but not full." I propose that some human institutions can be more than It-entities in human life, more than useful distillations from lived encounter. I propose they can also be, at

37. Berry, p. 64, here drawing on Smith's translation of *I and Thou,* p. 34.

least some of them, what Buber called "spiritual beings," mediating the presence of absolute Thou. This is an opening to the small Christian communities of liberation theology, to doctrines of church, to what Josiah Royce called beloved communities. Little of religion is lived at the extremes of what one believes in his or her solitude and what is readily knowable to everyone. Between the individual and all humanity are communities. I ask whether communities, recognized as so central in many religions, cannot under some conditions be the thou in whom I hope for us.

Such considerations may also be useful for Christology. Not only may the community be understood as the body of Christ, the empirical thou with whom one is linked in ways stronger than the empirical I and thou can explain; the relation of God to the historical Jesus can perhaps be conceived along these lines. Thus the Buberian and Marcellian doctrine of empirical thou and absolute Thou might help address the "scandal of particularity" whereby what is proposed as salvation open to all is available through some particular tradition, texts, group, person, or church.

Such are the bridges I sketch linking my argument on hope with some religious and theological thought. They may be too quickly drawn, overly dense, or doubtfully suited for carrying much traffic. I think they at least suggest promising lines of reflection. But perhaps it is better to rest with a variation on a well-known theme from *The Imitation of Christ*: I'd rather have hope than be able to define it.

* * *

SELECTED BIBLIOGRAPHY

Hope and General

Alves, Rubem A. *A Theology of Human Hope.* Washington and Cleveland: Corpus Books, 1969.

Barbour, Ian. *Myths, Models and Paradigms.* New York: Harper & Row, 1974.

Berry, Donald. *Mutuality: The Vision of Martin Buber.* Albany: State University of New York Press, 1985.

Boros, Ladislaus, S.J. *We Are Future.* Translated by W. J. O'Hara. New York: Herder and Herder, 1970. Orig. *Wir Sind Zukunft.* Mainz: Matthias-Grünewald-Verlag, 1969.

Boros, Ladislaus, S.J. *Living in Hope: Future Perspectives in Christian Thought.* Translated by W. J. O'Hara. Garden City, N.Y.: Doubleday, 1973. Orig. *Aus der Hoffnung leben.* Olten and Freiburg im Breisgau: Walter-Verlag, 1968.

Brandon, S. G. F. *A Dictionary of Comparative Religion.* New York: Charles Scribner's Sons, 1970.

Buber, Martin. "Distance and Relation." In *The Knowledge of Man: Selected Essays,* edited by Maurice Friedman, pp. 59-71. New York: Harper & Row, 1965.

Buber, Martin. *I and Thou.* Translation, prologue and notes by Walter Kaufmann. New York: Charles Scribner's Sons, 1970.

Capps, Walter H., ed. *The Future of Hope.* Philadelphia: Fortress Press, 1970.

Capps, Walter H. *Time Invades The Cathedral: Tensions in the School of Hope.* Philadelphia: Fortress Press, 1972.

Crowe, Frederick, S.J. "Complacency and Concern in the Thought of St. Thomas." *Theological Studies* 20 (1959): 1-39, 198-230, 343-395.

Davis, Wayne A. "The Two Senses of Desire." *Philosophical Studies* 45 (March 1984): 181-96.

Day, J. P. "Hope." *American Philosophical Quarterly* 6 (April 1969): 89-102.

Day, J. P . "Anatomy of Hope and Fear." *Mind,* n.s. 79 (July 1970): 369-384.

Despland, Michel. *The Education of Desire: Plato and the Philosophy of*

Religion. Toronto: University of Toronto Press, 1985.

Desroche, Henri. *The Sociology of Hope.* Translated by Carol Martin-Sperry. London, Boston, and Henley: Routledge & Kegan Paul, 1979. Orig. *Sociologie de l'espérance,* Calmann-Lévy, 1973.

Downie, R. S. "Hope." *Philosophy and Phenomenological Research* 24 (1963-64): 248-250.

Edmaier, Alois. *Horizonte der Hoffnung: Eine philosophische Studie.* Regensburg: Pustet, 1968.

Encyclopedia of Philosophy. Edited by Paul Edwards. S. v. "Bollnow, Otto Friedrich," by Friedrich Kümmel. New York: Macmillan and Free Press; London: Collier-Macmillan, 1967.

Erikson, Erik. "The Roots of Virtue." In *The Humanist Frame,* edited by Julian Huxley, 225-246. London: Allen and Unwin, 1961.

Erikson, Erik H. *Childhood and Society.* 2nd ed. New York: W. W. Norton; Toronto: George J. McLeod, 1963.

Erikson, Erik H. *Insight and Responsibility: Lectures on the Ethical Implications of Psychoanalytic Insight.* New York: W. W. Norton; Toronto: George J. McLeod, 1964.

Erikson, Erik H. "Life Cycle." In *International Encyclopedia of the Social Sciences.* Vol. 9: 286-292. Edited by David L. Sills. New York: Macmillan and Free Press, 1968.

Evans, Donald. *The Logic of Self-Involvement: A Philosophical Study of Everyday Language with Special Reference to the Christian Use of Language about God as Creator.* London: SCM, 1963; New York: Herder and Herder, 1969.

Evans, Donald. *Struggle and Fulfillment: The Inner Dynamics of Religion and Morality.* London: Collins, 1980; Philadelphia: Fortress, 1981.

Evans, Donald. *Faith, Authenticity, and Morality.* Toronto: University of Toronto Press, 1980.

Fackenheim, Emil. "The Commandment to Hope: A Response to Contemporary Jewish Experience." In *The Future of Hope,* edited by Walter H. Capps, 68-91. Philadelphia: Fortress Press, 1970.

Feuerbach, Ludwig. *Principles of the Philosophy of the Future.* Translated by Manfred H. Vogel. Indianapolis: Bobbs-Merrill, 1966.

Fichte, Johann Gottlieb. "On the Foundation of Our Belief in a Divine Government of the Universe." In *Nineteenth-Century Philosophy,* edited by Patrick L. Gardiner, 19-26. New York: Free Press, 1969. A translation by Paul Edwards of "Über den Grund unseres Glaubens an eine göttliche Weltregierung." *Philosophisches Journal* 8 (1798): 1-20.

Frost, William P. "A Decade of Hope Theology in North America."

Theological Studies, Vol. 39, No. 1 (March 1978): 139-153.

Gauthier, René Antoine, O.P., and Jolif, Jean Yves, O.P. *L'Éthique à Nicomaque: introduction, traduction, et commentaire.* 2ème édition. Louvain: Publications Universitaires de Louvain, and Paris: Éditions Béatrice-Nauwelaerts: 1959; 2ème édition 1970.

Geach, Peter. *The Virtues: The Stanton Lectures 1973-74.* Cambridge: Cambridge University Press, 1977.

Genovesi, Vincent J. *Expectant Creativity: The Action of Hope in Christian Ethics.* Washington, DC: University Press of America, 1982.

Gilkey, Langdon. *Reaping the Whirlwind: A Christian Interpretation of History.* New York: Seabury Press, A Crossroad Book, 1976.

Gilligan, Carol. *In a Different Voice: Psychological Theory and Women's Development.* Cambridge (USA) and London: Harvard University Press, 1982.

Gratton, Carolyn. *Trusting: Theory and Practice.* New York: Crossroad, 1982.

Gustafson, James M. "The Conditions for Hope: Reflections on Human Experience." *Continuum 7* (Winter 1970): 535-45.

Haight, Roger, S.J. "The Suppositions of Liberation Theology." *Thought* 58, No. 229 (June 1983): 158-169.

Haight, Roger, S.J. *An Alternative Vision: An Interpretation of Liberation Theology.* New York, and Mahwah, N.J.: Paulist, 1985.

Hayes, Zachary, O.F.M. *What Are They Saying About the End of the World?.* New York: Paulist, 1983.

Hefner, Philip, Carl E. Braaten, et al. *Hope and the Future of Man.* Philadelphia: Fortress Press, 1972.

Hellwig, Monika K. *What are They Saying About Death and Christian Hope?.* New York: Paulist, 1978.

Hick, John. *Philosophy of Religion.* Third Edition. Englewood Cliffs, NJ: Prentice-Hall, 1983.

Humphreys, Christmas. *A Popular Dictionary of Buddhism.* Third ed. London: Curzon Press, 1984.

James, William. *The Will to Believe and Other Essays in Popular Philosophy.* New York: Dover Publications, 1956.

Kadowaki, J. K., S.J. *Zen and the Bible: A Priest's Experience.* Transl. Joan Rieck. London, Boston, and Henley: Routledge & Kegan Paul, 1980. Orig. Japanese: *Koan to Seisho no Shindoku* (Body-Reading Koans and the Bible: A Christian's Experience with Zen). Tokyo: Shunjusha, 1977.

Kamenka, Eugene. *The Philosophy of Ludwig Feuerbach.* London: Routledge & Kegan Paul, 1970.

Kenny, Anthony. *Action, Emotion and Will.* London: Routledge & Kegan Paul; New York: Humanities Press, 1963.

Kerans, Patrick. "Hope, Objectivity, and Technical Culture." *Continuum* 7 (Winter 1970): 570-582.

Kierkegaard, Søren. *Fear and Trembling and The Sickness unto Death.* Translated with introductions and notes by Walter Lowrie. Princeton, N.J.: Princeton University Press, 1968.

Kübler-Ross, Elisabeth. *On Death and Dying.* New York: Macmillan; London: Collier-Macmillan, 1969.

Küng, Hans. *Does God Exist? An Answer for Today.* Translated by Edward Quinn. Garden City, N.Y.: Doubleday & Company, 1980. Orig. *Existiert Gott?,* München: R. Piper & Co., 1978.

Küng, Hans. *Eternal Life: Life After Death as a Medical, Philosophical, and Theological Problem.* Translated by Edward Quinn. Garden City N.Y.: Doubleday, 1984. Orig. *Ewiges Leben?* München: R. Piper & Co., 1982.

Loevinger, Jane. *Ego Development: Conceptions and Theories.* San Francisco: Jossey-Bass, 1976.

Lombardi, Joseph L., S.J., "Towards a Logic of Hope." Typescript, New York University, December 1970.

Lynch, William F., S.J. *Images of Faith: An Exploration of the Ironic Imagination.* Notre Dame, Ind.: University of Notre Dame Press, 1973.

Lynch, William F. *Images of Hope: Imagination as Healer of the Hopeless.* Notre Dame, Ind. and London: University of Notre Dame Press, 1974.

Mackie, J. L. *The Miracle of Theism: Arguments For and Against the Existence of God.* Oxford: Clarendon, 1982.

Macquarrie, John. *Christian Hope.* New York: Seabury Press, 1978.

Mannheim, Karl. *Ideology and Utopia.* Preface by Louis Wirth. International Library of Psychology, Philosophy, and Scientific Method. London: Routledge & Kegan Paul, 1966.

Maslow, Abraham H. *Toward a Psychology of Being.* 2nd ed. New York: D. Van Nostrand, 1968.

Maslow, Abraham H. *Motivation and Personality.* 2nd ed. New York: Harper & Row, 1970.

Maslow, Abraham H. "I-Thou Knowledge." In *Sources,* edited by Theodore Roszak, 81-93. New York: Harper & Row, Colophon Books, 1972.

McFadden, Thomas M., ed. *Liberation, Revolution, and Freedom: Theological Perspectives.* Proceedings of the College Theology Society. New York: Seabury, 1975.

Mendez-Flor, Paul R. "'To Brush History Against the Grain': The Eschatology of the Frankfurt School and Ernst Bloch." *Journal of the American Academy of Religion* 51 (December 1983): 631-650.

Menninger, Karl. "Hope." *American Journal of Psychiatry* 116 (December 1959): 481-491.

Merlan, Philip. "Eschatology, Sacred and Profane." *Journal of the History of Philosophy* 9 (April 1971): 193-203.

Mermall, Thomas. "Spain's Philosopher of Hope [Pedro Laín Entralgo]." *Thought* 45 (Spring 1970): 103-123.

Mills, Robert. "An Anatomy of Hope." *Journal of Religion and Health* 18 (January 1979): 49-52.

Moltmann, Jürgen. *The Experiment Hope.* Edited, translated, and Foreword by M. Douglas Meeks. Philadelphia: Fortress Press, 1975.

Muyskens, James Leroy. "Religious-Belief as Hope." *International Journal for Philosophy of Religion* 5 (Winter 1974): 246-253.

Muyskens, James Leroy. *The Sufficiency of Hope: The Conceptual Foundations of Religion.* Philosophical Monographs, Third Annual Series. Philadelphia: Temple University Press, 1979.

Nyanatiloka. *Buddhist Dictionary: Manual of Buddhist Terms and Doctrines.* Third rev. and enlarged edition, ed. Nyanaponika. Colombo, Ceylon [Sri Lanka]: Frewin and Co., 1972.

Oliver, Harold H. "Hope and Knowledge: The Epistemic Status of Religious Language." *Cultural Hermeneutics* 2 (1974): 75-88.

Owens, Joseph, C.Ss.R. *Human Destiny: Some Problems for Catholic Philosophy.* Washington: Catholic University of America Press, 1985.

Pannenberg, Wolfhart. "The God of Hope." *Cross Currents* 18 (Summer 1968): 284-295.

Pannenberg, Wolfhart. "The Question of God." *Basic Questions in Theology.* Collected Essays. Vol. II. Translated by George H. Kehm. Philadelphia: Fortress Press, 1971.

Pieper, Josef. *Hope and History.* Translated by Richard and Clara Winston. New York: Herder and Herder, 1969.

Radford, Colin. "Hoping, Wishing, and Dogs." *Inquiry* 13 (Summer 1970): 100-103.

Radford, Colin, and Hinton, J. M. "Hoping and Wishing." *Proceedings* of the Aristotelian Society for the Systematic Study of Philosophy, London. Supplementary Volume 44 (1970): 51-88.

Rahner, Karl. "The Theology of Hope." *Theology Digest* Sesquicentennial [of St. Louis University] Issue (February 1968): 78-87.

Rahner, Karl, S.J. *Zur Theologie der Zukunft.* München: Deutscher Taschenbuch Verlag, 1971.

Ratzinger, Joseph. *Introduction to Christianity.* Translated by J. R. Foster. New York: Herder and Herder, 1970. Orig. *Einführung in das Christentum.* Munich: Kösel-Verlag, 1968.

Ricoeur, Paul. "Hope and the Structure of Philosophical Systems." *Proceedings* of the American Catholic Philosophical Association, (1970): 55-69.

Ricoeur, Paul. "Fatherhood: From Phantasm to Symbol." Translated by Robert Sweeney. In Paul Ricoeur, *The Conflict of Interpretations: Essays in Hermeneutics,* edited by Don Ihde, 468-497. Evanston: Northwestern University Press, 1974.

Roman, Eric. "Will, Hope, and the Noumenon." *Journal of Philosophy* 72 (February 13, 1975): 59-77.

Rossi, Philip J., S.J. *Together Toward Hope: A Journey to Moral Theology.* Notre Dame and London: University of Notre Dame Press, 1983.

Rupp, George. *Beyond Existentialism and Zen: Religion in a Pluralistic World.* New York: Oxford, 1979.

Schacht, Richard. *Alienation.* Introduction by Walter Kaufmann. Garden City, N. Y.: Doubleday, 1970.

Schilpp, Paul Arthur, and Friedman, Maurice, eds. *The Philosophy of Martin Buber.* The Library of Living Philosophers, vol. 12. La Salle, Ill.: Open Court; London: Cambridge University Press, 1967.

Schrader, George A. "The Structure of Emotion." In *Invitation to Phenomenology,* edited by James M. Edie, 252-265. Chicago: Quadrangle, 1965.

Solomon, Robert C. *The Passions.* Garden City, N. Y.: Doubleday 1976.

Stotland, Ezra. *The Psychology of Hope: An Integration of Experimental, Clinical, and Social Approaches.* San Francisco: Jossey-Bass, 1969.

Tallon, Andrew. "Person and Community: Buber's Category of the Between." *Philosophy Today* 17 (Spring 1973): 62-83.

Thomas Aquinas. "Hope," *Summa Theologiae* II-II, 17-22. Blackfriars, with New York:McGraw-Hill, and London: Eyre & Spottiswoode, 1966.

Tillich, Paul. "The Right to Hope." *Neue Zeitschrift für systematische Theologie und Religionsphilosophie* 7 (1965): 371-377.

Wheatley, J. M. O. "Wishing and Hoping." *Analysis* 18 (June 1958): 121-131.

Wittgenstein, Ludwig. *Philosophical Investigations.* Translated by G. E. M.

Anscombe. 3rd. ed. Oxford: Blackwell, 1968.
Wood, Ernest. *Vedanta Dictionary*. New York: Philosophical Library, 1964.
Wood, Robert E. *Martin Buber's Ontology: An Analysis of "I and Thou."* Evanston: Northwestern University Press, 1969.
Wyschogrod, Michael. *The Body of Faith: Judaism as Corporeal Election.* New York: Seabury, 1983.

Bloch

Bloch, Ernst. *Gesamtausgabe.* Frankfurt a. M.: Suhrkamp, 1959 – .
Bloch, Ernst. "Angst und Hoffnung in unserer Zeit." In *Politische Messungen, Pestzeit, Vormärz,* pp. 425-499. *Gesamtausgabe* Bd. 11. Frankfurt a. M.: Suhrkamp, 1970.
Bloch, Ernst. *Atheism in Christianity: The Religion of the Exodus and the Kingdom.* Translated by J. T. Swann. New York: Herder and Herder, 1972.
Bloch, Ernst. *Atheismus im Christentum: Zur Religion des Exodus und des Reichs. Gesamtausgabe*, Bd. 14. Frankfurt a. M.: Suhrkamp, 1968.
Bloch, Ernst. *Differenzierungen im Begriff Fortschritt.* Edition "Arche Nova." Zurich: Verlag der Arche, 1970; Frankfurt a. M.: Suhrkamp, 1970.
Bloch, Ernst. "Kann Hoffnung enttäuscht werden?" In *Verfremdungen* I, pp. 211-219. Frankfurt a. M.: Suhrkamp, 1962.
Bloch, Ernst. "Man as Possibility." Translated by William R. White. *Cross Currents* 18 (Summer 1968): 273-283.
Bloch, Ernst. *Man on His Own: Essays in the Philosophy of Religion.* Translated by E. B. Ashton. Forward by Harvey Cox. Introduction by Jürgen Moltmann. New York: Herder and Herder, 1970. Translation of *Religion im Erbe,* an edition of selected chapters from several of Bloch's works.
Bloch, Ernst. *On Karl Marx.* Translated by John Maxwell. New York: Herder and Herder, 1971. Translation of *Über Karl Marx*, an edition of selected chapters from several of Bloch's works.
Bloch, Ernst. *A Philosophy of the Future.* Translated by John Cumming. New York: Herder and Herder, 1970. Translation of chapters 1-15 of *Tübinger Einleitung in die Philosophie,* Bd. 1.
Bloch, Ernst. *Das Prinzip Hoffnung. Gesamtausgabe,* Bd. 5. Frankfurt a. M.: Suhrkamp, 1959 & 1970.
Bloch, Ernst. "Studien zum Buch Hiob." In *Wegzeichen der Hoffnung: eine Auswahl aus seinen Schriften: Mythos, Dichtung, Musik.* Mit Einführung v. Iring Fetscher; Auswahl u. Zwischentexte v. Walter Strolz. Freiburg: Herder Bücherei, 1967.

Bloch, Ernst. *Tübinger Einleitung in die Philosophie.* Neue erweiterte Ausgabe. *Gesamtausgabe,* Bd. 13. Frankfurt a. M.: Suhrkamp, 1970.

Blain, Lionel. "Two Philosophies Centered on Hope: Those of G. Marcel and E. Bloch." In *Dimensions of Spirituality,* edited by Christian Duquoc, 91-100. Concilium: Theology in the Age of Renewal, vol. 59. New York: Herder and Herder, 1970.

Breines, Paul. "Bloch Magic." *Continuum* 7 (Winter 1970): 619-624.

Buhr, Manfred. "A Critique of Ernst Bloch's Philosophy of Hope." *Philosophy Today* 14 (Winter 1970): 259-271. A translation by Robert Schreiter of "Der religiöse Ursprung und Charakter der Hoffnungsphilosophie Ernst Blochs," *Deutsche Zeitschrift für Philosophie,* Heft 4 (1958), 576-98.

Buhr, Manfred. "Kritische Bemerkungen zu Ernst Blochs Hauptwerk 'Das Prinzip Hoffnung.'" *Deutsche Zeitschrift für Philosophie 8* (1960): 365-379.

Encyclopedia of Philosophy Ed. Paul Edwards. S. v. "Bloch, Ernst," by Franco Lombardi. New York: Macmillan & Free Press; London: Collier-Macmillan, 1967.

Furter, Pierre. "Utopia and Marxism according to Bloch." *Philosophy Today* 14 (Winter 1970): 236-249.

Green, Ronald M. "Ernst Bloch's Revision of Atheism." *Journal of Religion* 49 (1969): 128-135.

Gross, David. "Man on His Own." *Continuum* 7 (Winter 1970): 625-627.

Heim, Theodor. "Blochs Atheismus." In *Ernst Bloch zu ehren: Beiträge zu seinem Werk,* hrsg. von Siegfried Unseld, pp. 157-180. Frankfurt a. M.: Suhrkamp, 1965.

Holz, Hans Heinz. "Kategorie Möglichkeit und Moduslehre." In *Ernst Bloch zu ehren. Beiträge zu seinem Werk,* hrsg. von Siegfried Unseld, pp. 99-120. Frankfurt a. M.: Suhrkamp, 1965.

Hudson, Wayne. *The Marxist Philosophy of Ernst Bloch.* New York: St. Martin's, 1982.

Jäger, Alfred. *Reich ohne Gott: Zur Eschatologie Ernst Bloch.* Basler Studien zur historischen und systematischen Theologie, hrsg. von Max Geiger. Bd. 14. Zurich: EVZ-Verlag, 1969.

Kimmerle, Heinz. *Die Zukunftsbedeutung der Hoffnung: Auseinandersetzung mit Ernst Blochs "Prinzip Hoffnung" aus philosophischer und theologischer Sicht.* Bonn: H. Bouvier, 1966.

Metz, Johannes B. "God Before Us Instead of a Theological Argument." *Cross Currents* 18 (Summer 1968): 259-306.

Metzger, Arnold. "Utopie und Transzendenz." In *Ernst Bloch zu ehren. Beiträge zu seinem Werk,* hrsg. von Siegfried Unseld, pp. 69-82. Frankfurt a. M.: Suhrkamp, 1965.

Moltmann, Jürgen. "Hope without Faith: An Eschatological Humanism without God." In *Is God Dead?,* edited by Johannes Metz, pp. 25-40. Concilium: Theology in the Age of Renewal, vol. 16. New York: Paulist Press, 1966.

Roeder von Diersburg, Egenolf. *Zur Ontologie und Logik offener Systeme: Ernst Bloch vor dem Gesetz der Tradition.* Hamburg: Meiner, 1967.

Ruhle, Jürgen. "The Philosopher of Hope: Ernst Bloch." In *Revisionism: Essays on the History of Marxist Ideas,* edited by Leopold Labedz, 166-179. New York: Fredrick A. Praeger; London: George Allen and Unwin, 1962.

Schreiter, Robert. "Ernst Bloch: the Man and his Work." *Philosophy Today* 14 (Winter 1970): 231-235.

Times Literary Supplement. "The Principle of Hope," review of *Das Prinzip Hoffnung* by Ernst Bloch, 31 March 1961, pp. 193-94.

Über Ernst Bloch. Frankfurt a. M.: Suhrkamp, 1968.

Wren, Thomas. "An Ernst Bloch Bibliography for English Readers." *Philosophy Today* 14 (Winter 1970): 272-273.

Wren, Thomas. "The Principle of Hope." *Philosophy Today* 14 (Winter 1970): 250-258.

Kant

Kant, Immanuel. *Kants gesammelte Schriften.* Hrsg. von der Königlichen Preussischen Akademie der Wissenschaften. Berlin: Georg Reimer, 1902 – .

Kant, Immanuel. *Kritik der praktischen Vernunft. Kants gesammelte Schriften* 5: 1-163.

Kant, Immanuel. *Die Religion innerhalb der Grenzen der blossen Vernunft.*

Kants gesammelte Schriften 6: 1-202.
Kant, Immanuel. *Zum ewigen Frieden. Kants gesammelte Schriften* 8: 341-386.

Kant, Immanuel. *Critique of Practical Reason.* Translated by Lewis White Beck. Library of Liberal Arts. New York: Bobbs-Merrill, 1956.
Kant, Immanuel. *Critique of Pure Reason.* Translated by Norman Kemp Smith. London: Macmillan, 1929; New York: St. Martin's Press, 1965.
Kant, Immanuel. *On History.* Edited by Lewis White Beck. Translated by Lewis White Beck, Robert E. Anchor, and Emil L. Fackenheim. New York: Bobbs-Merrill, 1963.
Kant, Immanuel. *Religion Within the Limits of Reason Alone.* Transl. Theodore M. Green and Hoyt H. Hudson. New York: Harper & Row, Harper Torchbooks, 1960.
Kant, Immanuel. *Perpetual Peace.* Translated by Lewis White Beck. Library of Liberal Arts. New York: Bobbs-Merrill, 1957.

Beck, Lewis White. *A Commentary on Kant's "Critique of Practical Reason."* Chicago: University of Chicago Press, 1960.
Despland, Michel. *Kant on History and Religion, with a Translation of Kant's "On the Failure of All Attempted Philosophical Theodicies."* Montreal and London: McGill-Queen's University Press, 1973.
Fackenheim, Emil. "Kant and Radical Evil." *University of Toronto Quarterly* 23 (1954): 439-453.
Fackenheim, Emil. "Kant's Concept of History." *Kant-Studien* 48 (1956-57): 381-398.
Goldman, Lucien. *Immanuel Kant.* Translated by Robert Black. London: NLB, 1971.
Silber, John R. "Kant's Conception of the Highest Good as Immanent and Transcendent." *Philosophical Review* 68 (Oct. 1959): 469-492.
Wood, Allen W. *Kant's Moral Religion.* Ithaca and London: Cornell University Press, 1970.
Yovel, Yirmiahu. *Kant and the Philosophy of History.* Princeton: Princeton University Press, 1979.
Zeldin, Mary-Barbara. "The Summum Bonum, the Moral Law and the Existence of God." *Kantstudien* 62 (1971): 43-54.

Marcel

Marcel, Gabriel. *Being and Having: An Existentialist Diary.* New York: Harper & Row, Harper Torchbooks, 1965.

Marcel, Gabriel. *Creative Fidelity.* Translated with introduction by Robert Rosthal. New York: Farrar, Strauss, and Giroux, Noonday Press, 1964.

Marcel, Gabriel. "Desire and Hope." In *Readings in Existential Phenomenology,* edited by Nathaniel Lawrence and Daniel O'Connor, pp. 277-85. Englewood Cliffs, N.J.: Prentice-Hall, 1967.

Marcel, Gabriel. "Existence and Objectivity." In Marcel's *Metaphysical Journal,* translated by Bernard Wall, 319-39. London: Rockliff, 1952.

Marcel, Gabriel. *The Existential Background of Human Dignity.* Cambridge: Harvard University Press, 1963.

Marcel, Gabriel. *Homo Viator: Introduction to a Metaphysic of Hope.* Translated by Emma Craufurd. New York: Harper & Row, Harper Torchbooks, 1962; London: Victor Gollancz, 1951.

Marcel, Gabriel. *Homo Viator: Prolégomènes à une métaphysique de l'espérance.* Paris: Aubier, 1944, 1963.

Marcel, Gabriel. "I and Thou," translated by Forrest Williams. In *The Philosophy of Martin Buber,* edited by Paul A. Schilpp and Maurice Friedman, pp. 41-8. The Library of Living Philosophers, vol. 12. La Salle, Ill: Open Court; London: Cambridge University Press, 1967.

Marcel, Gabriel. *Man Against Mass Society.* Translated by G. S. Fraser. Foreward by Donald Mackinnon. Chicago: Henry Regnery, Gateway Edition, 1962.

Marcel, Gabriel. "Martin Buber's Philosophical Anthropology." In Marcel's *Searchings,* pp. 73-92. New York and Toronto: Newman, 1967.

Marcel, Gabriel. *The Mystery of Being.* Vol. 1: *Reflection & Mystery;* Vol. 2: *Faith & Reality.* Translated by G. S. Fraser. Chicago: Henry Regnery, Gateway edition, 1960; London: Harvill, 1950, 1951.

Marcel, Gabriel. *Philosophical Fragments 1904-1914* and *The Philosopher and Peace.* Translated with an introduction by Lionel Blain. Notre Dame, Ind.: University of Notre Dame Press, 1965.

Marcel, Gabriel. *The Philosophy of Existentialism.* Translated by Manya Harari. New York: Philosophical Library, 1949; Citadel Press, 1971.

Marcel, Gabriel. *Pour une sagesse tragique et son au-delà.* Paris: Plon, 1968.

Marcel, Gabriel. *Presence and Immortality.* Translated by Michael A. Machado. Revised by Henry J. Koren. Pittsburgh: Duquesne University Press, 1967.

Marcel, Gabriel. *Royce's Metaphysics.* Translated by Virginia and Gordon Ringer. Chicago: Henry Regnery, 1956.

Marcel, Gabriel. "Theism and Personal Relationships." *Cross Currents* 1 (Fall 1950): 35-42.

Marcel, Gabriel. *Tragic Wisdom and Beyond, Including Conversations between Paul Ricoeur and Gabriel Marcel.* Translated by Stephen Jolin and Peter McCormick. Evanston: Northwestern University Press, 1973.

Blain, Lionel. . . See Blain under Bloch.

Nowotny, Joan. "Gabriel Marcel's Philosophy of Hope." Ph.D. dissertation, University of Toronto, 1974.

Plourde, Simonne. *Gabriel Marcel, philosophie et témoin de l'espérance.* Montréal: Presses de l'Université de Québec, 1975.

Troisfontaines, Roger. *De l'existence à l'être: La philosophie de Gabriel Marcel.* Bibliothèque de la Faculté de Philosophie et Lettres de Namur, fasc. 16. Louvain: Nauwelaerts, and Paris: Vrin, 1953.

Widmer, Charles. *Gabriel Marcel et le théisme existentiel.* Cogitatio fidei 55. Paris: Cerf, 1971.

INDEX